Disaster Management

In recent times the frequency and severity of natural disasters has placed a clear emphasis on the ability of governments to plan, prepare and respond in an effective way. *Disaster Management in Australia* examines government coordination when faced with large scale crises, outlining the challenges in managing events such as the 2009 Victorian bushfires and 2011 Queensland floods.

The public sector is equipped to deal with policy and service delivery in more routine environments, but crisis management often requires a wider government response where leadership, coordination, social capital, organisational culture and institutions are intertwined in the preparation, response and aftermath of large scale crises.

As crises continue to increase in prevalence and severity, this book provides a tangible framework to conceptualise crisis management which can be utilised by researchers, emergency services and government officials alike. *Disaster Management in Australia* is an important contribution to the study of government coordination of crises and, as such, will be of considerable interest to students and scholars of disaster management, and to policy makers and practitioners looking to refine their approach.

George Carayannopoulos is Head of the Higher Degree Research Centre at the University of Sydney, Australia, and an Associate Member of the Bushfire and Natural Hazards Cooperative Research Centre. George has held a number of senior positions in management and research development. He has a background in policy development, analysis and evaluation and his research areas include public policy collaboration, interagency coordination and crisis management.

Routledge Humanitarian Studies

Series editors: Alex de Waal and Dorothea Hilhorst
Editorial Board: Mihir Bhatt, Dennis Dijkzeul, Wendy Fenton, Kirsten Johnson, Julia Streets, Peter Walker

The Routledge Humanitarian Studies series in collaboration with the International Humanitarian Studies Association (IHSA) takes a comprehensive approach to the growing field of expertise that is humanitarian studies. This field is concerned with humanitarian crises caused by natural disaster, conflict or political instability and deals with the study of how humanitarian crises evolve, how they affect people and their institutions and societies, and the responses they trigger.

We invite book proposals that address, amongst other topics, questions of aid delivery, institutional aspects of service provision, the dynamics of rebel wars, state building after war, the international architecture of peacekeeping, the ways in which ordinary people continue to make a living throughout crises, and the effect of crises on gender relations.

This interdisciplinary series draws on and is relevant to a range of disciplines, including development studies, international relations, international law, anthropology, peace and conflict studies, public health and migration studies.

Australia's Foreign Aid Dilemma
Humanitarian Aspirations Confront Democratic Legitimacy
Jack Corbett

Public Health Humanitarian Responses to Natural Disasters
Emily Chan

People, Aid and Institutions in Socio-economic Recovery
Facing Fragilities
Gemma van der Haar, Dorothea Hilhorst, and Bart Weijs

Anti-genocide Activists and the Responsibility to Protect
Edited by Annette Jansen

Disaster Management in Australia
Government Coordination in a Time of Crisis
George Carayannopoulos

Disaster Management in Australia

Government Coordination in a
Time of Crisis

George Carayannopoulos

LONDON AND NEW YORK

First published 2018
by Routledge
2 Park Square, Milton Park, Abingdon, Oxon OX14 4RN

and by Routledge
711 Third Avenue, New York, NY 10017

Routledge is an imprint of the Taylor & Francis Group, an informa business

© 2018 George Carayannopoulos

British Library Cataloguing in Publication Data
A catalogue record for this book is available from the British Library

Library of Congress Cataloging in Publication Data
Names: Carayannopoulos, George, author.
Title: Disaster management in Australia / George Carayannopoulos.
Description: New York : Routledge, 2018. | Series: Routledge
humanitarian studies | Includes bibliographical references and index.
Identifiers: LCCN 2017032013 | ISBN 9781138049123 (hardback) |
ISBN 9781315169774 (ebook)
Subjects: LCSH: Crisis management--Australia. | Disaster relief--Australia.
Classification: LCC HV551.5.A8 C37 2018 | DDC 363.34/80994--dc23
LC record available at https://lccn.loc.gov/2017032013

ISBN: 978-1-138-04912-3 (hbk)
ISBN: 978-1-315-16977-4 (ebk)

Typeset in Goudy
by Taylor & Francis Books

Contents

Illustrations

Figures

Tables

Acknowledgements

I would like to acknowledge the financial support that has been provided in order to conduct and present this research from the; School of Social and Political Sciences and the Faculty of Arts and Social Sciences at the University of Sydney, the Australian Political Studies Association (APSA), the Public Policy Network and the Bushfire & Natural Hazards Cooperative Research Centre.

I would like to sincerely thank Professor Allan McConnell for his support of the research. He has been a great mentor and colleague throughout the course of the project and has always provided telling insights and perspectives. Thanks also to Associate Professor Paul Fawcett for his advice during the early part of the project and in framing ideas around governance.

I would also like to thank my family for their support and assistance throughout the life of the research. They have been instrumental in helping me reach its completion and instilling in me the value of curiosity and perseverance needed to complete a large scale research project.

Finally, I would like to acknowledge the sorrow and destruction caused by the 2009 Victorian bushfires and 2011 Queensland floods to many innocent people, both residents and responders who were impacted by these events. These events should never be forgotten or lost from the national consciousness.

List of acronyms

Title	Acronym
Australian Government Disaster Response Plan	COMDISPLAN
Australian Public Service	APS
Bushfire Cooperative Research Centre	CRC
Central Government Response Committee	CGRC
Council of Australian Governments	COAG
Country Fire Authority	CFA
Department of Sustainability and Environment	DSE
Emergency Management Australia	EMA
Emergency Management Queensland	EMQ
Federal Emergency Management Agency	FEMA
Goods and Services Tax	GST
Integrated Emergency Coordination Centre	IECC
Natural Disaster Relief and Recovery Arrangements	NDRRA
New Public Management	NPM
Non-Government Organisations	NGOs
Queensland Police Service	QPS
Queensland Reconstruction Authority	QRA
Securities and Emergencies Cabinet Committee	SECC
State Disaster Management Committee	SDMG
State Emergency Response Coordinator	SERC
Victorian Bushfire Reconstruction and Recovery Authority	VBRRA
Victorian Emergency Management Council	VEMC

Preface

Over the past decade, there has been a global explosion in the number of crisis events. The spectre of terrorism, global financial meltdowns, nuclear accidents and natural disasters has loomed large over governments and the general public. As a nation, Australia has not been immune from these crises. As a large country with a diverse ecology and environment, Australia faces natural disasters on a yearly basis. From the floods and cyclones of the tropical north to the scorching fires of southern Australia, these events have shone a spotlight on how governments at different levels respond to natural disasters.

Within the context of increasing and higher stake events, there has been a clear emphasis on understanding the role of government in mitigating and responding to crises. Large scale natural disasters represent a significant test of the public sector's ability to respond in a coordinated and efficient way in the face of adversity. Crises and disasters also come against a backdrop in Australia where trust in government from its citizens continues to decline. The public also retain high expectations of government's ability to plan, prepare and respond to disasters. In many respects, the combination of more frequent and severe crises as well as heightened public expectation creates a perfect storm for politicians, bureaucrats and emergency managers looking for solutions.

An examination of crisis management reveals that it is occurring not in a vacuum but where changes in the public sector mean that whole of government or connected forms of working are a highly pervasive mantra. Crisis responses oblige the different layers of government – political, bureaucratic and operational response agencies – to work together to confront these events and require collective action. There is a strong recognition that the response to disasters is beyond the capacity of any single person, agency or department.

To date, there has been little work undertaken on how whole of government structures impact on the management and response to crises and how these may shape the overall perception of a 'successful' or 'failed' response. This book seeks to understand how and why approaches to crisis management are created and establish the pre-conditions which may lead to the 'successful' or 'unsuccessful' resolution of these events. It does so by placing a focus on a series of key inputs: leadership, coordination, organisational culture, social capital and institutions which mediate the outcomes. These key inputs have a strong resonance in the Australian context, from where the case studies are drawn but can also be applied more universally given they form the core of any response to large scale crisis events.

1   The challenge of managing crises

Overview

In recent times the frequency and severity of natural disasters has placed a
clear emphasis on the role of governments in responding to these crises. At
the international level events such as Hurricane Katrina, the Japanese Tsunami
and Nepal Earthquake have illustrated the challenges of managing disaster
responses. These events have indicated that there are a number of unifying
characteristics related to the management of crises which transcend national
borders and have resonance across different disaster events. Australia has
also not been immune to natural disasters; over the past decade there have
been large number of natural disasters in Australia – part of the cycle of life
in an extensive continent of diversity. Whilst accustomed to natural disasters,
recent events have had a significant impact on the relevant communities as
well as raising questions regarding the role of government in managing
planning and response processes. Public confidence in the ability of government to manage these events has been challenged, given some of the adverse
outcomes that have been experienced. Heightened public expectation and
media scrutiny have highlighted that there are serious challenges around the
preparation, response and overall management of crises.

Australia provides an interesting context in which to ground discussions
on the nature and management of crises given its diversity, size and history
of natural disaster events. The two case studies which will be used – the 2009
Victorian bushfires and the 2011 Queensland floods – were large scale
disasters managed at the state level. Under Australia's federal system, emergency
management has always been the domain of state governments. The delineation was established through the constitution and provides for state-based
management of disaster events. Disaster management arrangements have
largely remained unchanged over the past fifty years despite the punctuation
of major events such as Cyclone Tracey in 1974, the Ash Wednesday bushfires in 1983 and the 1989 Newcastle earthquake. In the context of Australian
emergency management there has been an increasing identification of the
importance of whole of government for managing large scale natural disasters. The rhetoric surrounding the importance of working across agency

boundaries increased markedly following the release of the 2002 Council of Australian Governments (COAG) Report "Natural Disasters in Australia". As one of its principal recommendations the report noted the need to establish a "national machinery ... to ensure effective collaboration and coordination of Commonwealth, State, Territory and Local Governments" (Council of Australian Governments, 2002, p. vii).

In the period following 2002, the focus on whole of government within emergency management was further sharpened by a series of large scale disaster events: the 2003 ACT bushfires, 2006 Cyclone Larry and the 2009 Victorian bushfires. In the wake of these events, significant scrutiny was placed on the response of government agencies. There was a strong shift away from command and control crisis management techniques towards more agile and integrated network approaches. The shift towards horizontal working was emphasised by the 2011 COAG Report "National Strategy for Disaster Resilience" which noted that "traditional government portfolio areas and service providers, with different and unconnected policy agendas may be attempting to achieve the outcome of a disaster resilient community individually" (Council of Australian Governments, 2011, p. 3). The 2011 COAG report placed a strong emphasis on the concept of shared responsibility where government agencies "contribute to achieving integrated and coordinated disaster resilience" and work in an inter-agency context (Council of Australian Governments, 2011, p. 3). The progression over the decade from the 2002 COAG report to the 2011 COAG report indicates that whilst coordination and collaboration were seen as important in 2002, by 2011 they were viewed as an imperative. The change in stance can largely be ascribed to the number and severity of the disaster events that occurred in the intervening decade and the political challenges which arose from 'failed' disaster responses.

Within the discussion of crisis management approaches in this book, a dichotomy is presented between two models: the traditional command and control approach and the network-based collaborative model. Whole of government approaches fall within the latter, given they emphasise the importance of system integration, multi-level coordination and inter-dependencies across networks. Over the past 10 years, and in the wake of major disasters, there has been an acknowledgement that command and control models cannot be used exclusively to manage complex events. As a result, there has been a shift to more horizontal approaches which harness and connect the capabilities of crisis management actors. This book seeks to examine the rise of whole of government approaches to emergency management in Australia as a new model for managing disaster events. The book explores whether commitments to this envisioned approach have been enacted in the face of wide ranging and large scale disasters.

This chapter provides an overview of the key questions that underpin this book. It provides a brief introduction to the case studies which have been selected in order to frame the key concepts to be examined. Chapter 2 reviews the literature to suggest a model through which we can understand crisis management and will be used as the basis for analysis of the case studies. Chapter 3 presents an overview of the 2009 Victorian bushfires and reviews these through the key themes of the book in order to understand the perception of a 'failed' crisis response. Chapter 4 provides an overview of the 2011 Queensland floods and also presents the case study as a vignette to better understand how disaster responses can be considered 'successful'. Chapter 5 presents a detailed comparison of the two case studies underpinned by a comparative method, highlighting synergies and differences in order to frame the implications of the cases for the broader study of crisis management. Finally, Chapter 6 concludes the book with reflections on the impact that high level characteristics related to disaster management have had on the case studies. Chapter 6 will also suggest future research directions for the study of connected crisis responses and consider future contributions which can be made in this area.

Rhetoric or reality: Can commitments to whole of government working be implemented during crises?

Universally there has been an acceptance that to manage large scale complex crises, there is a need to engage a range of actors such as government, private sector and non-government. Government agencies maintain a specific challenge around coordinating across organisational boundaries. The book provides a conceptual model through which to understand crises and specifically examines this model through two case studies from Australia. This book examines the case studies from a perspective that looks at the political and bureaucratic challenges of managing natural disasters. Given the rise of whole of government approaches to managing crises, the book seeks to understand whether commitments to connected working are rhetoric or whether they can become reality in the face of a crisis?

In attempting to unravel and understand whether large networks of actors are used effectively in the preparation and response to crises, numerous key themes emerge including: the importance of whole of government working, the nature of crisis management, the role of leadership, understanding coordination, the role of organisational culture, influence of social capital and the role of institutions. These themes are central to understanding how governments manage crisis situations and whether the overall outcomes are perceived as 'success' or 'failure' as depicted by Figure 1.1. The conceptual model provides for an examination of the key issues related to whole of government and crisis management, it allows for an exploration of similarities and differences between crisis events and provides explanatory power on why the outcomes to crises differ.

The key inputs can be understood further by analysing what each of them may tell us about the ability to solve problems and create solutions, governance methods (vertical and horizontal) and ideal versus practical action. Framing the thematic areas through the above matrix allows for an extra

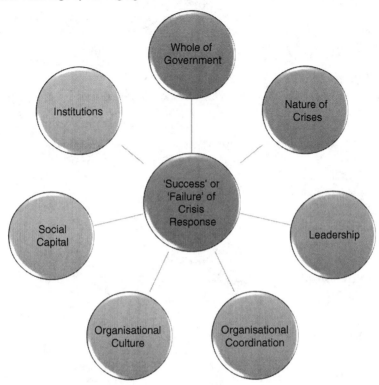

Figure 1.1 Crisis management inputs
Source: Author.

layer of analysis and is highly relevant to crisis management. At the heart of crisis management is an understanding that crises remain problematic, require immediate attention and engage a myriad of actors. Crises are also heavily shaped by the normative perception of what governments should and should not do. As a result, an identification of thematic areas allows for an examination of key mediators at the nexus of whole of government and crisis management including:

- Understanding the nature of whole of government working, how commitments to this are formed and how whole of government actually plays out in a crisis situation.
- Understanding the nature of managing a crisis or disaster and the narratives which emerge from this process. Identifying how the nature of a particular crisis itself shapes whole of government planning and responses.
- Examining the impact of leadership within whole of government arrangements and its impact on responses to crises.
- An analysis of the role of coordination within a crisis situation, including forms of coordination in inter-agency settings.

- Exploring the impact of organisational culture and motivation on coordination during crises.
- Examining whether moves towards increasing horizontality in the public sector have led to a culture where existing relationships and social capital are positively leveraged in times of crises.
- An analysis of the role of institutions and how these may mediate interactions or shape a crisis response.

Aims and scope

Given the conceptual model and the thematic areas outlined as part of this, the book has a number of aims and objectives that will be used to underpin both the conceptual and case study material used through the remaining chapters:

- To explicitly link the areas of whole of government and crisis management through the examination of two crisis events where little work has been done in this area.
- To understand and explore commitments to whole of government working and identify whether these commitments are upheld during a time of crisis.
- To provide a detailed overview and examination of the responses to the individual crisis events as well as provide a comparison of the events which allows a discussion of how these may have shaped outcomes.
- To understand how key themes related to whole of government impact on the horizontal response to crises and influence the interactions between different strands of government; that is, political, bureaucratic and operational agencies.
- To provide an opportunity to document the accounts and narratives arising from the events in a more unencumbered way than has previously been possible on the public record.
- To understand how overarching principles related to crisis management impact on the cases.

It is important to note that for the purposes of this book a normative or prescriptive position is not taken; that is to say that the purpose of the book is not to provide a list of recommendations or outcomes which might be enacted at either the political or bureaucratic level. Rather, the book seeks to explain and understand the response to crises through a conceptual model. It is intended that this research can then be used to inform discussion on the nature of whole of government responses to crises that may be a catalyst for further work in this area.

In terms of defining a scope for the research, it is important to note the parameters that guided the work towards the case studies. The case studies retain significant complexity and richness; as such it was fundamental to develop a distinct analytic framework that could allow for an in-depth analysis. Given this, it is important to note the following key aspects:

1   The scope of the research in each jurisdiction is to examine whole of government at the state level. That is to say, the discussion of whole of government is primarily intended to review the interactions within state government departments and response agencies. It is relevant to note that interactions between the federal, state and local level do remain important to the response of crises, they will be referenced as part of the analysis of the case studies; however, they are not the main focus of this research.

2   The scope of the research is to review the immediate lead up to and the response to the crisis events; within the first month of the response period. Information will be referenced beyond this period related to the emergence of the relevant commissions of inquiry and reconstruction authorities. These will be referenced on the basis that although operationalised beyond the initial scope of the reference period, the decisions to enact these were made in the immediate response period and as such can be seen as part of the institutional response to the crises.

3   The scope of the research is focused predominantly at the political and bureaucratic levels; that is, the emphasis is at these levels of response. Whilst the book does reference the operational response it does this within the context of understanding the interaction between the political, operational and bureaucratic levels. There is no intention to provide a detailed review of operational issues such as emergency response technology systems, operability or other more technical response issues. The choice not to explicitly review the technical response of the operational agencies is based on the orientation of the book in reviewing the political and bureaucratic challenges of crises rather than the 'hardware' which underpins disaster response.

Fire and flood in our states: Introduction to the case studies

In order to provide an application of the conceptual model which will be addressed in the book, the choice of two case studies – the Victorian bushfires (2009) and Queensland floods (2011) – best allows for a detailed examination of issues at the heart of crisis responses. The cases will provide the opportunity to explain and understand differences in the events and their outcomes, which can be used to reflect upon the key themes in the book. In this way, the cases are presented not as 'outliers' but as epitomising the challenges of large scale crisis management.

The first case study, the 2009 Victorian bushfires were collectively the worst fire events in Australian living memory surpassing the infamous 1983 Ash Wednesday fires. The scale, speed and dimensions of the fire meant that 173 people died on or around the 7th of February 2009. The fires were the culmination of an extreme dry period, high temperatures and strong winds which remain unprecedented in Victoria. As a result of the fires, significant scrutiny was placed on the emergency preparation and response capabilities within Victoria as part of the Victorian Bushfires Royal Commission. In subsequent years this had led to significant restructuring of the Victorian emergency management arrangements including the move towards an operationally focussed Emergency Management Victoria and review of contentious policies such as 'stay or go'. The event had a profound impact on the affected communities which is still evident more than seven years on as community recovery continues.

The second case study, the 2011 Queensland floods, were cumulatively the most significant series of flooding events in Queensland's history. The flooding event began in September 2010 and culminated in the flooding of Brisbane in January 2011. During the flood event there was significant impact on major centres such as Brisbane, Ipswich, Rockhampton and the Lockyer Valley, which were subjected to flooding. The wide-ranging floods were also accompanied by tragic flash flooding events in areas such as Grantham. The partial flooding of the Brisbane metropolitan area in January 2011 was the culmination of a period of extreme rainfall activity in a state that due to its geographical and meteorological characteristics is largely accustomed to natural disasters. As a result of the floods, significant scrutiny was placed over decision making in the run up to the flooding and to understand the impact of policy and structural arrangements with respect to dam management and land zoning practices. More than seven years on, there have also been moves to change the underlying structure of emergency management responses with the abolition of what was previously the peak government disaster body, Emergency Management Queensland (EMQ), with a shift towards a model that embeds coordination responsibility primarily within the emergency services.

These case studies were selected given that in terms of recent Australian history they represent the most significant disaster events in terms of social, economic and emotional impact. Both of these events are stories cf national significance and in many ways have had a profound impact both in the immediate aftermath and in the long term recovery process. More than eight years on from the events in Victoria and more than seven years on from the events in Queensland, relatively little has been written about the political consequences beyond the commission of inquiries which were conducted. The commissions of inquiry that were established after each event provide a detailed record but have limitations given they did not explicitly apply a whole of government lens. This book seeks to make a specific contribution by analysing the events and the factors that shaped their outcomes with specific reference to whole of government as an overarching framework. Contrary to other academic literature which has been written on these events (see Bajracharya & Hastings, 2015; Haertel & Latemore, 2011; Sturzenegger & Hayes, 2011; Whittaker & Handmer, 2010), this book does not provide an account of the technical operational response. The book makes a distinct contribution to the literature on both events by understanding the unique political and administrative challenges which arose.

The case studies were selected to demonstrate synergies as Australia's two most significant and recent disaster events. The nature of the events as major crises also allows for an examination of the political, bureaucratic and operational dimensions of whole of government in crises. The cases are drawn from different jurisdictions and hence allow for a comparison of how different whole of government systems and processes may have played out, given that in Australia's federal system, states have autonomy over their disaster management arrangements. State autonomy in disaster management enables discussion and analysis of how different characteristics may have impacted on the perceived 'failure' or 'success' of the responses. The events also occurred within a limited timeframe of each other (two years), allowing for a direct comparison of whole of government approaches within a com-parable political climate. It was felt that in the Australian context, there was no other event which could have usefully been used as a comparison to the Victorian bushfires and Queensland floods.

The choice of two case studies as opposed to a larger number is beneficial given that the cases will be examined in depth through a qualitative metho-dology providing a greater level of detail to explain and understand differences between the events. This is in contrast to a more quantitative approach which may have chosen a larger range of events and examined the role of different variables that could then be assessed for statistical significance to determine causal links. A large n sample would not have allowed for a thorough examination of the issues that arose in implementing whole of government in the response to each event. The selection of a qualitative case study approach is consistent with the use of case studies in public policy as well as disaster management research (Gerring, 2007; Nissen, 1998). With respect to the Victorian bushfires and Queensland floods this represents an opportune moment to hear directly from the protagonists in the events who due to the passage of time, completion of the commission of inquiry process, changes in government and changes in roles are less encumbered and able to provide a frank account of their experiences. In this way, there is an oppor-tunity to triangulate documentary evidence and secondary sources with the elite interviewing to create a rich narrative around the cases.

Understanding the cases: Research methodology

The following section provides an outline of the research methodology used to address the objectives of this book in reviewing the inputs for successful crisis management. It commences by providing an overview of case study methodology and its selection as the main framework for the research. Following on from this, will be an overview of the two main research tech-niques that will be used to operationalise the themes: document analysis and elite interviewing.

The research approach for the book is based on the case study methodology. Case studies provide a valuable means by which to assess conceptual constructs; they are particularly common within public policy and management research and also within crisis management. They have been used to examine government responses to events such as Hurricane Katrina, the Indian Ocean Tsunami and other significant happenings (see Deverell, 2010; Dunleavy, 1995; Kweit & Kweit, 2006; Meier, O'Toole, & Hicklin, 2010; Turner, 1976). As a result, case studies offer a valuable means by which to assess the interplay between whole of government approaches to governing and crisis management. Each case study whilst retaining its own unique value provides the possibility for a comparative analysis. In this way, there is an opportunity to assess whether similarities and differences may indicate a common set of features to a particular type of crisis (Millar & Heath, 2004). Indeed, case study research may be preferable as much of crisis research seeks to explore key events rather than creating generalisable outcomes and findings (Gerring, 2007, p. 39). Therefore, the case study's "unique strength is its ability to deal with a full variety of evidence-documents, artifacts, interviews and observations" (Yin, 2009, p. 11). Case study research is predicated on "analyzing a few cases in depth (that is looking at a large number of dimensions, usually within a historical perspective)" (Della Porta, 2008, p. 202). In this sense, when using cases "the challenge is to acknowledge and uncover its specific meaning" (Vennesson, 2008, p. 226). The case study method is strongly aligned to the scope and objectives of the book which are to conduct an in-depth analysis of events and better understand the factors that shaped the perceptions of 'successful' or 'failed' crisis responses.

Case studies can also be used when there is a developed logic as to why the research question is significant and there is no existing body of work which offers an explanation (Eisenhardt & Graebner, 2007; Patton, 1990). Understanding the cases in greater depth is highly relevant to the disaster events at the heart of this book; given there has been little empirical investigation of the political and administrative challenges raised by these crisis episodes. As a result, case studies have been suggested to be a strong research approach where the researcher seeks to explore and understand how or why a particular phenomenon occurred (Yin, 2009, p. 2). It is also relevant to note that case study research has been used about "topics as diverse as group process, internal organization and strategy", all themes similar to the topic of this book (Eisenhardt & Graebner, 2007, p. 25). Case studies are also appropriate where there is a focus on contemporary events that does not require behavioural or experimental control (Yin, 2009, p. 8). Finally, "a multi-case approach helps to ground the evidence in a variety of empirical settings, guarding against the dangers that findings are tied to a unique aspect of a single case" (Moynihan, 2009, p. 900). In this way, multiple cases "clarify whether an emergent finding is idiosyncratic to a single case" or more typical across a number of cases (Eisenhardt & Graebner, 2007, p. 27). Given the overview of case study research which has been provided above and the aims and scope of the book outlined earlier in this chapter, there are strong reasons to use this methodology given it provides the most conclusive means to elucidate the key themes.

It is however important to acknowledge critiques of the case study approach, which suggest that it may be less rigorous than other research techniques using large quantitative cohorts. The suggestion has often been made that such case study research may add little to the body of knowledge given its lack of generalisability. This however has been countered by establishing that context dependent knowledge that arises from case study analysis can be just as critical as generaliseable knowledge drawn from research (Flyvberg, 2006, p. 225). Indeed, critiques can also be countered by suggesting that "a priori (there is) no reason to regard case oriented research as methodologically soft, and indeed this approach can provide a far more rigorous and sophisticated response to some types of research questions" (Hopkin, 2010, p. 261). The argument can also be made that a highly quantitative approach to the research using significant statistical analysis could be undertaken. An approach which combines evidence from a number of sources provides a more suitable means to approach the themes and explore the richness of the case studies rather than a quantitative approach.

In order to ensure that the methodology used to underpin the research is robust and can address the criticisms noted above regarding the case study methodology, it has been underpinned by a model which seeks to provide a systematic framework for the conduct of this type of research. Two such models which epitomise this are presented by Crotty (2003) and by Munck (2004). Crotty suggests that in designing research there are four key considerations (Crotty cited in Creswell, 2003, p. 4): the epistemology, which informs the research; the theoretical perspective behind the methodology in question (e.g. behaviouralism, positivism etc.); the methodology, strategy or plan that links methods to outcomes and the methods, techniques and procedures that guide the research.

As a result of these frameworks, the research in this book was undertaken through the use of a methodology that utilised document analysis as well as elite interviewing to provide an in-depth understanding of the 2009 Victorian bushfires and the 2011 Queensland floods. It was felt that for the purposes of obtaining a thorough understanding of the outcomes, two cases were optimal particularly given the binary nature of the outcomes. The choice of two case studies was consistent with the notion that it is reasonable to "choose cases such as extreme situations and polar types in which the process of interest is observable" (Eisenhardt, 1989, p. 537). In terms of the application of case study methodology to this book, it was based on a comparative analysis to understand why the outcomes may have been different in the cases. This is consistent with most case study research which does not seek to "produce a general theory of crises" (Turner, 1976, p. 379). Rather, this research sought to understand the nature of the crises and provide explanation for the differences in outcomes that occurred (Meier et al., 2010, p. 984). The use of case studies was consistent with a cross-case analysis where "the research focuses on instances of the outcome being studied that are located in two or more different cases" (Collier, Mahoney, & Seawright, 2004, p. 92). The book did not attempt to judge or provide a prescriptive view of what the policy directions should have been, but sought to understand the impact of whole of government structures on crisis responses.

Data collection

As a result of the key constructs that are to be examined in the book and the case study approach explained above, the research data collection and analysis process sought to operationalise the research themes through the use of multiple data sources. This is consistent with the notion that data can be collected in multiple ways and used to sequentially build understanding and meaning through the course of the research. The data collection provided a general context in which to situate the case study events. Following on from this, it provides a deeper understanding of the individual disaster characteristics. This understanding was derived through an examination of the events as experienced by the key protagonists and through both primary and secondary sources. The research approach followed a sequential order, using document analysis followed by the conduct of elite interviews which allowed for "elaborating or expanding on the findings of one method with another method" (Creswell, 2003, p. 16). Hence, meaning was sequentially built to provide depth to the analysis of key research themes. In order to provide an overview of the data collection mechanisms, Table 1.1 below provides a summary of the primary and secondary data access mechanisms with specific reference to sources. After the table is a specific outline of each stage of the data collection process.

Table 1.1 Data access techniques

Research tool	How evidence is to be accessed	Specific actions
Document analysis	Through both publicly available sources such as Hansard, commissions and inquires, news reports and non-publicly available documents	1. Environmental scanning for media articles, commissions and inquiries and other relevant reports 2. Freedom of information requests for non-publicly available documents
In-depth interviews	Conduct of in-person interviews with key actors from the responses to each disaster	1. Acquisition of research ethics approval for the conduct of interviews 2. Invitation and acceptance by potential interviewees

Source: Author.

Document Analysis

The first step in the research methodology involved conducting a thorough document analysis of key documents related to each of the disaster events. Document analysis can include "newspapers to research reports, government records to personal diaries" (Burnham, Gillard, Grant, & Layton-Henry, 2008a, p. 165). Other sources such as, meeting documents, cabinet documents, plans, structures, legislation are also relevant. Documents can be useful in "providing background information prior to designing a research project" in order to set a general frame of reference for research (Yannow, 2007, p. 411). Document analysis is an appropriate research technique for this study as it offers the ability to "develop novel accounts and interpretations for significant events" (Burnham, et al., 2008a, p. 84). In terms of this research, the sampling frame for document analysis included the use of secondary sources such as official inquiry reports and primary sources such as Hansard records, minutes, reports and correspondence from key emergency units established to respond to the crises. Records were examined from the year preceding the crises to the release of the official inquiry outcomes. An example of the document analysis was the use of statements, proceedings and exhibitions from the 2009 Victorian Bushfires Royal Commission. The commissions, which were held for each of the disasters, provided a means in which to review the information that was provided about the cases through submissions, interviews and hearings, which provide important insights into the disaster responses.

Elite interviews

The second stage in the research methodology involved the conduct of in-depth interviews. It has been argued that an optimal way of approaching interviews is to use "numerous and highly knowledgeable informants who view the focal phenomena from diverse perspectives" (Eisenhardt & Graebner, 2007, p. 28). Interviews have been argued to be invaluable in order to understand the "experiences, opinions, feelings and knowledge" of the informants (Patton, 1990, p. 10). Interviews are a "great vehicle for bringing a research topic to life and it is also an excellent method of obtaining data about contemporary subjects which have not been extensively studied and for which there is little literature" (Stedward cited in Harrison, 2001, p. 90). In the case of the interviews in this research, the main objective was to "provide an insight into the mind of that particular political actor" (Harrison, 2001, p. 94).

With regard to the research, the views and accounts of key actors involved in the responses were central to understanding the events in each of the jurisdictions. In terms of the sampling frame for the interviews, the focus was on senior figures in the political, bureaucratic and operational response agencies. The choice of senior figures as interview participants was based on their importance as part of the strategic response to the crises. At the senior executive level, the research sought input from ministers and premiers. At the bureaucratic level, this involved the heads of government departments and at the emergency response agency level senior officers of response agencies. Interviewees were also provided the opportunity to indicate whether they wished for their comments in the interview to be formally attributed or de-identified and this has been indicated accordingly in the empirical chapters with either attribution by name or use of a general position to retain anonymity.

The interviews provided significant depth to the research study and the understanding of meaning by individual actors; this was strongly complementary to the document analysis which was undertaken. The interviews were pivotal in capturing insights that may not have been captured through the document analysis or through quantitative analysis techniques if these had been adopted. They were also central in creating a more holistic understanding of the events which occurred in order to understand the "complex system as more than the sum of its parts" (Patton, 1990, p. 49). Given that the interviewing followed on from the document analysis it was also highly beneficial in terms of data triangulation. Triangulation in this research study involved the review of documents in the sample period (one year prior to the completion of inquiries), against secondary sources such as media reports as well as interview data. This allowed for a comparison of the official account of the events presented in the inquiries (with the benefit of hindsight) against the sentiment arising at the time through the media to the lived experiences of individual actors pivotal in the responses. This represented a sound approach to the research given that the triangulation process "entails using more than one method or source of data in the study of social phenomena" (Bryman cited in Burnham, Gillard, Grant, & Layton-Henry, 2008b, p. 232) and that interviews are "essential sources of case study information" (Yin, 2009, p. 106). In order to counter one of the potential difficulties related to memory and recollections of events can often diminish over time (Deverell, 2010, p. 73), information established from the interviews has been reviewed against the document analysis by comparing and contrasting the relevant material.

Conclusion

This chapter has provided an overview and introduction to the case studies, the aims and scope of the research, key themes and the methodology to be used to operationalise key questions. Governments now face more pressure than ever in terms of responding to crises and it is an appropriate time to review how rhetoric is supported by whole of government working. The chapter has outlined that the research is premised on a multi-tiered approach that uses both document analysis and elite interviewing as a means to provide a contextual understanding of the two events. Through a process of document analysis (including primary and secondary sources) and elite interviewing a comprehensive review of the events is possible which allows for the generation of new insights and a contribution to the literature.

The research has been framed to understand whether the commitments to whole of government working were applied during periods of crisis or whether these were put aside given the complexity of events – that is, whether they were 'rhetoric' rather than 'reality'. The book seeks to address concepts such as executive leadership, the fabric of coordination, organisational values and state structures which need to exist in order to implement whole of government. The following chapter provides a review of the literature relevant to the conceptual model and key themes which are central to the book, including whole of government and crisis management. The chapter to follow serves as a basis to provide a theoretical grounding for the empirical material to be presented around the case studies and the broader reflection on crisis management. Chapter 2 will frame the key thematic issues in a way which acknowledges how debates about whole of government working can be seen to be complementary to crisis management and provides an opportunity to integrate these bodies of literature.

References

Bajracharya, B., & Hastings, P. (2015). Public–private partnerships in emergency and disaster management: Examples from the Queensland floods 2010–11. *Australian Journal of Emergency Management*, 30(4), 30–36.

Burnham, P., Gillard, K., Grant, W., & Layton-Henry, Z. (2008a). Documentary and archival analysis. In *Research Methods in Politics* (2nd ed., pp. 165–188). Basingstoke, UK: Palgrave.

Burnham, P., Gillard, K., Grant, W., & Layton-Henry, Z. (2008b). Elite interviewing. In *Research Methods in Politics* (2nd ed., pp. 231–247). Basingstoke, UK: Palgrave.

Collier, D., Mahoney, J., & Seawright, J. (2004). Claiming too much: Warnings about selection bias. In H. Brady & D. Collier (Eds.), *Rethinking Social Inquiry: Diverse Tools, Shared Standards* (pp. 85–102). Lanham, MD: Rowman & Littlefield.

Council of Australian Governments (2002). *Natural Disasters in Australia: Reforming Mitigation, Relief and Recovery Arrangements*. Canberra: Commonwealth of Australia.

Council of Australian Governments (2011). *National Strategy for Disaster Resilience*. Canberra: Commonwealth of Australia.

Creswell, J. (2003). *Research Design: Qualitative, Quantitative and Mixed Methods Approaches* (2nd ed.). Thousand Oaks, CA: Sage.

Della Porta, D. (2008). Comparative analysis: Case oriented versus variable oriented research. In D. Della Porta & M. Keating (Eds.), *Approaches and Methodologies in the Social Sciences* (pp. 198–223). Cambridge: Cambridge University Press.

Deverell, E. (2010). *Crisis-induced Learning in Public Sector Organizations*. Stockholm: Elanders Sverige.

Dunleavy, P. (1995). Policy disasters: Explaining the UK's record. *Public Policy and Administration*, 10, 52–70.

Eisenhardt, K. M. (1989). Building theories from case study research. *Academy of Management Review*, 14(4), 532–550.

Eisenhardt, K. M., & Graebner, M. E. (2007). Theory building from cases: Opportunities and challenges. *Academy of Management Journal*, 50(1), 25–32.

Flyvberg, B. (2006). Five misunderstandings about case study research. *Qualitative Inquiry*, 12(2), 219–245.

Gerring, J. (2007). *Case Study Research: Principles and Practices*. New York: Cambridge University Press.

Haertel, C. E. J., & Latemore, G. M. (2011). Mud and tears: The human face of disaster – A case study of the Queensland floods, January 2011. *Journal of Management & Organization*, 17(6), 864–872.

Harrison, L. (2001). Conducting interviews in political research. In *Political Research: An Introduction* (pp. 89–104). London: Routledge.

Hopkin, J. (2010). The comparative method. In D. Marsh & G. Stoker (Eds.), *Theory and Methods in Political Science* (3rd ed., pp. 249–267). Basingstoke, UK: Palgrave.

Kweit, M. G., & Kweit, R. W. (2006). A tale of two disasters. *Publius – The Journal of Federalism*, 36(3), 375–392.

Meier, K. J., O'Toole, L. J., & Hicklin, A. (2010). I've seen fire and I've seen rain: Public management and performance after a natural disaster. *Administration & Society*, 41(8), 979–1003.

Millar, D., & Heath, L. (2004). *Responding to Crisis: A Rhetorical Approach to Crisis Communication*. Mahwah, NJ: Lawrence Erlbaum.

Moynihan, D. P. (2009). The network governance of crisis response: Case studies of incident command systems. *Journal of Public Administration Research and Theory*, 19(4), 895–915.

Munck, G. (2004). Tools for qualitative research. In H. Brady & D. Collier (Eds.), *Rethinking Social Inquiry; Diverse Tools, Shared Standards* (pp. 105–121). Lanham, MD: Rowman & Littlefield.

Nissen, S. (1998). The case of case studies: On the methodological discussion in comparative political science. *Quality & Quantity*, 32(4), 399–418.

Patton, M. (1990). *Qualitative Evaluation and Research Methods*. Thousand Oaks, CA : Sage.

Sturzenegger, L., & Hayes, T. (2011). Post Black Saturday: Development of a bushfire safety system. *Australian Journal of Emergency Management*, 26(2), 54–59.

Turner, B. (1976). The organisational and interorganisational development of disasters. *Administrative Science Quarterly*, 21(3), 378–397.

Vennesson, P. (2008). Case studies and process tracing: Theories and practices. In D. Della Porta & M. Keating (Eds.), *Approaches and Methodologies in the Social Sciences* (pp. 223–240). Cambridge: Cambridge University Press.

Whittaker, J., & Handmer, J. (2010). Community bushfire safety: A review of post-Black Saturday research. *Australian Journal of Emergency Management*, 25(4), 7–13.

Yannow, D. (2007). Qualitative-interpretive methods in policy research. In F. Fischer, G. Miller & M. Sidney (Eds.), *Handbook of Public Policy Analysis: Theory, Politics and Methods* (pp. 405–415). Boca Raton, FL: CRC Press.

Yin, R. (2009). *Case Study Research: Design and Methods* (4th ed.). Thousand Oaks, CA: Sage.

2 Crisis management and whole of government – comfortable bedfellows*

* Parts of this chapter have previously been published as Carayannopoulos, G. (2016), Whole of government: The solution to managing crises? *Australian Journal of Public Administration*. vol. 76, no. 2, pp. 251–265. doi:10.1111/1467-8500.12227

Overview

This chapter provides a review of the literature crucial to understanding the impact of key inputs into the success or failure of crisis management. The chapter commences by providing a brief review of engagement with whole of government within public sector discourse in order to frame discussions about this mode of working when applied to crisis situations. It posits the paradigm shift arising through moves towards whole of government working and considers the preconditions or characteristics which enable its implementation. To this end, the chapter presents an overview of six key thematic areas fundamental to understanding collaborative disaster management responses: crisis management, leadership, coordination, organisational culture, social capital and institutions. It considers what these distinct areas may tell us about the ability of the public sector to solve the numerous problems created by crises. Further, the chapter reflects on how changes in governing around vertical and horizontal forms of governance occur and considers whether normative or prescriptive views of management are possible during complex crisis events.

The objective of the literature review is to provide a basis to underpin the conceptual model brought to life in the later chapters through the case studies. The literature review through its focus on the key characteristics related to crises also helps explain why the outcomes of disaster events differ and what the implications are for future practice. Finally, the review of the literature allows for an explicit link to be made between whole of government approaches and crisis management. The link between the aforementioned remains highly relevant given that there are strong similarities around the core issues but relatively little has been done to link them in the international context.

Whole of government: The paradigm shift

There has been a significant amount of literature written regarding whole of government and its application in various countries and contexts, where it has been posited as a paradigm shift in public administration. Whole of government or joined-up government entails the creation of "mutually consistent objectives, mutually consistent means, and means which support objectives consistently" (6, Leat, Seltzer, & Stoker, 2002, p. 34). Hood (2005) further defines whole of government where the "aim is for the various units of government to present a single face to those they are dealing with and operate as a unit on problems that are interrelated" (Hood, 2005, p. 19). For the purpose of this book, the definition of whole of government from the 2004 Connecting Government report will be used:

> Whole of government denotes public service agencies working across portfolio boundaries to achieve a shared goal and an integrated government response to particular issues. Approaches can be formal and informal. They can focus on policy development, program management and service delivery.
>
> (Management Advisory Committee, 2004, p. 1)

The above definition allows for an examination of whole of government practices across specific issues, accounts for a variety of implementation mechanisms (formal and informal) and provides for all stages in the policy cycle from policy design to implementation. In the context of this book, whole of government refers to the interactions between the political, bureaucratic and operational agencies which provide preparation, response and recovery from disaster events at the state government level. The concept of whole of government is an important guiding framework given there is an increasing understanding in both crisis management and other complex policy domains that there has been fragmentation in the public sector. Whole of government has been posited as a counter doctrine to a silo mentality which has been described where "problems are defined, processed and handled on the basis of the intellectual and physical resources of the particular organisation that is handling it" (Page, 2005, p. 141). One of the most interesting frameworks provided regarding whole of government is by Ling (2002), who suggests a list of key characteristics for connected working, including: recognition of organisational change; merged structure and budgets; joint teams; shared budgets; joint customer–interface arrangements; shared objectives and policy indicators; consultation to enhance synergies and manage tradeoffs and sharing information to increase mutual awareness. The characteristics listed above represent a tangible set of criteria by which whole of government can be understood. This allows for an understanding of whether activities related to policy making and service delivery can be defined as joined-up.

Joined-up or connected government has become a very powerful discourse within the public sector and there has been a strong move for government agencies and departments to interact in a more horizontal way. It is important to note however that there are counter-doctrines that critique the feasibility of whole of government. A number of critiques have been presented regarding whole of government including that "separate units of bureaucracy should operate independently at least for some purposes, each with its own financial resources, information systems and command structures" (Hood, 2005, p. 36). It has also been argued that "dividing up government into discrete organisations or units is an effective way to provide for effective exercise of managerial capacity" (Hood, 2005, p. 36). Finally, political barriers such as 'turf wars' have been cited, where this refers to conflict as agencies maintain the desire to expand their own power within the bureaucracy. Turf wars are one of the most widely cited mechanisms "preventing departments or sections within them from working together" (Page, 2005, p. 141). The following section provides further background on the application of joined-up government in Australia, to help understand how this may impact on the disaster responses in the case studies.

Whole of government in Australia

Whilst whole of government or joined-up government remains a phenomenon in a number of countries such as the United Kingdom and New Zealand, the Australian view of whole of government retains its own uniqueness and characteristics. In the Australian context, whole of government policy development and delivery has been defined as "developing policy in a coordinated way, to manage its seamless delivery and to ensure that policy development is informed by the experience of those delivering it" (Shergold, 2005, p. 44). The development of whole of government approaches in Australia has been characterised by the nature of its federal system as well as by institutional elements – for example, task forces, committees and the alignment of government departments and agencies and informal approaches which rely upon the network of contacts and public servants in the Australian Public Service (APS) (Management Advisory Committee, 2004, p. 2).

The issue of addressing government coordination in Australia is not a new one, given the federal system and the division of responsibilities that exists between levels of government. Indeed, inter-organisational coordination was addressed as early as 1977, through the Royal Commission on Australian Government Administration. The 1977 review was followed by the Connecting Government Report three decades later which signalled a clear intent on behalf of the federal government to see better connection across government, noting that "although whole of government working is costly and time consuming, it can be suitable for complex and longstanding policy issues" (Australian Public Service Commission, 2007b, p. 18). Whole of government has been seen as particularly relevant to Australia where there "are no less than 955 Australian

Government bodies" and where the federal nature of the political system means that coordination is required at a number of levels (Shergold, 2005, p. 43).

The Connecting Government report also echoes a number of the key characteristics or pre-conditions established by Ling (2002) as being important to whole of government arrangements including: supportive structures and processes, a supportive culture and skills base, facilitative information management and infrastructure, appropriate budget and accountability frameworks (Australian Public Service Commission, 2007b, p. 19). Whole of government has itself been described as a paradigm shift or as a new way of working. The Australian Public Service Commission (2007a, p. 224) defines the difference between older ways of working and new whole of government approaches dichotomously where older forms are focussed on individual agency outcomes undertaken at single agency level, whereas new ways are focussed on whole of government outcomes managed across portfolios with an emphasis on collaborative working.

There is however an acute understanding that facilitating whole of government interaction is a complex activity that will take a considerable period of time to embed as part of the cultural practice of the public service. Whole of government can also be seen as a highly political process, with an acknowledgement of the importance of the political dimensions that occur in whole of government arrangements consistent with understanding the importance of process in politics (Aulich, Halligan, & Nutley, 2001; Hay, 2002). Whole of government arrangements necessitate a cultural shift where agency specific goals and objectives are superseded by whole of government considerations, requiring major cultural change within the Australian Public Service (Australian Public Service Commission, 2007a, p. 223). Whole of government is seen as means to unlock untapped potential within the public service that is greater than the sum of its individual parts. As such, it is interesting to understand what agency individual actors have within this system and the power relationships that exist in whole of government arrangements. This may include the centrality of coordinators who may need to drive or champion collaborative working. The political aspects of whole of government are particularly noted in the realm of crisis management. In a crisis there is a strong political dimension given the need to be seen to be effectively dealing with these events and where coordinated responses are seen as a solution.

Given the context that has been provided above, the following section provides an overview of six key thematic areas which provide explanatory power around the success or failure of crises: the nature of crisis management, leadership, coordination, organisational culture, social capital and the role of institutions. These thematic areas have been selected as they allow for a thorough examination of the whole of government construct across the political, bureaucratic and operational divides. The themes are entwined with debates in public management about the moves away from hierarchical government to more plural forms of working in the public sector. These themes have universal resonance in the management of crises at the global level as well as within the Australian context. The first theme, crisis management is included to reflect on the way that the specific context of a crisis provides a unique lens through which to understand the operation of whole of government. Considering crises as a unique public policy challenge allows us to understand the potential impact of whole of government. Secondly, leadership provides an important reference point to whole of government management of crises, given that during crises the public looks to its leaders to maintain security and safety. The third theme of coordination cuts across public policy debates around whole of government and command and control approaches to crisis management by positing whether hierarchy has been supplanted by networks. Inter-agency coordination is the common pillar between whole of government and crisis management and provides a unifying thread across the research. A major focus of this book is the way that the institutions of government work during a crisis. In reviewing how institutions work, the underpinning organisational culture provides a frame of reference to understand the motivation and values that exist within public sector organisations. The fifth theme social capital represents a multi-dimensional concept and provides insight into the nature of professional relationships within response agencies. Social capital also refers to the degree of disaster resilience that exists within communities prone to disaster events. The final theme, institutions, reaches directly to the heart of the whole of government challenge, given the centrality of institutions in modern political life. In the crisis realm, there are serious challenges to system integration where effective responses are not merely the sum of the individual parts but require a higher order of integration.

To provide an extra layer of analytic capability the abovementioned thematic areas are examined through a focus which seeks to understand what each may tell us about the ability to solve problems and create solutions, governance methods (vertical and horizontal) and ideal versus practical action. Each of the thematic areas is examined with a view to what they may be able to tell us about the kinds of problems faced by governments and the contribution they can make to resolving these. The themes also provide a contribution to debates around governance including vertical and horizontal forms of governance. The thematic areas reflect on normative approaches and the constraints and limitations on government action. The constraints and limitations on normative action are highly relevant in the field of crisis management, where there are strong views on what should be done that often neglect the difficulty of managing these situations. As such, reviewing the thematic areas against these three categories allows us to better understand what crises, leadership, coordination, organisational culture, social capital and institutions contribute to broader debates in public policy.

Crises in our states: The Victorian bushfires and Queensland floods

In the Australian context, whole of government has increasingly been used as a reference point for understanding the management of crises. Whole of government provides a potential solution to managing the complexity of effective inter-agency coordination during crises. The 2009 Victorian bushfires and 2011 Queensland floods represent the most significant natural disaster events in recent Australian history. The literature which has been written on these disaster events has to date been framed from an operational perspective. This book, however, provides a unique contribution in assessing the political and bureaucratic challenges of crisis management across the entire spectrum of government (political, bureaucratic and operational streams). In framing the case studies for the empirical work to follow, it is important to acknowledge that the cases exemplify a number of key debates including: the nature of community resilience, multi-agency collaboration in emergency management and the nature of 'success' or 'failure' in handling disaster events.

Developing community resilience in order to prepare and respond to natural disasters has become a significant commitment from all levels of government. The 2011 report from the Council of Australian Governments on Disaster Resilience highlighted the need for "a national, coordinated and cooperative effort to enhance Australia's capacity to withstand and recover from emergencies and disasters" (Council of Australian Governments, 2011, p. 4). The emphasis on inter-agency collaboration comes against a backdrop where there have been moves away from command and control towards horizontal approaches. Under horizontal approaches there is recognition that "decentralisation can have a number of practical benefits for crisis management policy" (Stark & Taylor, 2014, p. 300). Within the field of disaster resilience "shared responsibility" (McLennan & Handmer, 2014) has emerged as a pervasive idea to describe responsibility for disaster preparation and recovery between governments, the private sector and the community. Communities have been positioned as playing a powerful role in disaster resilience where there is "real community participation in crisis management" (Stark & Taylor, 2014, p. 301). If we look at the context underpinning the Victorian bushfires and Queensland floods, it is clear that the level of community engagement in the lead up to both events was problematic. In terms of Victoria and its susceptibility to fires, there does not appear to have been the degree of preparation required at community level in order to face fire threats. This came despite efforts from organisations like the Country Fire Authority (CFA) who delivered comprehensive programs that developed community preparedness for bushfire. There was acknowledgement that "programs were not delivered through a comprehensive systems approach but were targeted in an ad-hoc way to communities perceived as at risk" (Sturzenegger & Hayes, 2011, p. 57) leading to gaps in overall preparation. Lack of community engagement in disaster preparation was also noted in terms of the Queensland floods, particularly with regard to Brisbane where "the majority of Brisbane respondents were aware that their home was vulnerable to flood yet very few tried to protect their house with sandbags" (Bird, Box, Okada, Haynes, & King, 2013, p. 37).

A notable part of the development of enhanced community resilience in Australia is the use of communication where "communicating risk is vital so that communities can prepare to meet approaching natural hazards" (Boon, 2014, p. 17). In both the Victorian bushfires and Queensland floods communication of threats was complex and provided a major challenge to the emergency response agencies. The cases demonstrate that community needs vary and that "communities are inherently different and need targeted emergency communications, tailored to the disaster type and community composition" (Boon, 2014, p. 17). The reality of effective communication can be contrasted against the rhetoric of a linear process which involves "identifying the best, most suitable channel for emergency information for an intended audience is critical for emergency management planning, particularly in an age of evolving communication technologies" (Boon, 2014, p. 18). Social media has arisen as a means to connect communities through real time communication "in Australia, we saw the emergence of social media as an effective method of disseminating information during the 2011 floods in Queensland and Victoria" (Bird, Ling, & Haynes, 2012, p. 28). Social media is now seen as pivotal to the management of crises since its large scale uptake from 2008 onwards given that "it can be used to effectively and efficiently disseminate emergency information on: the occurrence of hazards; location of evacuation centres and road closures; fundraising opportunities; volunteering; and, reassure people about the safety of family and friends" (Bird et al., 2012, p. 32). In terms of the 2009 Victorian bushfires, social media represented an emergent yet still nascent technology. The breakdown of the telecommunications network that occurred also limited its potential to positively impact on community resilience. On the other hand by the time of the 2011 Queensland floods, the development of social media usage had increased and it was successfully used in mobilising volunteers. The mobilisation of volunteers occurred through the 'mud army' which "highlighted the important and rapidly emerging role of social media in emergency communications" (Posetti, 2012, p. 34).

A feature of enhancing community resilience and improving preparation and response to natural disasters is multi-agency and multi-sector collaboration. Prior to both the 2009 Victorian bushfires and 2011 Queensland floods, there was an increasing emphasis on the need to better connect agencies involved in natural disasters across different sectors – public, private and Non-Government Organisations (NGOs). In a state such as Victoria highly prone to bushfires which involves a number of government agencies as well as the forestry industry "there is a challenge for assessors undertaking land-use planning bushfire assessments, such as planners, ecologists, foresters and fire officers, to develop a deeper understanding of bridging multiple aspects of bushfire risks" (Owen, Scott, Adams, & Parsons, 2015, p. 15). The type of collaborative arrangement in minimising bushfire risk in Victoria is related to the concept of shared responsibility where it "applies not only to emergency management agencies, but requires action by different sectors including government, business, communities and individuals" (March & Rijal, 2015, p. 11).

Collaboration across the private and public sector in disaster responses has been seen as difficult where there are "significant challenges to establishing and maintaining effective public–private partnerships in this context [crises]" (Bajracharya & Hastings, 2015, p. 35). Difficulties in working across public and private sectors are predicated on "diverging interests and expectations of partners (e.g. duty of care versus profitability), problems of spanning organisational boundaries and scales, managing perceived roles and outcomes, negotiating information-sharing, establishing trust and certainty in service delivery" (Bajracharya & Hastings, 2015, p. 35). In Queensland, the issue of disaster preparation and competing tensions between the public and private sector can be exemplified through land planning and development in Brisbane. In the intervening period between the 1974 flood and 2011, Brisbane had undergone significant change and urban development which meant that there was increased susceptibility across a larger population base. In reviewing the response to the 2011 floods, a number of key factors have been identified as critical to recovery: "direct experience, outcome expectancy, communication and information, governance and physical protection, insurance, financial restraint and relief assistance, housing including design/ construction" (Bird et al., 2013, p. 43). In the case of Brisbane, it is also important to recognise the role of local government. Brisbane City Council is a large well-resourced council that spans the entire metropolitan area of Brisbane. In the wake of the crisis, the council was able to mobilise its significant resources in line with best practice where "local governments become effective emergency managers when they are able to recognise opportunity in risk; when they can envisage beyond the initial chaos of response and lay solid foundations for relief and recovery operations" (Saaroni, 2015, p. 58). The role of Brisbane City Council can be juxtaposed against the role of regional councils in other areas across Queensland during the floods and in the Victorian bushfires. The degree of response capacity and recovery potential which existed in many regional areas was highly variable and dependent on individual context rather than any overarching drivers of success or failure.

Whilst there has been analysis of the Victorian bushfires as a 'failed' crisis response and the Queensland floods as a 'successful' response, there is not a comprehensive analysis that critically examines these outcomes and understands the key drivers in these events. If we look at the events of Victoria in 2009, serious breakdowns and deficiencies of the emergency management were highlighted in the wake of the disaster. However, if we consider the role of shared responsibility and the degree to which institutions of state can influence individual behaviour there is a disjuncture. The degree to which individual behaviour about risk can be mediated is demonstrated here: "the disparity between intentions and actions is a major issue for fire and emergency services. Research demonstrates that what people intend to do and what they actually do during a bushfire can vary considerably" (Whittaker & Handmer, 2010, p. 12). In this way, it is relevant to consider the interaction between state institutions and individuals in understanding the perceived success or failure of a disaster response.

If we look at the Queensland floods, this event has generally been described as an example of a successful disaster response (Arklay, 2012). It has been noted that Queensland due to its tropical latitude and history of disaster events was well positioned to face threats such as flooding and cyclones. This view of a successful response can be juxtaposed against more critical views such as Stark and Taylor (2014) who point to the failure of Local Disaster Management Groups in some areas (e.g. Lockyer Valley and Somerset) characterised by "doing little to establish, review and improve its capabilities over time" (Stark & Taylor, 2014, p. 305). The critique of regional responses can be juxtaposed against the urban response in Brisbane and points to the need to assess the impact of these events on different parts of the community: "governments and policy makers need to make provision to alleviate the economic impacts of natural disasters on the disadvantaged" (Boon, 2013, p. 16).

The nature of major disaster events such as the Victorian bushfires and Queensland floods provide an opportunity to assess the nature of whole of government and interactions between government and the community: "the activation of the Community Development and Recovery Package in Queensland created a unique and unprecedented opportunity to evaluate perceptions of participants as to whether a community development approach, delivered by local government post-disaster, has been successful in helping communities recover" (Dean, 2015, p. 25). This research specifically contributes to the existing literature on the Victorian bushfires and Queensland floods by considering the key characteristics which drove to the perception of a 'failed' or 'successful' political response. The research also specifically addresses these events not as outliers but as events which epitomise the challenges of crisis management in Australia.

When the unexpected happens: Crises and disaster management

At a broad level, the events which occurred in Victoria in 2009 and Queensland 2011 can be seen to be typical of the complexities of managing crises. An analysis of crisis responses has indicated that over the past century there has been both an increase in the prevalence and impact of crises with trends suggesting that they will continue to increase in their severity (Lai, He, Tan, & Phua, 2009; United Nations – International Strategy for Disaster Reduction, 2010). The human, economic and developmental losses occasioned by these events have brought crisis management to the forefront of international attention. The literature on crisis management has been characterised by "a strong orientation towards technical, managerial and organizational studies which tend to be rational, positivistic and designed for the practitioners of crisis management" (Stark, 2010, p. 2). Much of the analysis surrounding crisis management has tended to focus on the "'hardware' (formal structures;

technical equipment; legal frameworks) ... which distracts attention from the often more salient and cost-effective, yet symbolically powerful 'software' factors (leadership, training, network building and organizational culture)" (Boin and 't Hart cited in McGowan, 2012, p. 7). In contrast, this book provides a review on the literature on crisis management that is framed with a more political orientation, given that the emphasis of the research is on the political-administrative challenges raised by crises.

As a starting point, it is important to note that the literature surrounding crisis management suggests that the identification of crises is highly contested and subject to the creation of meaning. As a result, the term crisis management is itself a contentious one with a variety of definitions surrounding its meaning. A common definition is where crisis management has been described as "mobilizing and directing resources in order to create a capacity to manage crisis when it occurs" (Odlund, 2010, p. 96). Other definitions have described crisis management as managing "the perceptions of an unpredictable event that threatens important expectancies of stakeholders and can seriously threaten an organization's performance" (Coombs, 2007, p. 3). The meaning making and narratives developed during the crisis period may actually be more significant to the perceived ending than the event itself. Crises also represent a unique situation where public expectation around action is heightened and there is vulnerability where the public must trust government as the major body responsible to act in their interests. This has been described as a situation where "public trust in government is intrinsically linked to the ability to hold decision makers accountable for the crucial decisions they make in crises" (Svedin, 2012, p. 1). The increasing number of crises also comes against a backdrop where in countries such as Australia there has been a decline in overall levels of trust towards government. The Organisation for Economic Co-operation and Development has identified increasing scepticism regarding the ability of governments to meet citizens' needs in line with trends in other economically developed countries (Organisation for Economic Co-operation and Development, 2015). An interesting juxtaposition is created based on higher expectations but lower trust by citizens, which impacts how and why some crisis responses are defined as a 'success' or a 'failure'. The conceptualisation of success and failure within the policy community has been well described by McConnell (2010) through the identification of: process, programs and politics as central to the 'success' or 'failure' of policy (McConnell, 2010, p. 350). In later work specifically oriented at understanding success or failure in crisis management, McConnell (2011) "disaggregates crisis management into three strands: processes, decisions and politics" (p. 64). These three categories are usefully applied to the discussion of policy making in disaster management, given the multi-dimensional nature of crises. The first dimension of process represents an approach to understand actions undertaken in the preparation and response to crises. A fundamental assumption which arises is that the impact of crises can be "prevented, prepared for, managed, recovered from and learned about,

through adherence to certain principles which should be embedded in institutional structures, rules and procedures, as well as the cognitive processes
of actors" (McConnell, 2011, p. 64). The second strand, decisions and in
particular the decision making that occurs at the political-strategic level
during a crisis is focal point of the book. This dimension indicates the
inherent tensions which exist in decision making under highly pressured
circumstances where information may be limited. Finally, the third category
politics demonstrates that the design and implementation of policy is not an
apolitical event but occurs within a political context (McConnell, 2010).
Politics is particularly relevant to the discussion of crisis management where
there is an intrinsic struggle between the nature of the event and the perception of how it has played out. Given the context established above, the
following section presents an analysis of the literature on crisis management
framed within a context of understanding problems and solutions, governance
methods and ideal versus practical modes of working.

Problems and solutions

Crises represent a significant problem in a practical and political sense with
the ability to frame a crisis a key political concern. Crises represent a complex
policy problem which often requires agencies to work outside norms. Crisis
management has often been seen as a unique area of public policy where the
public retains a high degree of expectation that governments will respond to
crisis in a timely and efficient manner. Under these situations, leaders are
required to manage emergency responses and situations without full operational knowledge (Boin, Stern, Sundelius, & 't Hart, 2007). Consequently,
they are placed under extreme pressure and scrutiny to make the correct
decisions in an environment where there is a "serious threat to the basic
structures or the fundamental values and norms of a social system which are
under time pressure and highly uncertain circumstances – which necessitates
making critical decisions" (Rosenthal, Charles, & 't Hart, 1989, p. 10).

Crises can be problematic in a political sense given that public pressure
for action and policy reform is heightened during these times and that a
failure to act can cause adverse political consequences (Seeger, Sellnow, &
Ulmer, 2003). This pressure is compounded by the "fragmentation of
authority that is inherent to crises and disasters" as "a crisis brings unique
problems that rarely fall neatly within the domain of one agency or leader"
(Boin, 2009, p. 373). In this way, governments are under pressure to justify
their responses to natural disasters, which represent a unique public policy
challenge. During crises the public retain strong expectations that government will plan for prevention, act swiftly and review the causes of crises for
the future avoidance. This has been described by Svedin (2009, p. 2) as part
of the "social contract" between government and society in that "governments and public agencies do their utmost to keep the public out of harm's
way" (Boin et al., 2007, p. 7).

It has been noted that if crises are not adequately handled by politicians they may face "'a media, citizen or stakeholder backlash" (Drennan & McConnell, 2007, p. 160) and that crises "provide an ultimate test for the resilience of political systems" (Boin et al., 2007, p. 2). As a result of these expectations from the public surrounding the management of disasters, ensuring a performance gap is not established or false expectations are not raised is critical (Coombs, 2007; Landy, 2008; Schneider, 1992, p. 135). Solutions and responses to crises that are well handled can provide an enormous political boost and solutions which utilise well-functioning coordination mechanisms can have significant benefit to future resilience. There are numerous examples of where public perception of a leader or government has been heightened as a result of the way in which they responded to a crisis; most notably Mayor Rudolph Giuliani received a significant boost in popularity during and immediately after the 9/11 attacks for his handling of the response in New York city. It can be argued that it is useful to view the response to a crisis in terms of a narrative, given that it has been argued, that "telling a story is a culturally typical response to crisis" (Millar & Heath, 2004, p. 168). Particularly in relation to leadership, the narrative which is created regarding the actions of leaders in a crisis situation can often represent "a turning point in an unstable situation" and define perceptions of an event and can be seen to represent a solution to a complex policy and perception problem (Nye, 2008, p. 102).

Governance methods (horizontal and vertical)

Arguments surrounding the benefits of horizontal and vertical modes of governance can be seen to be directly applicable to the realm of crisis management. Traditional models have focussed on top-down vertical structures, while increasingly there has been an acknowledgement that there needs to be more of an emphasis on horizontal approaches. This has been highlighted by recent disaster failures such as Hurricane Katrina and the Fukushima nuclear disaster, where agencies or organisations have acted in isolation as opposed to in a more coordinated or unified way. In many respects, the governance surrounding these cases has been one of the key exacerbating factors. In the case of Hurricane Katrina the relationship between the city, state and the Federal Emergency Management Agency (FEMA) is one of the key elements that was blamed for the failure of the response. The coordination and interaction between levels of government was noted as a key failure in the immediate response period, including the in ability to mobilise resources and meet basic necessities. The suggested failure was complicated by the multiple levels of government involved and the inability to successfully coordinate across these layers.

Traditional approaches to crisis management have been based on "top-down or command and control" (Helsloot, 2008, p. 173; Sabatier, 1986, p. 22) and "centralized decision making" (Rosenthal, 't Hart, & Kouzmin, 1993, p. 12) models which have reinforced the importance of hierarchy (Wise, 2006). However, given notable disaster and crisis management failures such as Hurricane Katrina (Comfort, 2007), a strong case and argument has been made for the failure of top-down responses to crises with the argument that traditional models are not created to respond appropriately to crisis situations (Boin & McConnell, 2007). Indeed, it has been suggested that traditional government agencies are simply not "designed nor prepared to deal with the dynamics and escalating effects of trans-boundary crises" (Kettl cited in Boin, 2009, p. 370). In this way "complex bureaucracies are not designed or ideally suited to deal with non-routine events" (Wilson cited in Boin, 2009, p. 370). This argument is premised on the notion that the use of hierarchy in crises is problematic given that "tasks cannot be programmed and the creative collaboration that they require cannot simply be commanded" (Wise, 2006, p. 311).

As a result of the above, horizontal arrangements involving cooperation amongst "horizontally organized actors" (Svedin, 2009, p. 1) have been positioned as providing a more adaptive approach to resolving the difficult task of coordination and collaboration required in multi-organizational and multi-sector responses to crises (Birkland, 2006; Boin & McConnell, 2007; Kapucu, Arslan, & Collins, 2010). The argument has been made that "there is a need for a new focus on shared responsibility ... to contribute to achieving integrated and coordinated disaster resilience" (Council of Australian Governments, 2011, p. 2). Hence, decision making in emergencies requires a non-traditional approach and tools characterized by non-hierarchical structure and flexibility (Kapucu, 2008). Further, it has been noted that "crisis response inevitably depends on collaborative processes to succeed" (Moynihan, 2009, p. 897). Views which suggest that lateral structures should be adopted in crises differ from those that argue that there should be a powerful assertion of centralised power in crisis management responses. Kweit and Kweit (2006) have suggested that "traditional inter-governmental responses should give way to a more dominant role for the national government" (Kweit & Kweit, 2006, p. 375). Arguments in favour of hierarchy however tend to be less prevalent in the literature, with a growing understanding that horizontal structures are preferable to hierarchy. Indeed, it has even been suggested that appropriate crisis response depends on inter-agency coordination despite the difficulties that occur through collaborative responses (Goode et al., 2011, p. 17).

Ideals and realities

In the realm of crisis management debates about the ideal vs. practical modes of working and responding are critical. In a crisis situation and through crisis planning, ideal types of response patterns are suggested, which can be difficult to put into effect once the crisis situation itself emerges. At the heart of the crisis management literature is the understanding that the identification of crises is "inherently contested" (Dunleavy, 1995, p. 53). Crises are based on the social construction of events as opposed to statements of fact, more "a creation of the language used to depict it, its creation is a political act, not a recognition of fact" (Brandstrom & Kuipers, 2003, p. 280). So, it is often difficult to objectively identify the nature of the crisis itself and to separate ideals regarding crisis management from the reality of what occurs. Crises cannot be seen as discrete events but rather as a process with a number of competing variables which shape and design crisis outcomes (Rosenthal, 2003, p. 132; Rosenthal, Boin, & Comfort, 2001) and where "symbols, emotions, language and expressions of power" are important to the dynamics of crises" (Brandstrom & Kuipers, 2003, p. 280). The understanding of crises and the narratives that have been ascribed to these events are a critical part of understanding the impact of crisis management. In essence this relates to the way in which the 'villains' and 'victims' of a crisis (Mitroff, 2001, p. 19) are established and who plays a critical role in determining the status of key actors.

This identification of blame is also a key point in understanding disaster responses. Traditionally natural disasters have represented a less threatening type of crises to governments given that they are "not caused by internal decisions or management oversight" (Seeger et al., 2003, p. 48). Natural dis-asters may be considered "acts of God" subject to less criticism than other types of manmade disasters (Comfort, 2002, p. 32). This may be a result of the perception that natural disasters are seen as beyond the sphere of control of organisations and are externally imposed as opposed to internally created. The view however of natural disasters being distinct from other forms of crises is slowly beginning to change, as the public recognise the wide array of decisions that can often lead to a crisis. Mitroff and Anagnos (2003) have noted that there has been an increasing understanding that although governments may not be responsible for natural disasters, they are key in creating the human factors which may either mitigate or perpetuate the crises (Mitroff and Anagnos cited in Seeger et al., 2003).

As a result, there is a disconnect which occurs between the rhetoric of joined-up or connected modes of working and the reality of a crisis situa-tion. Crisis situations have a strong political imperative and blame avoidance can be seen as crucial to the political survival of government of the day. In this way, a clear divide emerges between ideals and practicalities of managing these situations.

Leadership in the face of crises

The discussion of leadership is pivotal to how governments manage crises. Leaders are at the forefront of the public and political response that occurs in the wake of a crisis event. The challenge that occurs, however, is to define leadership characteristics that are effective in crisis situations. The difficulty in defining successful crisis leadership characteristics is consistent with the broader leadership literature. There are a wide range of views regarding what can be considered appropriate and effective leadership. Indeed, there are multiple theoretical approaches which suggest that leaders need to play a number of different roles and need to be able to select the right approach as a situation arises. In many ways, leaders can be seen to play the role of a symbolic figurehead, mentor, coach, motivator and chief keeper of the narrative that drives an organisation. Leaders are often tasked with leading groups or organisations which may have fragmented and inconsistent goals at the organisational level, given the tendency to disaggregate goals and performance metrics to the individual rather than collective level. As a result, one of the most significant challenges is creating an emphasis on collective rather than individual in an environment that increasingly prioritises the role of the individual leader (Kefford, 2013, p. 135). Given the importance of leadership in the modern political landscape, the following section presents an analysis of the literature on leadership framed within a context of understanding problems and solutions, governance methods and ideal versus practical modes of working.

Problems and solutions

Leadership has been identified as both a problem and solution and can be viewed both positively and negatively. Leadership is often cited as a key determinant for success, with positive leadership styles and behaviours being considered as important in successful outcomes. Conversely, leadership can also be seen to be problematic, as it is often used in scapegoating activities and dysfunctional leadership is often blamed for the failure of organisations. The trend of ascribing an important role to leadership can be seen to be increasingly relevant in modern political life. It is also highly relevant in regards to the response to crisis situations and emerging forms of emergency management. New models in emergency management are increasingly moving away from top-down hierarchical structures and towards network based approaches where "the complexity of the mobilization of emergency management networks has raised important questions about the management and leadership of these networks" (Robinson, Eller, Gall, & Gerber, 2013, p. 347).

Leadership can often be seen to be conceptualised as a problem where there is a breakdown or failure of an organisational system. There have been multiple cases in the previous decade where the failure of leadership has been seen to be a central element of a crisis, the Japanese tsunami and ensuing Fukushima nuclear disaster being one of the most cited international examples. In this instance whilst the tsunami was unfolding, the nuclear event at Fukushima was also occurring and there were serious questions raised about the ability of leadership to respond to both events. The Japanese government faced significant criticism for its inability to communicate the unfolding events at Fukushima and to provide an adequate response to what was an unprecedented disaster. At a domestic level, the ACT bushfires in January 2003 is a prominent example of where leadership failure has been named as a key element in the response to a crisis situation. In this large fire event, it was asserted that key leaders did not do enough to avoid the possible crisis. The burden of blame arising from the crisis was in many ways placed squarely with key individuals in the ACT government and public service.

It has also been noted in the leadership literature that there are some instances in which coercive leadership should be used in times where it is absolutely crucial, as a possible solution to difficult problems (Goleman, 2000, p. 82). That is to say, that in the face of a crisis moves towards more plural forms of working may need to be put aside in order to have a strong and swift resolution which emanates from the top down. Increasingly however, critiques of coercive leadership suggest that it does little to understand or promote a strong organisational growth beyond the leader (Goleman, 2000, p. 82). The move towards re-asserting the importance of hierarchical or top-down leadership runs in parallel to the understanding that network based approaches may be more adaptive. It has been suggested that more plural forms of leadership can provide better, less individual centric responses and address the issue of how team based networks form rapidly in crisis situations (Hossain & Kuti, 2008, p. 68).

Leadership can also be viewed positively as a means to solve problems and create value in the area of public policy development and implementation. As a result, the leadership literature also provides for a heightened understanding of where leadership may emanate from and what value can be created. A solution to the leadership dilemma has been put forward by Moore, who through his work provides for a heightened role for those in public management to value add in the public sector (Moore, 1995, p. 28). Moore's theory of public value adding suggests that apart from the value added by top leadership there is a responsibility for those at managerial levels of bureaucracy to contribute in the public policy sphere through their day to day activities. It is interesting to note that through his work Moore places the onus on the manager to create and implement public value.

An interesting counter-point to the value building approach provided by Moore lies in the body of leadership literature that sees the role of leader as facilitating change based on a more ground up approach. Heifetz and Laurie (1997) position the leader as instrumental in the creation of the change environment but firmly places the onus on followers to implement change, in essence "giving the work back to the people" (Heifetz & Laurie, 1997, p. 129). As such, there is a more network oriented approach to change and management, although one that still gives the leader a strong degree of control in terms of agenda setting. Given the above, it is evident that there are numerous competing leadership theories which can provide insights into leadership during a crisis.

Governance methods (horizontal and vertical)

With regard to leadership there are various schools which posit that leadership is 'best' undertaken in a hierarchical way or as a more diffuse structure where leadership is embedded through network forms as opposed to vertical structures. This is reflected in a continuum of leadership, which on one hand suggests that command and control leadership is necessary in order to manage a difficult situation such as a crisis. On the other hand are more de-centralised or horizontal approaches which suggest that diffusing power and authority within a network provides the most appropriate means to foster collaboration and coordination. Within this continuum are other approaches which suggest mixed or balanced models where de-centralised power and authority are moderated by a core executive who maintain control of the overall agenda (Bell & Park, 2006, p. 64).

In terms of viewing leadership through its relationship with governance methods, questions inevitably arise about the roles that leaders may have in relation to those who follow them or those who work within their leadership framework. Thrasher (1960) in his seminal work suggests that the exercise of leadership is the result of the interaction between leaders and followers and that leaders often embody the characteristics of the group, a challenge to traditional notions of top-down leadership. Debates surrounding vertical and horizontal forms of leadership are relevant to broader governance debates, which suggest that strong leadership may be a pre-condition for the successful use of networks in joined-up arrangements. The argument has been made that without the incentive to join-up activities, it can often be difficult for agencies to decide to work in a more collective way (Ling, 2002, p. 629). It has been noted that this is often a result of the emphasis on individual performance metrics that have arisen as a consequence of new public management (Kloot & Martin, 2007, p. 485). As such, it can be seen that leadership forms and types and the conceptualisation of leadership may be closely linked to governance methods and debates surrounding horizontality and verticality in public policy.

Ideals and realities

Idealised forms of leadership have gained significant prominence with the view that leaders should retain very specific characteristics and mannerisms, yet it is often the case that the reality of leadership and leading organisations is very difficult. There are deep questions which can be raised about idealised forms of leadership and how these actually play out, particularly in a time of crisis or stress. The point has been made that in contemplating that leaders can have authority without necessarily having role based or positional power, that there are certain characteristics or traits which are pivotal in leadership, most of which point to the individual level (Grint, 2005, p. 19). There are a variety of characteristics which may be important in leaders, particularly in a crisis situation. These may include the ability to transfer or pass on a narrative and ability to demonstrate empathy with a population who may be passing through difficult period. Two prominent examples in recent times include President Bush's decision not to visit New Orleans via an on the ground visit during Hurricane Katrina and Premier Anna Bligh's "We are Queenslanders" address during the Queensland floods in 2011. These two instances reflect the dichotomy that can exist between ideal and practical forms of leadership. On one hand in the example of President Bush, we have a practical decision being taken not to tour a disaster prone area. On the other hand in the case of Premier Bligh we in essence have a call to arms for Queenslanders to rally. It is interesting to note within the contexts of discussion of ideals and practicalities that the political impacts of these leadership acts may have been similar, although the general public appraisal was different. President Bush retained consistently low approval ratings throughout his terms in office, whereas the Bligh government was deemed to have very good public appraisal immediately after the floods. In the end, this was not important enough to affect voting and the government was ultimately defeated comprehensively in the next general election following on from the floods.

Coordination in the face of complexity

Coordination is a highly pervasive concept within public management which can refer to both a process and an outcome. As well as this, coordination can refer to a variety of approaches which attempt to integrate the activities of a group; this can mean that coordination can be upward, downward and horizontal as well as take on less tangible and rigid forms. Coordination can refer to activities that involve individuals, small groups, large groups, departments, states and nations. The term is generally used to describe a state where positive coordination occurs as a process, or that the outcomes of interactions are such that a coordinated outcome has been achieved. Coordination has been cited as part of broader processes that exist such as consultation, collaboration and other types of partnership arrangements that may occur within collaborative governance arrangements. The argument has been made that discussions regarding coordination need to consider moves towards a more collaborative governance characterised by "public policy decision making and management that engages people constructively across the boundaries of public agencies and levels of government" (Emerson, Nabatchi, & Balogh, 2011, p. 2). The following section presents an analysis of the literature on coordination framed within a context of understanding problems and solutions, governance methods and ideal versus practical modes of working.

Problems and solutions

Coordination has been seen as problematic in many ways given that it has a wide range of applications and that the process of reaching a coordinated outcome or coordinating at different levels has traditionally been viewed as difficult. On the other hand, coordination is often cited as being able to 'cure' concerns such as fragmentation which occur through isolated and silo forms of working in the public service. It is within this context that discussions regarding whole of government and more horizontal forms of working within the public sector have become more prominent. Suggestions have been made that as a result of changes which are occurring to the state and in governments, that working collaboratively across government provides the 'best' possible means by which to face complex policy formulation and service delivery issues requiring "multi-organisational and multi-sector interaction for successful solutions and implementation" (Kapucu et al., 2010, p. 223). Indeed, network models have been presented dichotomously to hierarchical modes to suggest that more horizontal coordination may be more effective (Moynihan, 2008, p. 205). In recent times, it has been suggested that the "unitary, rationalist, understanding of coordination has been challenged by a more pluri-centric understanding of coordination in public governance" (Pedersen, Sehested, & Sorensen, 2011, p. 375). These concepts whilst not new have received more attention in the last 20 years due to attempts to connect parts of government which have been argued to have become fragmented. Reforms in "joining-up government" prominently came to the fore in the Blair government in Britain (6 et al., 2002l, p. 19) and have been applied in a number of other countries such as Australia and New Zealand as a means of achieving better coordination.

Given the above, coordination initiated through whole of government approaches to policy and service delivery may serve as a counter to fragmentation in the public service and assist to "focus beyond agency specific outcomes and on the government's overall agenda" (Australian Public Service Commission, 2005, p. 1). It has been noted that whole of government initiatives can assist in the resolution of policy matters that "cannot be solved-or be easily solved by a single organization" (McGuire cited in O'Flynn, 2009, p. 113). They are based on the coordination of multiple actors and premised on the idea that "lateral structures can outperform hierarchy" (Considine, 1992, p. 309). Moves towards emphasising whole of government approaches have arisen because of the perceived problem of fragmentation that has occurred in the public sector through New Public Management (NPM) (Bouckaert, Peters, & Verhoest, 2010; Peters, 1998; Shergold, 2005). NPM has been suggested to represent a fundamental paradigm shift in policy design and service delivery based on notions which suggested that states needed to pursue neoliberal economic practices and to create a public service more interested and able to meet the needs of service users (Ling, 2002, p. 618). The argument has been made that under the NPM paradigm, government through hierarchy was superseded by notions of governance with the emergence of "a pattern of small politically controlled, policy focused core departments", with supervision responsibilities for organisations both within and external to government (Aulich et al., 2001, p. 15). Given NPM reforms, which have tended to prioritise individual performance measures, there have been few incentives for collaboration and coordination in the public sector. A strong argument has been made that through NPM a culture was created where each government department has been keen to improve its individual outcomes rather than outcomes for the public service as a whole (Ling, 2002, p. 618). Further, decision making in public agencies has been made through "closed decision processes" and with little collaboration (Ansell & Gash, 2008, p. 547). Hence, more lateral forms of coordination have been cited as a potential solution to the problem of fragmentation that has occurred in the public sector.

Governance methods (horizontal and vertical)

There are a range of debates surrounding how coordination best occurs. The suggestion has been made that coordination may occur when there is an overarching framework or direction from the top that retains importance in overseeing the coordination of actors. On the other hand, network approaches to coordination can occur through networks where coordination is embedded throughout a group in a more organic way. Debates surrounding how coordination may occur or be achieved can be seen to be firmly located within concepts surrounding the role of government in policy formulation and service delivery, in particular the governance methods in place. As such, understanding the governance models in place becomes central to understanding how "all or many parts of government should interconnect, complement each other and pool related information" as part of a coordination process (Hood, 2005, p. 19).

It has been argued that moves towards understanding and improving coordination are "far from new" (6 et al., 2002, p. 9) and follow a cyclical pattern where the "slogan of joined-up government provides a convenient label for an old doctrine in the study of public administration" (Bogdanor, 2005, p. 2). As such, it can be seen that the assertion of the importance of coordination can also be linked to changes in governance and more broadly related to the move from hierarchy towards more pluralised or network modes of working. Hood has suggested that whole of government represents a counter to departmentalism "the tunnel vision, mutual export of problems and preoccupation with ... vertical silos" (Hood, 2005, p. 22; Mulgan, 2005). In these silos "policy problems are defined, processed and handled on the basis of the intellectual and physical resources of the particular organization handling it" as opposed to a more collective response (Page, 2005, p. 141). Traditional views of policy making suggest that the state has retained a primacy in setting policy directions and through the implementation of service delivery. These notions have however been strongly challenged through reforms and moves towards governance in the Anglophile countries. It has been noted that in countries such as Australia, governance scenarios have been created. Under these governance scenarios governments must negotiate with a variety of interest groups and power is seen as more dispersed throughout government and in governance networks. As such, there is a movement away from an analysis at "individual parts of a system to the system as a whole: as a network of elements that interact and combine to produce systematic behavior that cannot be broken down merely into the actions of its constituent parts" (Cairney, 2012, p. 346).

The moves noted above represent a shift away from hierarchical government where the central state retains the key role in setting policy directions to a more pluralised arrangement. Indeed, in recent times, arguments have been made that the state is in decline, challenged by globalisation and governance (Marinetto, 2006, p. 4). Moves towards more horizontal and network forms of governance mean that the state and governments are at risk of becoming "swallowed up by global forces" (Marinetto, 2006, p. 120) and "obsolete" (Hay, Lister, & Marsh, 2006, p. 14). Arguments regarding horizontal modes of governance have been extended further to indicate that coordination may take shape in a more plural form where "coordination is about striking the right balance between fixation and flexibility, between control and autonomy, between unity and diversity and between simplicity and complexity" (Pedersen, et al., 2011, p. 388). There have of course also been powerful arguments used to negate the suggested decline of the state, which argue that the state still retains a position of primacy in network arrangements and that the central core executive is still "more highly resourced in terms of authority, finance and control of domestic institutions" (Marinetto, 2006, p. 63). The influence of path dependency has also been noted meaning that "institutions become deeply embedded" and unable to stray from a dependent course (Tavan, 2012, p. 549). Therefore, understanding coordination through the lens of debates surrounding governance can be seen to be an important analytic tool with respect to the management of crises.

Ideals and realities

Frameworks surrounding collaboration and coordination suggest that coordination is an ideal process and outcome that organisations should strive to achieve. In reality, obtaining and achieving coordinated practice requires significant effort and can be complex to implement. Coordination is generally seen as highly sought after, however with inherent difficulties in having different individuals or groups work together. Critiques have suggested that "despite considerable collaborative activity there is little evidence that clearly links collaboration to improvements in service-user outcomes" (Dickinson & Sullivan, 2013, p. 161). One of the main barriers cited has been that individuals or groups may tend to prioritise their own goals over collective goals and that certain pre-conditions may need to exist in order to promote collective action. On the other hand and more idealistically there is a notion that some situations such as crises drive a coordinated approach as people band together for a common good or cause. However, there are critiques of this type of rhetoric which suggest that changes in behaviour are unlikely and may be temporary at best and politically driven.

It has been noted that whole of government approaches and initiatives that seek to promote effective coordination represent a remedy to the perceived fragmentation that has occurred in the public sector. The rhetoric surrounding whole of government approaches argues that effective coordination can assist to address "wicked problems" (Rittel & Webber, 1973). The suggestion has been made that it represents a powerful means by which to improve policy outcomes and promote "horizontally and vertically coordinated thinking and action" (Pollitt, 2003, p. 35). Traditional views regarding coordination note that "coordination is the outcome of processes within coherent institutionally or functionally demarcated units" (Pedersen et al., 2011, p. 375). A linear view of coordination is increasingly being challenged by views which suggest that coordination can be seen as the "outcome of a messy pluri-centric process that involves a plurality of endogenously constructive interpretive logics of action that are linked through loosely coupled interactive arenas" (Pedersen, et al., 2011, p. 376). It is evident that there is a strong disjuncture between ideal modes of working and the realities of coordinating across government.

There remain strong institutional drivers for coordination; it has been noted that agencies are often brought together through formal means such as task forces to focus on policy development and service delivery improving "effectiveness, efficiency and quality" (O'Flynn, 2009, p. 112). Coordination can be seen to be a process as opposed to an outcome consistent with the notion that moves towards whole of government approaches are part of the third generation of NPM reforms where "system integration" is critical to the mode of governance (Halligan, 2007, p. 217). In the crisis management context, cases of perceived whole of government success such as the response to the Indian Ocean Tsunami have been used to suggest that whole of government approaches develop a sense of shared responsibility and accountability that each department belongs to the broader public service (Shergold, 2005). The discussion above tends to indicate that there may be different and competing views surrounding the rhetoric of coordination in connecting government and the reality of achieving coordinated actions and outcomes across government.

Understanding internal cooperation: Organisational culture

Organisational culture refers to the nature and behaviour of an organisation and how this manifests itself. Organisational culture has often been cited as the root cause of failure where an organisation underperforms or suffers a crisis or as a cause of success where successful outcomes are achieved. It is suggested that organisational culture can be more than the sum of its parts and that organisational culture where negative can become difficult to shift and moderate change. Organisational culture has been described in the following way:

> the pattern of basic assumptions that a given group has invented, dis-
> covered, or developed in learning to cope with its problems of external

adaptation and internal integration, and that have worked well enough to be considered valid, and, therefore, to be taught to new members.

(Schein cited in Hatch, 1993, p. 658)

Broadly, studies of organisational culture recognise that "although organizations are themselves embedded within a wider cultural context, the emphasis of researchers here is on socio-cultural qualities that develop within organizations" and the patterns and types of interactions that occur (Smircich, 1983, p. 344). As a result, the literature on organisational culture has been seen as pivotal to understanding the functioning of organisations and the ways in which organisations can optimise their performance. This is particularly the case in the public sector, where over the past 20 years there have been a number of significant changes through moves away from hierarchy towards markets and networks. Moves towards different forms of governing have had a significant impact on the culture of the public service, both at the individual agency level as well as at the general over-arching level. The following section provides an analysis of the literature on organisational culture framed within a context of understanding problems and solutions, governance methods and ideal versus practical modes of working.

Problems and solutions

Organisational culture can be framed in a positive and negative way as both a problem and a solution to the functioning of agencies in the public sector. More and more it has been noted that there are significant challenges to the creation and maintenance of a positive organisational culture. Organisational culture or the construction of a store of goodwill within an organisation can be seen to be problematic, given that the drivers of behaviour are increasingly seen as individual rather than collective. This is particularly the case in the public sector, where moves towards NPM have increasingly focussed on individual outcomes and metrics as opposed to collective outcomes. Consequently, it may be that there has been a climate which has emphasised metrics over the ability to achieve coordination and joint outcomes. Key to the literature on organisational culture is the concept of change and the assumption that the culture of an organisation is malleable and subject to change. This proposition itself has been subject to debate given that "the barriers might be substantial, and some would doubt the feasibility of changing an organization's culture" (Jennings, 2012, p. S94). It has often been noted that to impact or influence broad change it may be necessary to look at the individual level where "the failure of planned organizational change may be due to many factors, few are so critical as employees' attitudes towards the change event" (Jones, Jimmieson, & Griffiths, 2005, p. 362). This is particularly seen in the realm of responding to crises and attempts to instigate joined-up modes of working. Indeed, recent reviews and inquiries into major disasters such as the ACT bushfires have suggested that organisations may not have been adept at adapting to change and cultural changes are required in order to better prepare organisations to respond to crisis situations.

On the other hand, organisational culture can also be seen to be the driver of change and as a solution to problems which may arise, given that organisational culture has been seen as a possible remedy to build organisational performance. It has been suggested that: "organizational culture is widely considered to be one of the most significant factors in bringing about organizational change and modernizing public administration and service delivery" (Jung et al., 2009, p. 1087). In this way, it can be seen that a more positive, less pessimistic approach to organisational culture exists which posits that the culture of an organisation is more malleable and can be positively changed. An interesting example is the suggested paradigm shift that has occurred towards connected government. The APS has highlighted that the move towards more connected ways of working represents a shift in the culture of the public service. In the new era of collaborative working there is an emphasis on having high level leadership support for changes in culture and practices. This is consistent with literature which suggests that "decade's worth of leadership studies have examined the relationship between leadership styles of top management teams and organizational performance" (Wilderom, van den Berg, & Wiersma, 2012, p. 836). More specifically there is a strong link between the role of senior leadership and support for change and the ability for positive changes to organisational culture to be implemented through collaborative processes (Ansell & Gash, 2008, p. 554). The section below considers how organisational culture may be influenced by governance methods and modes of working and the role that vertical and horizontal approaches may have in shaping organisational culture.

Governance methods (horizontal and vertical)

In looking at the way that organisational culture can impact upon an organisation, the governance model in place can be seen as fundamental. The argument can be made that more vertical forms of governance would tend to prioritise the role of the core executive in setting the agenda for the culture of an organisation. More horizontal or network based approaches would tend to suggest that organisational culture may be a more organic quality that arises through the interactions of members of a group, rather than being set or pre-defined from the top-down.

In terms of a more vertical conceptualisation of organisational culture, it can be understood as being able to be set from the top-down in order to effect change throughout an organisation. In regards to whole of government working, the argument has been made that strong leadership is required to create a culture where collective outcomes and means of working are prioritised over individual goals. The role of leaders and in particular the senior leadership is seen as pivotal, given that they have the ability to set the tone for the organisation. In many instances leaders also have control over the resources required in order to shape the culture of an organisation. It can be seen that the leadership of an organisation may have a significant capacity by which to shape and influence the culture of an organisation.

Conversely it can be argued that the building of organisational culture is more about the way in which this organically arises as opposed to being set from the top-down. Organic approaches are more consistent with horizontal views of governance which suggest that the culture of an organisation may be less about what is implemented from the top-down and more about the characteristics that organically emerge through the organisation. Changes in organisational culture may be the result of interactions between groups and individuals that occur outside the formal line management or hierarchical structures. As such, the agency or departmental culture which includes "norms, beliefs, and routine patterns of action that guide the behaviour of organizational members" (Jennings, 2012, p. S93) can be seen as emergent from the group itself rather than set in a more prescriptive way. This provides an interesting way in which to view the building of culture in the public service, given that the development of these norms can be traced to the development of interactions across the organisation rather than being prescriptively set from the top echelons of the organisation.

There is also a suggestion that perhaps looking at organisational culture through a vertical/horizontal dichotomy may negate or fail to acknowledge the interaction between the support for a culture set from the top and validated across a group. Conversely, an organic culture may be generated from within a group and then validated by the senior leadership who may have the ability to adequately resource such arrangements. As a result, the development of organisational culture is in itself an activity which requires coordination and can be seen to typify debates surrounding governance.

Ideals and realities

Finally, organisational culture is itself subject to conceptualisation in both idealised and practical forms, that is to say it is important to understand where the disjuncture may be between the rhetoric and reality surrounding the ways in which organisations function. In many respects, the changing or aligning of organisational culture has been recommended as part of a solution to improving organisational functioning. The reality may be however that given the pressures faced by organisations, an in-depth review or analysis of culture may not be high on a list of priorities given other key items which may be seen as more pressing on the agenda.

In an ideal sense, organisational culture has been described as "the shared meanings, shared understandings and shared sense making that result from the process of reality construction that allows people to see and understand particular events and processes in distinctive ways" (Martin cited in Kloot & Martin, 2007, p. 487). Culture is created as an overarching characteristic of an organisation that pervades through different levels and drives the interactions of its members. Organisational culture can also be seen to be the product of organisational memory and learning that occurs through an organisation. In many instances the learning of the past can be implemented in order to change or shift the organisational culture; however it must be noted that this may occur with varying degrees of success. This can often be based on the people to people links and the human capital in place in an organisation. Given this, it can often change or shift quickly when these people or human capital links change or disappear completely.

The conceptualisation of a unitary organisational culture which pervades across an organisation can be seen to be problematic given that sub-culture may play a critical role in the formation of an overall culture (Denison, 1996, p. 628). Increasingly it also needs to be acknowledged that individual rather than collective goals may drive activities and implementing a positive organisational culture may also fail to acknowledge the importance of politics. Motivation around action is particularly important in the discussion of whole of government management of crises. In these situations there is a strong political dimension involved, where an organisation may or may not have a motive to contribute to the growth of a positive culture. Given this, there is often a disjuncture that may emerge between the idealised forms of a positive organisational culture and the complexity of ensuring that such a model is established and maintained.

The ties that bind us: Social capital

Social capital is a concept which has emerged to describe the bonds which are built at different levels of relationships (individual or groups). Social capital refers to the store of goodwill which is created through interactions and which can be harnessed at different points of time. The development of social capital has been identified as pivotal, as the people to people links which exist are often the key mediating factor to outcomes which arise for organisations and society in general. The concept of social capital is broadly based on the notion that involvement and participation in groups "can have positive consequences for individuals and the community" (Portes, 1998, p. 2). In broad terms, it has been defined as "the social networks and the norms of reciprocity associated with these networks" (Putnam & Goss, 2002, p. 3). Social capital can be seen to be a challenge to rationalist theories such as rational choice, as it extols the importance of non-monetary social ties and links. As a result, the linkages which are formed are the main resource that is obtained through social capital. In recent times, the understanding of social capital has been extended from "an individual asset to a feature of communities and even nations" (Portes, 1998, p. 1). Social capital has also been used to consider patterns of relationships within and across organisations. At the organisational level, organisational social capital has been described as being "realized through members' levels of collective goal orientation and shared trust, which create value by facilitating successful collective action" (Leana & Van Buren, 1999, p. 538). In terms of its usage in this book, social capital will be used to describe professional relationships that existed within and across response agencies as well as to describe community disaster resilience. The following section provides an analysis of the literature on social capital framed within a context of understanding problems and solutions, governance methods and ideal versus practical modes of working.

Problems and solutions

Social capital has been seen as being important to the individual to individual links that occur in organisations. Building a strong sense of the collective and social capital has been argued to be pivotal to reaching positive outcomes. Social capital provides a powerful counter argument to rational choice theories. Rational choice theory is based on a positivist approach which suggests that the natural sciences provide a model to which the social sciences can follow based on empirical testing of hypothesis (Hay, 2002). Under rational choice actors will follow their own self-interest and paradoxically there is an incentive not to participate in collective action that will secure mutual benefits across actors (Hay, 2002). As a result, political behaviour is rendered predictable in a given context and there is a strong degree of predictability regarding how actors will behave (Hay, 2004). Critiques of rational choice have noted that actors can be motivated by other factors such as emotions or higher order moral or ethical concerns (Elster, 2000, p. 692). In more general terms, rational choice has also been critiqued as not allowing for the impact of human agency and the ability for individuals to act outside the frame of reference provided by rational choice (Hay, 2004, p. 40).

Social capital and the links built between individuals have been cited as central to the development of organisations and organisational culture. Increasingly though there is an understanding that there may be limitations to the way in which this can be applied and changes which are taking place more generally at the societal level which may impact. In recent times, arguments have been made around a problematic decline in the level of social capital in the community. The decline in the level of social capital has been posited as a result of the lack of engagement in community groups and public participation as part of a broader trend in civic disengagement. Whilst social capital is generally presented as a positive feature, it can also be seen to potentially have negative consequences. The argument has been made that the creation of strong social capital amongst particular individuals or groups may lead to exclusionary practices, the formation of strong bonds in a group may impede strong functioning if behaviours are not adaptive and finally the formation of a group may create a conformity which does not allow for dissent (Portes, 1998, p. 17).

Governance methods (horizontal and vertical)

Discussions regarding social capital can also be viewed within a framework that reflects upon governance models and the means by which horizontal or vertical approaches may impact upon the culture of an organisation and people to people links. Vertical approaches to social capital building suggest that it is through the use of incentives and targets set from above that people to people links are created. This however would be more consistent with a rational choice perspective which suggests actors will only act in line with their own goals and objectives. On the other hand more horizontal approaches to building social capital suggest that capital building needs to be more embedded through an organisation. In this way, the creation of people to people links and relationships can be more in line with the stated objectives of social capital and more consistent with a philosophy which indicates that these links emerge organically and in a more altruistic way.

The argument has been made that moves towards horizontal policy making arrangements in a range of policy areas mean that government departments are now more connected and able to form stronger bonds that can be harnessed in times of crises. Inter-organisational relationships which emerge through crisis response networks mean these arrangements are more than the sum of their parts but rather that these networks possess a macro-culture (Hillyard, 2000). It has also been noted that relationships formed in a time of crisis can represent a positive which can then also be used in other policy relationships. During a time of crisis a collective social capital may be created that leads to a sense of camaraderie through and extending beyond the crisis period that may be appropriately harnessed in other policy domains. In Australia a number of examples of this have been cited, most notably in Queensland where a series of disaster events Cyclone Larry, Cyclone Yasi and the Queensland floods led to the development of strong links between the key actors engaged in responding to crises. It is also clear that social capital plays a central role in community resilience towards preparation and response to natural disasters.

Ideals and realities

Social capital plays an important role with respect to community resilience and preparation and recovery from disaster situations. Social capital can be seen to be an idealised form of building relationships and links between individuals and organisations based on the notion that involvement and participation in groups "can have positive consequences for individuals and the community" (Portes, 1998, p. 2). The linkages which are formed are the resource that is obtained through social capital. The argument has been made that through social capital the individual interests of actors may be deferred in favour of collective goals based on the existence of social capital (Leana & Van Buren, 1999).

The practicalities of creating strong social capital remain complex. Part of the difficulty surrounding the implementation of social capital can be seen to be based on the key concept of "associability." Associability has been defined as "the willingness and ability of participants in an organization to subordinate individual goals to collective goals and actions" (Leana & Van Buren, 1999, p. 541). An important point here is that an organisation and its members must not only agree to the collective goals, but also be responsible for collective actions which bring these goals towards implementation. The argument has been made that for there to be successful collective implementation, actors in a network must maintain a resilient trust where "trust can survive the occasional transaction in which benefits and costs are not in equilibrium". This can be contrasted to fragile or transactional trust which is likely to dissolve where there is not equilibrium between costs and benefits (Leana & Van Buren, 1999, p. 543). It is evident that there are often significant hurdles or barriers in trying to implement a framework which prioritises individual over collective goals. This also represents a challenge to the notion that social capital leads to a sense of camaraderie given that levels of trust and reciprocity need to be high which is often difficult in highly politicised environments.

The institutional framework: Institutions in action

Institutions have been cited as a key mediating factor in the public service and the way in which policy development and service delivery occurs. At the government level, bureaucratic coordination is reliant upon the existence of institutions with their own norms and protocols in order to carry out the everyday business of government. The way institutions are created, validated and interact provides an insight into bureaucracies and how they function at the basic level. This is acutely evident in the realm of crisis management, where timeframes for action are short and the response to events relies on leveraging existing government frameworks. When considering the management of crises, there are a number of key institutions: cabinet, emergency management authorities, special purpose committees, disaster authorities, state government departments and local government that are positioned centrally to respond to these events.

At the heart of disaster management lies a fundamental tension in understanding whether it is the strength of institutional arrangements or individuals which lead to successful responses. In contrast to arguments that highlight the importance of institutional arrangements in responding to crises are approaches which cite individual agency in shaping action. Arguments in support of individual agency suggest that individual action may be more than pre-determined by the practices, norms and values of the institutions in which they are embedded. As a result of these different viewpoints on the role of institutions, there are a series of interesting debates which are created that can be directly applied to understanding the implementation of whole of government during crises. The following section provides an analysis of the literature on institutions framed within a context of understanding problems and solutions, governance methods and ideal versus practical modes of working.

Problems and solutions

Debates surrounding structure and agency can be understood with regard to institutions and individual actors. In a discussion of the relationship between whole of government and crisis management, institutions of government with their norms, values and practices play a central role in the management of large scale events. During natural disasters, institutions can be seen to be important to the core tasks of crisis management such as framing, sense making and the acute response to crises. Given the importance of institutions in political life, there a number of questions which arise in understanding their role in crisis management. If we examine the literature, institutionalism has been seen as a means to explain political life and can be seen to provide explanations for problems and solutions across the bureaucratic and political spheres. Accounts that prioritise institutions "draw their power and distinctiveness largely from an explicit rejection of traditional adaptation theories, and from an emphasis on institutional rather than technical environments" (Kraatz & Zajac, 1996, p. 812). Institutionalism does itself follow a continuum where historical institutionalism has been based on "an older tradition in political science that assigned importance to formal political institutions but developed a more expansive conception, regarding which institutions matter and of how they matter" (Hall & Taylor, 1996, p. 937). Indeed, it has been noted that "most of the major actors in modern economic and political systems are formal organisations and the institutions of law and bureaucracy play a dominant role in contemporary life" (March & Olsen, 1984, p. 734). During crises there is a sense that institutions represent a bedrock and reference point in unstable times. If, and when these institutions fail to adequately respond to crises, they are placed under strong scrutiny with demands for remediation.

Further along the continuum of discussions re institutionalism, there is recognition that there has been a move from the old institutionalism characterised by "issues of influence, coalitions, and where competing values were central, along with power and informal structures" to the new institutionalism characterised by "its emphasis on legitimacy, the embeddedness of organizational fields, and the centrality of classification, routines, scripts, and schema" (DiMaggio and Powell cited in Greenwood & Hinings, 1996, p. 1023). It has been noted that new institutionalism is concerned with "the difficulties of ascertaining what human actors want when the preferences expressed in politics are so radically affected by the institutional contexts in which these preferences are voiced" (Immergut, 1998, p. 25). The move towards new institutionalism does not however detract from the traditional institutionalist narrative which posits that "institutions matter more than any other factor in explaining political decisions" (McConnell, 2013, p. 15).

Within the framework of new institutionalism, there are a number of different approaches that have been suggested, each of which provides a different explanation of the institutionalist approach. Three broad versions of new institutionalism have been presented: rational choice institutionalism, historical institutionalism and sociological institutionalism (Keating, 2008, p. 104). Rational choice institutionalism posits that institutions provide the relevant incentives, and disincentives that shape the rational responses of actors. Historical institutionalism addresses the role of institutions through path dependence and the difficulties in moving into new directions. Sociological institutionalism is based on the impact of the institutions on individuals lives with respect to values and socialisation (Keating, 2008, p. 104). Hence, a key level of analysis is the effect of institutions and their interactions with individuals which addresses core issues surrounding structure and agency.

There is also recognition that new institutionalism may indeed be broader including other forms such as; normative, empirical, network, constructivist and feminist models (McConnell, 2013, p. 17). In many respects, the normative stream provides interesting insights into the relationships between individuals and institutions given that it "focuses on the norms and values of institutions and the ways in which they shape individual behavior and decision making" (McConnell, 2013, p. 17). With regard to how organisations function during a crisis there is a heightened awareness that institutions have their own values, norms and practices. Consequently it can be seen that crisis management systems are more than the sum of their individual parts. This is highly relevant when considering whole of government approaches to crises where system integration between relevant institutions is more important than the functioning of individual components. The new institutionalism framework can also be seen to provide an intermediary point to accounts that provide for the agency of individuals as it seeks to understand the impact of institutional norms on individual behaviours. Accounts of individual agency on the other hand tend to prioritise the role of the individual and the agency of individuals in which to shape responses through factors such as leadership (Kefford, 2013). These individual behaviours are central to the management of crises at the operational and political levels. In the operational response agencies, senior emergency management officials are often charged with decision making that may fall outside accepted operating procedures given the instability of crisis scenarios. At the political level, senior figures need to make decisions without full operational knowledge and often have to act decisively at times against the formal advice which is provided to them.

Governance methods (horizontal and vertical)

The interactions between institutions can also be viewed through the lens of governance methods. It may be suggested that the institutions of government have a vertical control over individuals and that the agency of individuals is constrained by the verticality of institutions. On the other hand, it is possible that there is a nexus around how individuals and organisations integrate at the horizontal level which follows a less hierarchical model that accounts for factors outside institutions such as ties, links and social networks. Therefore, these two approaches suggest different means by which public policy problems can be faced and how solutions can be found particularly when confronting the complexities which emerge through a crisis.

Institutional accounts are in contrast to narratives that emphasise individual agency. Given moves towards more horizontal relationships in the public sector there has been a diffusion of authority and power in comparison to hierarchical approaches (Kapucu et al., 2010). Hierarchical government and command and control have increasingly been replaced by networks with much more diffuse power structures. Hence key questions emerge surrounding the way in which power and politics are distributed in crises and the structures that are used to manage relationships. This can include how actors coordinate, the communication mechanisms used, including commitments to work collaboratively and how structures mediate the relationships in place.

If we reflect back on the key phases of the crisis management cycle, steps such as sense making and meaning making can be seen to be highly contingent on individual cognition; that is, generating an understanding from an on the ground experience of events. If a strictly institutionalist account was to be taken to explain the management of crises, it would be argued that the behaviour and interactions between actors would be constrained by the institutional context, which asserts the importance of institutions in shaping individual action. Conversely more horizontal approaches would tend to suggest that there may be interplay between individuals and institutions. Indeed, through a new institutionalism framework the informal conventions and relationships which occur through the interactions of individuals can be seen to be critical to the overall functioning of the organisation. In this sense there is strong interplay between key concepts in institutionalism and governance and an understanding that there is a role for individual agency. Individual agency is particularly relevant in a crisis situation where actors are often asked to work outside established norms. This also occurs against a backdrop where there is a unifying crisis culture distinct from regular operations.

Ideals and realities

At the institutional and individual levels there exists a range of ideals which merit consideration. Given the discussion on governance methods noted above, the main challenge remains to understand how institutions meet their objectives and the process they use to do so including the roles that individuals play. Reflecting on the nature of ideals allows us to assess the practicalities of the relationship between institutions and individuals.

The structure and agency debates occasioned by looking at institutions suggest that these may be mutually exclusive. It may be the case however that there is a more flexible continuum between the two and that individuals may exercise agency within institutional settings. New institutionalism emphasises the role of institutions in mediating political behaviour and the impact of path dependency on mediating behaviour (Hay, 2002, p. 11). New institutionalism asserts a stronger role for political institutions and presents a critique to criticisms of institutional analysis which have argued for the "downgrading of the role of the state as an independent cause" (Rhodes, 1995, p. 53). Traditional institutional accounts have suggested that institutions represent a key variable in understanding politics and administration through structures, rules, norms and traditions (Greenwood & Hinings, 1996, p. 1023; March & Olsen, 1984, p. 735). New institutionalism is broadly encompassing, however there is still a strong recognition that the state has a role in affecting the conduct of society. It also allows for the importance of more informal elements, including the relationships which form between individual actors. If this account is validated as an ideal position, questions arise surrounding how this may be implemented in what are increasingly more plural approaches to governance. This is strongly applicable to the realm of crisis management, where professional relationships are a fundamental characteristic of the emergency management system. In conclusion, debates surrounding institutions can be understood through a framework of understanding how these may be mapped at an ideal and a practical level. These debates can be seen to be highly relevant to the field of crisis management and whole of government. Crisis management systems are strongly shaped by the interactions between institutions, component organisations and individual actors where the sum of these is different from the individual parts. As a result there is a strong need not to view institutionalism and agency as dichotomous but rather to understand a more nuanced interaction between these dimensions in crisis management.

Conclusion

The literature review presented in this chapter has sought to frame a number of key areas relevant to understanding how whole of government arrangements are perceived to support the responses to crisis situations. To this end, an overview of key concepts surrounding: crisis management, leadership, coordination, organisational culture, social capital and institutions has been framed through understanding what each of these bodies of literature may tell us about problems and solutions, governance models and the ideal versus practical modes of working. From the review of the thematic areas, there are a number of key messages emanating that provide focus for further empirical investigation through the cases including:

- The uniqueness of managing crises and the challenges faced by those responsible for responding to crises, with the understanding that crisis events are subject to contestation.
- The complexity of leadership and its importance in a crisis as well as views regarding what represents appropriate leadership.
- The importance of understanding how coordination occurs and the challenges to coordination that exist in the public sector and the way that these have been shaped by public management doctrines.
- Understanding the drivers for building organisational culture and coop-eration in an inter-agency context, albeit with divergent views on how these influence organisations and individuals.
- The impact of the store of social capital which exists within the emergency response community and recognition of how this can be positively leveraged.
- The impact of conceptualising action at the institutional level and the constraints that may exist for both institutions and individuals.

Subsequent chapters seek to provide reflections on the thematic areas through the use of case studies to better understand how they impacted on each event. It is important to note that aside from the thematic areas covered in the review of the literature, there are deeper questions which arise regarding trust towards government and between organisations and how these mediate interactions. Crises represent a unique set of circumstances to assess whole of government and understand whether these events alter patterns of individual and agency behaviour.

References

6, P., Leat, D., Seltzer, K., & Stoker, G. (2002). *Towards Holistic Governance*. Hound-mills, Hampshire, UK: Palgrave.

Ansell, C., & Gash, A. (2008). Collaborative governance in theory and practice. *Journal of Public Administration Research and Theory*, 18(4), 543–571.

Arklay, T. (2012). Queensland's State Disaster Management Group: An all agency response to an unprecedented natural disaster. *Australian Journal of Emergency Management*, 27(3), 9–19.

Aulich, C., Halligan, J., & Nutley, S. (2001). *The Australian Handbook of Public Sector Management*. Sydney: Allen & Unwin.

Australian Public Service Commission (2005). *State of the Service Report 2004–2005*. Canberra: Commonwealth of Australia.

Australian Public Service Commission (2007a). *State of the Service Report 2006–2007*. Canberra: Commonwealth of Australia.

Australian Public Service Commission (2007b). *Tackling Wicked Problems: A Public Policy Perspective*. Canberra: Commonwealth of Australia.

Bajracharya, B., & Hastings, P. (2015). Public–private partnerships in emergency and disaster management: Examples from the Queensland floods 2010–2011. *Australian Journal of Emergency Management*, 30(4), 30–36.

Bell, S., & Park, A. (2006). The problematic metagovernance of networks: Water reform in NSW. *Journal of Public Policy,* 26(1), 63–83.

Bird, D., Box, P., Okada, T., Haynes, K., & King, D. (2013). Response, recovery and adaptation in flood-affected communities in Queensland and Victoria. *Australian Journal of Emergency Management,* 28(4), 36–43.

Bird, D., Ling, M., & Haynes, K. (2012). Flooding Facebook – the use of social media during the Queensland and Victorian floods. *Australian Journal of Emergency Management,* 27(1), 27–33.

Birkland, T. A. (2006). *Lessons of Disaster: Policy Change After Catastrophic Events.* Washington, DC: Georgetown University Press.

Bogdanor, V. (2005). Introduction. In V. Bogdanor (Ed.), *Joined-Up Government.* Oxford: Oxford University Press.

Boin, A. (2009). The new world of crises and crisis management: Implications for policymaking and research. *Review of Policy Research,* 26(4), 367–377.

Boin, A., & McConnell, A. (2007). Preparing for critical infrastructure breakdowns: The limits of crisis management and the need for resilience. *Journal of Contingencies and Crisis Management,* 15(1), 50–59.

Boin, A., Stern, E., Sundelius, B., & 't Hart, P. (2007). *Politics of Crisis Management: Public Leadership under Pressure.* Cambridge: Cambridge University Press.

Boon, H. (2013). Preparedness and vulnerability: An issue of equity in Australian disaster situations. *Australian Journal of Emergency Management,* 28(3), 12–16.

Boon, H. (2014). Investigation rural community communication for flood and bushfire preparedness. *Australian Journal of Emergency Management,* 29(4), 17–25.

Bouckaert, G., Peters, B., & Verhoest, K. (2010). *The Coordination of Public Sector Organisations: Shifting Patterns of Public Sector Organisations.* Houndmills, Hampshire, UK: Palgrave McMillan.

Brandstrom, A., & Kuipers, S. (2003). From normal incidents to political crises: Understanding the selective Politicization of policy failures. *Government and Opposition,* 38(3), 279–305.

Cairney, P. (2012). Complexity Theory in political science. *Political Studies Review,* 10, 346–358.

Comfort, L. K. (2002). Managing intergovernmental responses to terrorism and other extreme events. *Publius-the Journal of Federalism,* 32(4), 29–49.

Comfort, L. K. (2007). Crisis management in hindsight: Cognition, communication, coordination, and control. *Public Administration Review,* 67, 189–197.

Considine, M. (1992). Alternatives to hierarchy – the role and performance of lateral structures inside bureaucracy. *Australian Journal of Public Administration,* 51(3), 309–320.

Coombs, T. (2007). *Ongoing Crisis Communication: Planning, Managing and Responding.* Thousand Oaks, CA: Sage Publications.

Council of Australian Governments (2011). *National Strategy for Disaster Resilience.* Canberra: Commonwealth of Australia.

Dean, S. (2015). Resilience in the face of disaster: Evaluation of a community development and engagement initiative in Queensland. *Australian Journal of Emergency Management,* 30(3), 25–30.

Denison, D. R. (1996). What is the difference between organizational culture and organizational climate? A native's point of view on a decade of paradigm wars. *The Academy of Management Review,* 21(3), 619–654.

Dickinson, H., & Sullivan, H. (2013). Towards a general theory of collaborative performance: The importance of efficacy and agency. *Public Administration,* 92(1), 161–177.

Drennan, L., & McConnell, A. (2007). *Risk and Crisis Management in the Public Sector*. London: Routledge.

Dunleavy, P. (1995). Policy Disasters: Explaining the UK's record. *Public Policy and Administration*, 10(2), 52–70.

Elster, J. (2000). Rational choice history: A case of excessive ambition. *American Political Science Review*, 94(3), 685–695.

Emerson, K., Nabatchi, T., & Balogh, S. (2011). An integrative framework for collaborative governance. *Journal of Public Administration Research and Theory*, 22(1), 1–29.

Goleman, D. (2000). Leadership that gets results. *Harvard Business Review*, 78(2), 78–90.

Goode, N., Spencer, C., Archer, F., McArdle, D., Salmon, P., & McClure, R. (2011). *Review of Recent Australian Disaster Inquiries*. Melbourne: Monash University.

Greenwood, R., & Hinings, C. R. (1996). Understanding radical organizational change: Bringing together the old and the new institutionalism. *Academy of Management Review*, 21(4), 1022–1054.

Grint, K. (2005). *Leadership: Limits and Possibilities*. Houndmills, Hampshire, UK: Palgrave Macmillan.

Hall, P. A., & Taylor, R. C. R. (1996). Political science and the three new institutionalisms. *Political Studies*, 44(5), 936–957.

Halligan, J. (2007). Reintegrating government in third generation reforms of Australia and New Zealand. *Public Policy and Administration*, 22(2), 217–238.

Hatch, M. J. (1993). The dynamics of organizational culture. *The Academy of Management Review*, 18(4), 657–693.

Hay, C. (2002). *Political Analysis: A Critical Introduction*. Basingstoke, UK: Palgrave Macmillan.

Hay, C. (2004). Theory, stylized heuristic or self-fulfilling prophecy? The status of rational choice theory in public administration. *Public Administration*, 82(1), 39–62.

Hay, C., Lister, M., & Marsh, D. (Eds.). (2006). *The State: Theories and Issues*. Basingstoke, UK: Palgrave Macmillan.

Heifetz, R. A., & Laurie, D. L. (1997). The work of leadership. *Harvard Business Review*, 75(1), 124–135.

Helsloot, I. (2008). Coordination is a prerequisite for good collaboration isn't it? *Journal of Contingencies and Crisis Management*, 16(4), 173–176.

Hillyard, M. (2000). *Public Crisis Management*. Lincoln, NE: Writers Club Press.

Hood, C. (2005). The idea of joined-up government: A historical perspective. In V. Bogdanor (Ed.), *Joined-Up Government* (pp. 19–42). Oxford: Oxford University Press.

Hossain, L., & Kuti, M. (2008). CordNet: Toward a distributed Behaviour model for emergency response coordination. *Project Management Journal*, 39(4), 68–94.

Immergut, E. M. (1998). The theoretical core of the new institutionalism. *Politics & Society*, 26(1), 5–34.

Jennings, E. T. (2012). Organizational culture and effects of performance measurement. *Public Administration Review*, 72(s1), S93–S94.

Jones, R. A., Jimmieson, N. L., & Griffiths, A. (2005). The impact of organizational culture and reshaping capabilities on change implementation success: The mediating role of readiness for change. *Journal of Management Studies*, 42(2), 361–386.

Jung, T., Scott, T., Davies, H. T. O., Bower, P., Whalley, D., McNally, R., & Mannion, R. (2009). Instruments for exploring organizational culture: A review of the literature. *Public Administration Review*, 69(6), 1087–1096.

Kapucu, N. (2008). Collaborative emergency management: Better community organising, better public preparedness and response. *Disasters*, 32(2), 239–262.

Kapucu, N., Arslan, T., & Collins, M. L. (2010). Examining intergovernmental and interorganizational response to catastrophic disasters: Toward a network-centred approach. *Administration & Society*, 42(2), 222–247.

Keating, M. (2008). Culture in social science. In D. Della Porta & M. Keating (Eds.), *Approaches and Methodologies in the Social Sciences* (pp. 99–117). Cambridge: Cambridge University Press.

Kefford, G. (2013). The presidentialisation of Australian politics? Kevin Rudd's eadership of the Australian Labor Party. *Australian Journal of Political Science*, 48(2), 135–146.

Kloot, L., & Martin, J. (2007). Public sector change, organisational culture and financial information: A study of local government. *Australian Journal of Public Administration*, 66(4), 485–497.

Kraatz, M. S., & Zajac, E. J. (1996). Exploring the limits of the new institutionalism: The causes and consequences of illegitimate organizational change. *American Sociological Review*, 61(5), 812–836.

Kweit, M. G., & Kweit, R. W. (2006). A tale of two disasters. *Publius – The Journal of Federalism*, 36(3), 375–392.

Lai, A. Y., He, J. A., Tan, T. B., & Phua, K. H. (2009). A proposed ASEAN disaster response, training and logistic centre enhancing regional governance in disaster management. *Transition Studies Review*, 16(2), 299–315.

Landy, M. (2008). Mega-disasters and federalism. *Public Administration Review*, 68, S186–S198.

Leana, C. R., & Van Buren, H. J. (1999). Organizational social capital and employment practices. *Academy of Management Review*, 24(3), 538–555.

Ling, T. (2002). Delivering joined-up government in the UK: Dimensions, issues and problems. *Public Administration*, 80(4), 615–642.

Management Advisory Committee (2004). *Connecting Government: Whole of Government Responses to Australia's Priority Challenges Summary of Findings*. Canberra: Commonwealth of Australia.

March, A., & Rijal, Y. (2015). Interdisciplinary action in urban planning and building for bushfire: The Victorian case. *Australian Journal of Emergency Management*, 30(4), 11–16.

March, J. G., & Olsen, J. P. (1984). The new institutionalism – organizational-factors in political life. *American Political Science Review*, 78(3), 734–749.

Marinetto, M. (2006). *Social Theory, the State and Modern Society: The State in Contemporary Social Thought*. Maidenhead, Berkshire, UK: Open University Press.

McConnell, A. (2010). Policy success, policy failure and grey areas in-between. *Journal of Public Policy*, 30(3), 345–362.

McConnell, A. (2011). Success? Failure? Something in-between? A framework for evaluating crisis management. *Policy and Society*, 30(2), 63–76.

McConnell, A. (2013). Institutionalism. In R. Smith, A. Vromen, & I. Cook (Eds.), *Contemporary Politics in Australia: Theories, Practices and Issues* (pp. 14–24). Cambridge: Cambridge University Press.

McGowan, J. (2012). A missed opportunity to promote community resilience? The Queensland floods commission of inquiry. *The Australian Journal of Public Administration*, 71(3), 1–9.

McLennan, B., & Handmer, J. (2014). *Sharing Responsibility in Australian Disaster Management: Final Report for the Sharing Responsibility Project*. Melbourne: Bushfire Cooperative Research Centre.

Millar, D., & Heath, L. (2004). *Responding to Crisis: A Rhetorical Approach to Crisis Communication*. Mahwah, NJ: Lawrence Erlbaum.

Mitroff, I. (2001). *Managing Crises Before They Happen*. New York: American Management Association Press.

Moore, M. (1995). *Creating Public Value: Strategic Management in Government*. Cambridge, MA: Harvard University Press.

Moynihan, D. P. (2008). Combining structural forms in the search for policy tools: Incident command systems in US crisis management. *Governance-an International Journal of Policy Administration and Institutions*, 21(2), 205–229.

Moynihan, D. P. (2009). The network governance of crisis response: Case studies of incident command systems. *Journal of Public Administration Research and Theory*, 19(4), 895–915.

Mulgan, G. (2005). Joined-up government: Past, present and future. In V. Bogdanor (Ed.), *Joined-Up Government*. Oxford: Oxford University Press.

Nye, J. (2008). *The Powers to Lead*. New York: Oxford University Press.

O'Flynn, J. (2009). The cult of collaboration in public policy. *The Australian Journal of Public Administration*, 68(1), 112–116.

Odlund, A. (2010). Pulling the same way? A multi-perspectivist study of crisis cooperation in government. *Journal of Contingencies and Crisis Management*, 18(2), 96–107.

Organisation for Economic Co-operation and Development (2015). Trust in government. Retrieved 15 July 2015, from http://www.oecd.org/gov/trust-in-government.htm

Owen, C., Scott, C., Adams, R., & Parsons, D. (2015). Leadership in crisis: Developing beyond command and control. *Australian Journal of Emergency Management*, 30(3), 15–19.

Page, E. (2005). Joined-up government and the Civil Service. In V. Bogdanor (Ed.), *Joined-Up Government* (pp. 139–156). Oxford: Oxford University Press.

Pedersen, A. R., Sehested, K., & Sorensen, E. (2011). Emerging theoretical understanding of pluricentric coordination in public governance. *American Review of Public Administration*, 41(4), 375–394.

Peters, B. (1998). Managing horizontal government: The politics of coordination. *Public Administration*, 76(Summer), 295–311.

Pollitt, C. (2003). Joined-up government: A survey. *Political Studies Review*, 1(1), 34–49.

Portes, A. (1998). Social capital: Its origins and applications in modern sociology. *Annual Review of Sociology*, 24, 1–24.

Posetti, J. (2012). The Twitterisation of ABC's emergency and disaster communication. *Australian Journal of Emergency Management*, 27(1), 34–39.

Putnam, R., & Goss, K. (2002). Introduction. In *Democracies in Flux: The Evolution of Social Capital in Contemporary Society*. New York: Oxford University Press.

Rhodes, R. (1995). The institutional approach. In D. Marsh & G. Stoker (Eds.), *Theory and Methods in Political Science*. Basingstoke, UK: Macmillan.

Rittel, H., & Webber, M. (1973). Dilemmas in a general theory of planning. *Policy Sciences*, 4(2), 155–169.

Robinson, S., Eller, W., Gall, M., & Gerber, B. (2013). The core and periphery of emergency management networks. *Public Management Review*, 15(3), 344–362.

Rosenthal, Charles M., & 't Hart, P. (1989). *Coping with Crises: The Management of Disasters, Riots and Terrorism*. Springfield, IL: CC Thomas.

Rosenthal, U. (2003). September 11: Public administration and the study of crises and crisis management. *Administration & Society*, 35(2), 129–143.

Rosenthal, U., 't Hart, P., & Kouzmin, A. (1993). Crisis decision making – The Centralisation Thesis revisited. *Administration & Society*, 25(1), 12–45.

Rosenthal, U., Boin, A., & Comfort, L. (2001). *Managing Crises, Threats, Dilemmas, Opportunities*. Springfield, IL: Charles Thomas Publishing.

Saaroni, L. (2015). Managing spontaneous volunteers in emergencies: A local government perspective. *Australian Journal of Emergency Management*, 30(3), 56–59.

Sabatier, P. (1986). Top-down and bottom up approaches to implementation research: A critical analysis and suggested synthesis. *Journal of Public Policy*, 6(1), 21–48.

Schneider, S. K. (1992). Governmental response to disasters – the conflict between bureaucratic procedures and emergent norms. *Public Administration Review*, 52(2), 135–145.

Seeger, M., Sellnow, T., & Ulmer, R. (2003). *Communication and Organisational Crisis*. Westport, CT: Greenwood Publishers.

Shergold, P. (2005). Coping with crisis personal reflections on what the public service learned from the tsunami disaster. *Public Administration Today*, October–December, 43–48.

Smircich, L. (1983). Concepts of culture and organizational analysis. *Administrative Science Quarterly*, 28(3), 339–358.

Stark, A. (2010). Legislatures, legitimacy and crises: The relationship between representation and crisis management. *Journal of Contingencies and Crisis Management*, 18(1), 2–13.

Stark, A., & Taylor, M. (2014). Citizen participation, community resilience and crisis management policy. *Australian Journal of Political Science*, 49(2), 300–315.

Sturzenegger, L., & Hayes, T. (2011). Post Black Saturday: Development of a bushfire safety system. *Australian Journal of Emergency Management*, 26(2), 54–59.

Svedin, L. (2009). *Organisational Cooperation in Crises*. Surrey: Ashgate Publishing.

Svedin, L. (2012). *Accountability in Crises and Public Trust in Governing Institutions*. New York: Routledge.

Tavan, G. (2012). No going back? Australian multiculturalism as a path-dependant process. *Australian Journal of Political Science*, 47(4), 547–561.

Thrasher, F. (1960). *The Gang* (2nd ed.). Chicago, IL: University of Chicago Press.

United Nations – International Strategy for Disaster Reduction (2010). Disaster Occurrence. Retrieved 1 August 2010, from http://www.unisdr.org/disaster-statistics/occurrence-trends-century.htm

Whittaker, J., & Handmer, J. (2010). Community bushfire safety: A review of post-Black Saturday research. *Australian Journal of Emergency Management*, 25(4), 7–13.

Wilderom, C. P. M., van den Berg, P. T., & Wiersma, U. J. (2012). A longitudinal study of the effects of charismatic leadership and organizational culture on objective and perceived corporate performance. *The Leadership Quarterly*, 23(5), 835–848.

Wise, C. R. (2006). Organizing for homeland security after Katrina: Is adaptive management what's missing? *Public Administration Review*, 66(3), 302–318.

3   Black Saturday – a state in ashes

Overview

An important part of the earlier chapters of this book has been the identification of key themes regarding the intersection of whole of government working and crisis management. The identification of these themes has occurred with a view to understanding how the literature may be drawn together to better understand the challenges of whole of government implementation. This chapter and the chapter to follow on the Queensland floods provide case studies whereby the conceptual model can be brought to life and reviewed in real world scenarios. The case studies are intended to operationalise the key themes as two instances of whole of government responses to natural disasters. Through the examination of the cases, it is possible to better understand the bi-directional relationship between these natural disasters and crisis management principles.

In order to contextualise the case study, this chapter presents an overview of the disaster management arrangements which were in place at the time of the 2009 bushfires in Victoria. The chapter provides insights into the way that whole of government functioned through the use of both primary and secondary sources including interviews across the political, bureaucratic and operational levels. The analysis occurs by examining the key themes of the book: crisis management, leadership, coordination, organisational culture, social capital and institutions through the lens of problems and solutions, verticality and horizontality and ideals vs. practical forms of working. The insights generated from this chapter will then be used as part of a comparative analysis with the 2011 Queensland floods to understand the implications of the case studies relative to broader principles surrounding crisis management.

The Australian disaster management system in 2009: Understanding integration and fragmentation through the impact of federalism

Since federation in 1901, Australia's system of government has been marked by a delineation of responsibilities between the Commonwealth and the states across the six states and two territories. The Australian Constitution outlines the responsibilities of the federal government and stipulates that the federal government has responsibility for the following areas: defence and foreign affairs; trade, commerce and currency; immigration; postal services, telecommunications and broadcasting; air travel; most social services and pensions. On the other hand, states have primary responsibility for schools; hospitals; conservation and environment; roads, railways and public transport; public works; agriculture and fishing; industrial relations; community services; sport and recreation; consumer affairs, police, prisons and emergency services as well as other areas not listed in the constitution (Parliament of NSW, 2014). The separation of powers and responsibilities was originally created to articulate the areas which would be handled at the federal level and the matters which would be handled by the states in the newly created Commonwealth. The separation of powers also accounted for historical legacy issues prior to federation where each of the states had developed their own bureaucracies and systems of government based on their history, size and scale.

The experience of federalism in Australia does have its difficulties, challenges and constraints particularly with regard to the delineation of roles and responsibilities between the Commonwealth and the states through the negotiation of funding flows. Indeed, funding flows have been described as "the Achilles heel of Australian federalism" which makes "the Commonwealth the predominant tax collector and the states dependent on handouts to fund their tasks" (Kasper, 2007, p. 35). Issues of the financial inequality between states were particularly highlighted in the period around 2009 where "the GFC has highlighted structural problems with the financial dimensions of Australian federalism both in terms of the equalisation regime currently under review as well as the inefficient and in some cases inadequate nature of State taxation" (Eccleston, Warren, & Woolley, 2013, p. 27). Traditionally the main financial flows between the Commonwealth and state governments have been through Special Purpose Payments that are tied funding grants related to specific purposes, the distribution of Goods and Services Tax (GST) revenue and National Partnership Payments.

There have often been complex and difficult financial negotiations between the Commonwealth and the states, although it has been argued that Australian states are less confrontational than others in federal systems (Lecours & Beland, 2013, p. 109). Difficulties in the current funding model are largely based on GST revenue. In particular Western Australia has been an outspoken critic. The level of dissent is highlighted by a recent example around funding arrangements. The then West Australian Premier Colin Barnett controversially linked GST revenue to previous support of disasters: "when Victoria had those tragic fires a few years back, Western Australia was the first state and the most generous state to provide financial assistance" (Barnett cited in ABC 7:30, 2015). Barnett was suggesting that Western Australia should receive its fair allocation of GST revenue given it had supported other states in disasters. He further extended with regard to the Queensland floods: "when Queensland was in trouble, Western Australia was the first state to provide assistance during the Queensland floods" (Barnett cited in ABC 7:30, 2015). These exchanges indicate that national responses to crises are often influenced by broader funding arrangements and relationships between the Commonwealth and states.

In terms of disaster management arrangements, federalism has also had a profound impact on the way disaster management responses in Australia are structured at the legislative, financial, institutional and political levels. State governments retain a high degree of autonomy in the way they manage disasters, given that they maintain control of legislation and are responsible for disaster responses. States do however have the ability to call upon resources from the Commonwealth level and from other states should capacity be exhausted. The following section considers the influence of legislative, financial and political frameworks in responding to crises.

With regard to the legislation which underpins the interaction of the Commonwealth and states on disaster management matters, this has traditionally been based on administrative arrangements. The reliance on administrative arrangements is a result of the fact that no direct legislation exists as an overarching structure. Rather disaster management procedures are covered through the national emergency response arrangements. The Australian Government Disaster Response Plan (COMDISPLAN) is the main guiding document that existed at the time of both the Victorian bushfires 2009 and Queensland floods 2011. COMDISPLAN allows for the provision of "Australian Government physical assistance to the Australian states in an emergency or disaster" (Attorney General's Department: Emergency Management Australia, 2008, p. iv). The arrangements in place through COMDISPLAN mean that there is a clear delineation between the role of the Commonwealth and the role of the states with regard to preparation for and response to disasters. Disaster management arrangements in place in 2009 and 2011 at the Commonwealth level are indicated in Figure 3.1 below.

The detail provided below illustrates that broadly the Commonwealth provides a planning framework through Emergency Management Australia (EMA) and support for preparation and planning prior to a disaster. In the wake of a disaster, the Commonwealth can provide support where local capacity is overwhelmed in the response period through the defence force and other national mechanisms. These support mechanisms would usually be requested where the relevant state or territory could not reasonably cope with the needs of the crisis situation and where capacity may be exhausted (Attorney General's Department: Emergency Management Australia, 2008, p. 10). As such, at the Commonwealth level, EMA plays a role in coordinating inter-state assistance in times of disaster and through advocating emergency management training and education (Emergency Management Australia, 2004, p. 9).

Given the lack of a national coordinating body in the direct response to crises, state governments have significant autonomy in the way in which they

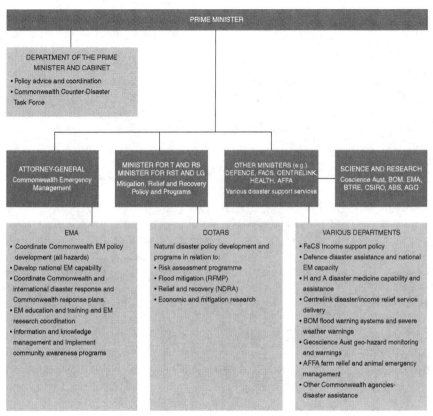

Figure 3.1 Commonwealth disaster management arrangements
Source: Council of Australian Governments, 2002, p. 110

manage disasters through their own state level legislation and administrative procedures. States also maintain autonomy in setting the strategic and operational arrangements that exist in regards to disaster management. States such as Victoria and Queensland have developed significantly different arrangements around disaster planning, response and recovery. At the intersection of the Commonwealth and the states with regard to disaster management, there are however some overarching concepts which influence the nature of disaster management including: recovery funding arrangements, use of national resources such as the defence force and the Council of Australian Governments. It is noted (although not within the scope of this book) that the analysis of whole of government across the tiers of government would itself be an interesting point to understand how disaster management systems can be operationalised across the different tiers of government, keeping in mind the delineation of responsibilities set out in the federal system.

One of the key elements at the financial intersection between the Commonwealth and states in dealing with disasters are the Natural Disaster Relief and Recovery Arrangements (NDRRA). The NDRRA mechanisms are fundamental as they indicate the degree to which the broad and large scale recovery arrangements are to be funded by the Commonwealth, given that under the federal system the Commonwealth retains control of revenue through taxation. In the Victorian bushfires, the nature and scale of recovery required meant that this was beyond the capacity of the state to address through its budget cycle but rather needed federal input. The NDRRA represents a tangible way in which the Commonwealth was required to provide support and assistance for the large scale reconstruction required. Ultimately however it was the states through their reconstruction authorities that undertook this response and provided acquittals back to the Commonwealth.

In considering institutional arrangements that support disaster management policy, COAG has played a key role in outlining the key sets of principles related to the management of disasters in Australia. COAG has attempted to try and bring about a more coherent approach to disaster management planning. The report "Natural Disasters in Australia" commissioned in 2002 by COAG had as its stated objective, the production of a new national framework to disaster mitigation and response. At its heart and "central to the new approach is a systematic and widespread national process of disaster risk assessment and most importantly a fundamental shift in focus towards cost-effective evidence based disaster mitigation" (Council of Australian Governments, 2002, p. 6). The report re-iterated that the arrangements for disaster response were based on primary responsibility for natural disaster preparedness and response lying with the states and that Commonwealth support or assistance follows when state or territory resources are insufficient (Council of Australian Governments, 2002, p. x). Through the course of the COAG report, it was also noted that there was a need for an increasingly whole of government approach to disaster mitigation where all levels of government need to ensure disaster mitigation strategies are in place (Council of Australian Governments, 2002, p. 11). Whole of government approaches were suggested given the recognition that Australia "lacks any machinery at a national level for Commonwealth, state and territory ministers to oversee emergency management and natural disaster matters" (Council of Australian Governments, 2002, p. 54).

The arrangements between the Commonwealth and states around disaster management are also underpinned by an all hazards approach, where the risk to "safer, sustainable community lies in the potential and actual interactions between the hazards to which that community is exposed and the vulnerability of that community's elements at risk" (Emergency Management Australia, 2004, p. 2). Under an all hazards approach natural disaster management is viewed as one aspect of emergency management, where preparations and responses are to be planned and implemented not on the basis of a specific threat but rather in a more generic way that may cover any eventuality (Council of Australian Governments, 2002, p. 4). Consistent with the all hazards approach and whole of government working, the Council of Australian Governments released the National Disaster Resilience Statement in 2011 which affirmed a commitment to working across government: "a national, coordinated and co-operative effort is required to enhance Australia's capacity to withstand and recover from emergencies" (Council of Australian Governments, 2011, p. iv). The strategy also outlined that collective means of working are preferable to avoid the problem that: "traditional government portfolio areas and service providers, with different and unconnected policy agendas and competing priority interests may be attempting to achieve the outcome of a disaster resilient community individually" (Council of Australian Governments, 2011). Further, it extended the idea of collaboration beyond government and acknowledged the importance of "building better links with the private sector, as infrastructure is often owned or managed by private interests" (Council of Australian Governments, 2011). The National Disaster Resilience Statement (Council of Australian Governments, 2011, p. iv) also outlined the role of government in strengthening disaster resilience by: having effective risk management practices in place, strategies to communicate risk, providing education around hazard response, supporting preparation for disaster events, ensuring effective inter-agency coordination in the emergency response groups, assisting in the recovery phase and leveraging past learning.

The final part of the federalist context that may have impacted the response to the 2009 bushfires and 2011 floods relates to the political dimensions. Fenna (2007) has suggested that in the lead up to 2009 and 2011 and from the election of the Rudd government in 2007, there was a stronger sense to build a more cooperative federalism and a move away from the Howard era. In the Howard era, Fenna suggests that the federal "government had proven so willing to extend Commonwealth power over the states since coming to power in 1996" (Fenna, 2007, p. 302). In many respects, the election of the Rudd government led to a renewed emphasis on the dialogue between the Commonwealth and the states and through the role of COAG where "the Rudd Government is giving an unprecedented role to COAG, which has been made an engine room of reform and now meets several times a year" (Grattan, 2009). Indeed, the hyperbole around this further extended to the suggestion that "a new era of cooperative federalism had begun in Australia. This era offers an ideal and rare opportunity to make lasting improvements in the functioning of our federal system in a way that delivers greater efficiencies and better services" (Wanna, Phillimore, Fenna, & Harwood, 2009, p. 3). It is perhaps the case that this renewed sense of purpose may have been as a result of the political composition of the Commonwealth and state governments at the time. If we look at the situation in 2009 the Australian Labor Party was in power at the federal level and was also in power in Victoria and a majority of other states. It is reasonable to assume that relationships between the Commonwealth and the states are often better and more harmonious where there is a party of the same political persuasion in power. Therefore, the political dimension at the time of the 2009 and 2011 crises meant that there was a renewed sense of cooperation between the Commonwealth and state governments.

This section has suggested that Australia's federal system is an important overall consideration when undertaking an analysis of disaster management arrangements, given that the response to disasters remains largely state driven. States do however rely upon the Commonwealth for support where capacity is exhausted and where funding for recovery is sourced through the NDRRA. COAG has played a key role in setting the national agenda around disaster policy and planning and provided an overarching policy structure. Despite COAG's reform agenda, states do however continue to independently define their own arrangements based on geography, risk profile and other factors. Finally, there is a strong political dimension that exists at the intersection of the Commonwealth and the states which can impact on the nature of the relationships and outcomes that can be achieved. Given the context provided above, the section below considers the detailed disaster management arrangements which existed at the time of the Victorian bushfires in 2009 as a precursor to understanding how whole of government may have worked during the crisis itself.

Victoria in February 2009: Ready or not?

Victoria has traditionally positioned itself as a state with a strong emergency management system, well prepared to deal with eventualities arising from bushfires and floods. In the years prior to 2009, there had been a number of major fire events which had been subject to inquiries. These inquiries suggested that there was fine-tuning rather than systematic change needed in the state's approach to managing disasters. Broadly speaking there were no major concerns with the nature of the emergency management system moving into 2009, which is reflected in the government rhetoric from the time.

There was however a disjuncture between the government's public rhetoric and internal critiques of the emergency management arrangements in place. At an internal level, there were concerns particularly from the emergency response agencies about the nature of the emergency management arrangements and the degree to which disparate agencies could be coalesced into a coherent response in the face of a major disaster. The concerns around the level of coordination and alignment between agencies indicate that the state was not as well prepared at it had envisaged. Indeed, it points to the fact that the state was not sufficiently prepared to confront a catastrophic event of the magnitude of the Black Saturday. Whilst with the benefit of hindsight it is easy to reflect on this, at the time it was challenging to bring the diverse viewpoints together into a coherent framework that could have been used to improve preparation and reaction to the events of February 2009.

In the immediate response to Black Saturday, it became apparent that there had been fundamental failures in the emergency response system, particularly with regards to cooperation between key agencies. Following on from Black Saturday the narrative of a mishandled response quickly took hold, especially when information regarding the whereabouts of key leadership figures came to public attention. In many ways, the outcomes which occurred from Black Saturday reflected specifically on the internal concerns that had been raised from the emergency response agencies but that not been acted upon. A narrative of confusion, lack of coordination and an overall loss of control led to the perception of a 'failed' disaster response. Overall, the emergency response has been characterised as a failure with breakdowns in individual components as well as a sense that the entire system failed to deal with the severity and scale of the disaster.

Whole of government was implicitly and explicitly part of the Victorian emergency management system at the time of Black Saturday and represented a viable means to prepare for and respond to natural disasters. What has become apparent is that a commitment to whole of government working is not in itself sufficient to invoke a successful response. The lessons learned from the Victorian bushfires demonstrate that for whole of government to be successful, horizontal structures need to be supported by leadership coordination mechanisms, organisational values, existing relationships and institutional structures. In the Victorian case study, whilst many of the preconditions were notionally in place, there were a number of reasons which meant that this was not able to be enacted appropriately when needed. The remainder of this chapter considers the Victorian disaster management arrangements in place and the impact of the abovementioned themes in shaping the outcomes to Black Saturday.

Victorian disaster management arrangements at Black Saturday: Pressure in the face of fire

Given the federal context that existed at the time of the 2009 bushfires, the following section provides an overview of the state disaster management arrangements which were in place in Victoria and guided the immediate response to the Black Saturday bushfires. It is important to note that in the aftermath of the bushfires, these structures have subsequently changed and now new disaster management arrangements led by Emergency Management Victoria exist. Changes in Victoria's emergency management arrangements have occurred as a direct result of the events in 2009 and provide a clear lead for Emergency Management Victoria to oversee and coordinate the emergency response in Victoria.

At the time of the February 2009 bushfires, the Victorian emergency management system was underpinned by the Emergency Management Act (Parliament of Victoria, 1986), which described the role of key actors. The creation of this Act followed on from the establishment of a working party in 1985 to review emergency management arrangements in Victoria in the wake of the "Ash Wednesday" bushfires in 1983 (Office of the Emergency

Services Commissioner, 2009, p. 1). Ash Wednesday represented the most significant event prior to the 2009 fires. The Victorian approach to disaster management at the time of Black Saturday embraced a "whole of government and whole of the community approach" (Government of Victoria, 2010, pp. 1–4) in connecting different agencies, departments and the state and local level.

A notable part of the disaster arrangements was that there was a strong delineation between the policy roles undertaken in regards to emergency management through the Office of the Emergency Services Commissioner and operational responsibilities undertaken by the emergency response agencies. The Emergency Services Commissioner, whose role was based on establishing standards for prevention and management of emergencies, was charged with creating relationships in the emergency management sphere and making relevant recommendations to the minister (Parliament of Victoria, 1986, p. 29). The Emergency Services Commissioner position and its related office were the central source of policy for emergency management in Victoria (Office of the Emergency Services Commissioner, 2009, p. 3). The Emergency Services Commissioner at the time was to provide policy advice and information through the Victorian Emergency Management Council (VEMC). Responsibility for operational responses to fire fell predominantly with the Country Fire Authority (CFA), Department of Sustainability and Environment (DSE) and Victoria Police in terms of coordinating the overall emergency management response. This approach is supported by the emergency management structure outlined in the State Emergency Response Plan and depicted in Figure 3.2 (Government of Victoria, 2010).

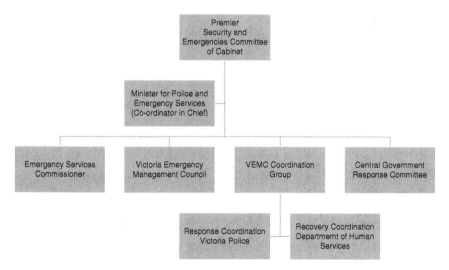

Figure 3.2 Emergency Response Arrangements in Victoria
Source: Adapted from State Emergency Response Plan

It is also notable that there is a significant delineation between the political and bureaucratic levels as indicated by the number of different committees and groups which existed at different levels. Despite the existence of the Victorian Emergency Management Council there was no real means to bring together the three strands of government. Within this context, the role of the Minister was to "ensure that satisfactory emergency management arrangements are in place to facilitate the prevention of, response to and recovery from emergencies" as opposed to "operational matters in relation to emergency management" (Parliament of Victoria, 1986, p. 9). The State Emergency Response Coordinator (SERC) was primarily charged with providing the minister with information related to actual or imminent events which may lead to emergencies and the response to emergencies. The role at the time was to be occupied by the Chief Commissioner of Police (Parliament of Victoria, 1986, p. 9).

At the political and government level there were two key elements of the emergency management structure in Victoria which were not mandated in legislation: the Securities and Emergencies Cabinet Committee (SECC) and the Central Government Response Committee (CGRC). The SECC was established as a cabinet committee to oversee whole of government decision making during a disaster. The CGRC was established to support the SECC with senior representatives from government departments – it did not have a role in managing the deployment of emergency services (Office of the Emergency Services Commissioner, 2009, p. 9). Also at the intersection between the political and bureaucratic level, the VEMC was intended to be the key body involved in providing advice to the Minister on all matters related to elements of a disaster response including the coordination of activities of government and non-government agencies, relating to the prevention of, response to and recovery from emergencies. This committee consisted of agencies whom the Minister believed should be represented (Parliament of Victoria, 1986, p. 9). The Act did not specify which agencies were represented, however membership was usually comprised of "police, emergency services and sections of government closely involved with emergency prevention response and/or recovery" (Office of the Emergency Services Commissioner, 2009, p. 8). Below the VEMC, the VEMC Coordination Group was also created to support the Minister in providing coordination for response and recovery activities and in providing an information flow during significant emergencies. The VEMC Coordination Group consisted of the Minister, State Disaster Coordinator, State Recovery Coordinator and the Emergency Services Commissioner (Government of Victoria, 2010, pp. 1–8). Below the Emergency Management Act and at the operational level, the State Emergency Response plan outlined the practical nature of emergency preparation response and recovery as well as the onus on municipal councils to "prepare and maintain a municipal emergency management plan" (Parliament of Victoria, 1986, p. 25). The State Emergency Response Plan also outlined the role of the State Crisis Centre as being central to whole of government arrangements by facilitating strategic advice and support to the relevant government committees and coordinating internally within the Victorian government as well as with counterpart agencies at the federal and state levels (Government of Victoria, 2010, pp. 3–25).

Finally, in the aftermath to the events of 7 February 2009, a non-legislated authority not included as part of the above arrangements was also central in the immediate response to the bushfires. The Victorian Bushfire Reconstruction and Recovery Authority (VBRRA) reporting directly to the Premier was a key whole of government body tasked with the immediate response to the bushfires including to "advise governments, coordinate efforts and develop an overarching plan for the restoration and recovery of regions, towns and communities affected by the 2009 bushfires" (Victorian Bushfire Reconstruction and Recovery Authority, 20010d, p. ii). The decision to establish the authority was made three days after the Black Saturday fires, as a key part of the response to the crisis. The VBRRA was to be co-funded by both the state and federal government as part of disaster management funding arrangements (Padula, 2011, p. 3).

Black Saturday: The tragic aftermath

The Black Saturday bushfires of 2009 were one of the most extensive natural disaster events in Australian history. During the disaster, 173 people were killed, 414 people were injured, 2029 homes were destroyed throughout the course of what was collectively 400 fires (Attorney General's Department, 2012). The fires that occurred in February 2009 came against a backdrop of an extreme heatwave that produced highly dangerous conditions. Figure 3.3 indicates the geographical spread of the fires and the scale of events that were faced in February 2009 (15 discrete large scale fires). The nature and scale of the fires meant that there was serious pressure on response capacity and moving into recovery. As a result many of the hardest hit localities became the focal point for recovery efforts once the scale of the crisis was known. Conditions at the time of the events in Victoria meant that "only a combination of wind and an ignition source was required to touch off potentially devastating fires" (Leonard & Howitt, 2010, p. 372). The Black Saturday bushfires were the most significant in a series of large bushfires that have affected Victoria, most notably Ash Wednesday in 1983, and events in 2002–2003 and 2006–2007. As a result of these events, a number of other inquiries and evaluations had been held as a point of review. In 2003 an inquiry was launched into the 2002–2003 bushfires, which also raised key issues such as the efficacy of the "stay or go policy" (Office of the Emergency Services Commissioner, 2003, p. 129) and the lack of formal structure to ensure consistency across agencies or to gain endorsement from government. In this sense very similar criticisms would also emerge from the Victorian Bushfires Royal Commission in the wake of the 2009 fires.

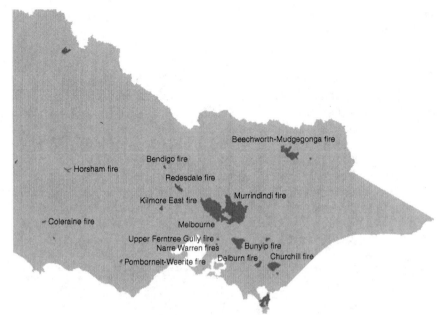

Figure 3.3 The Victorian bushfires location map
Source: Victorian Bushfires Royal Commission (Reproduced by permission of the Honourable Speaker of the Legislative Assembly, Victoria Australia)

As a result of the Black Saturday bushfires, there was significant scrutiny regarding the events that had occurred and whether adequate systems and policies were in place that could have averted the large scale loss of life and destruction. Critical to this review process was the Bushfires Royal Commission. The decision to create a commission of inquiry was made two days after Black Saturday. It was strongly felt at the time of the events, that given the scale and magnitude of what had unfolded there was a need for a Royal Commission to examine the events including the systems and structures which supported emergency management in Victoria as well as the actions of senior leaders in the face of the crisis. The Commission was provided a wide-ranging brief to review all elements of the preparation and response to the events of Black Saturday. It provided a detailed series of recommendations 18 months after its establishment that highlighted the need to review Victoria's safety policy (stay or go), reconfiguration of emergency management arrangements, land management planning and changes to building codes (Victorian Bushfires Royal Commission, 20010d). The forensic review which occurred as part of the inquiry also identified a "number of systemic and leadership failures" (Au, 2011, p. 28). One of the key criticisms which emerged as a result of the Royal Commission was that: "poor decisions were made by people in positions of responsibility and by individuals seeking to protect their own safety" (Victorian Bushfires Royal Commission, 2010d, p. 4).

This scrutiny was further extended to suggest that senior personnel "adopted a management style, which depended solely on problems being brought to their attention from the bottom up, rather than any active steps being taken to search out problems" (Victorian Bushfires Royal Commission, 2010b, p. 4). There was also an acknowledgment that Victoria's Emergency Management Framework is "nearly 30 years old and no longer meets the needs of the state" (State Government of Victoria, 2011, p. 1). The report noted that there was a lack of "clear responsibility for the control of the response to major bushfires" (Victorian Bushfires Royal Commission, 2010d, p. 76) as well as "poor coordination efficiency in the incident command system" (Au, 2011, p. 20).

Also at the core of findings emanating from the Royal Commission were issues regarding centralisation and decentralisation with an acknowledgement that on Black Saturday: "the roles of the most senior personnel were not clear, and there was no single agency or individual in charge of an emergency" (Victorian Bushfires Royal Commission, 2010d, p. 8). Individual failures of leadership were also identified with an acknowledgement that the "approach to emergency coordination was inadequate" (Victorian Bushfires Royal Commission, 2010d, p. 8). Strong concerns were also noted with the state government's reluctance to advance certain policy positions such as advocating community refuges and bushfire shelters (Victorian Bushfires Royal Commission, 2010d, p. 5). The Royal Commission also noted that the institutional arrangements in place "highlighted serious deficiencies in top-level leadership as a result of divided responsibilities and that the operational response was hindered by differences between agencies' systems, processes and procedures". The Commission recommended wide scale reform noting that "when considered collectively the problems illustrate systematic failings that led the commission to contemplate organizational change" (Victorian Bushfires Royal Commission, 2010d, p. 18).

To a significant degree the findings and criticisms which emanated from the Royal Commission have also been replicated in other work around the bushfires particularly from the Bushfire Cooperative Research Centre (CRC). Research undertaken through the Bushfire CRC has indicated that the role of government has been cited as one of the most contentious issues surrounding the response to the crisis events and that many people felt that there were serious flaws and deficiencies in the way that coordination worked across government. The excerpt below provides an indication of the tone of the sentiment from an affected householder that existed following on from the bushfires and what can be seen to have become the narrative around the response to the crisis itself.

> It seemed that the various government agencies responsible for the maintenance of the roadsides either had insufficient funds to clean up or lacked the will to do so. Dealing with DSE, Vicroads, Council and an array of other agencies with an interest in not doing anything proved an

impossible challenge for locals. From the 'outside' it appeared that these agencies just would/could not work together.

(Householder cited in McLennan & Handmer, 2014, p. 117)

Black Saturday: The response and whole of government in action

Having established the context around the Victorian bushfires, the case was examined through primary and secondary sources such as the Royal Commission report, internal government documents obtained through freedom of information requests, media reports and the conduct of interviews with key protagonists. Broadly, respondents were asked for their views on the key themes that may have shaped the response to the Victorian bushfires: whole of government, crisis management, leadership, coordination, organisational culture, social capital and role of institutions in the response to the event. The following section provides the empirical evidence related to the key thematic areas in order to support the comparative analysis that follows later in the book.

Whole of government in action

Prior to the Black Saturday fires there was an understanding that Victoria was facing unprecedented weather conditions, which would strongly challenge the ability of government to respond given the nature of the looming threat. In documents obtained through a freedom of information request, the Victorian Emergency Management Council (VEMC) noted in a dire prediction only days prior to the event that "14 out of 20 locations have the maximum fire index ... statistics show that conditions for every location are worse than Ash Wednesday and that this kind of weather has been unprecedented in the country" (Victorian Emergency Management Council, 2009, p. 2). There was an understanding in the lead up to the events that Victoria was facing a problem of significant magnitude, although the scenario which unfolded was beyond worst fears. Given the context around the fires, one of the key areas of analysis was the way in which whole of government worked; the advantages and disadvantages of whole of government working and how it could potentially solve the significant problems that arise in a crisis. There was a strong sense from all the participants interviewed that the whole of government response was critical and worked well in the immediate unfolding of the crisis as well as in the aftermath moving into recovery mode:

I remember sitting thinking what an experienced government we are. We'd been through a number of things and the things that you know how to do and how to get through. With any emergency you have to have cooperation, no one agency is capable of doing it on their own because they all have their own core focus. They all have to work together.

(Former Police Minister, Bob Cameron)

In terms of the response, I certainly felt a very well-oiled machine that kicked into action very quickly. The second response fairly immediately afterwards (was assessing) the situation we are dealing with, what were the needs and the resources required.

(Former Senior Bureaucrat)

There was also an understanding that whole of government working more generally required authority from the top down in order to encourage horizontal working as a means of solving fragmentation within government:

The biggest single one is leadership, leadership from the Premier and Treasurer or PM and Treasurer. So a commitment to doing things across government, breaking down silos you need it at that level, it permeates all the ways in which you do things particularly budget process.

(Former Premier, John Brumby)

I think that's the key really, each individual agency still has its core business that they need to undertake, it is about how you promote that idea of sharing accountability, collective responsibility – that is a leadership task. It is really about how you get that and how you get effective decision-making in that environment.

(Former Secretary Department of Justice, Penny Armytage)

There were also reflections that in the context of the scale of the unfolding disaster that coordination through whole of government was pivotal across agencies, particular where the disaster had been so severe:

You need to have cooperation between emergency agencies. You need to have cooperation between agencies more broadly who will be part of assisting. You have to have cooperation in government and whole of government. Some of those whole of government things in a big crisis don't actually affect the emergency in the here and now or immediately afterwards but nevertheless you have to attend to them straight away.

(Former Police Minister, Bob Cameron)

It is clear, however, that there were a series of challenges around whole of government working and indeed some of these constraints may have been due to the nature of disaster management arrangements in Australia's federal system. An example of this related to the creation of a national integrated telephone alert system which had been stymied in the lead up to 2009 due to differences between states and the Commonwealth regarding funding and costing for such a scheme. The Australian newspaper reported this in the following way "Canberra and the states baulked at the $20 million cost of a telephone-based alert system that would have given early warning of the deadly Black Saturday bushfires" even though the "test run of Telstra's Community Information and Warning System was for flooding, the Victorian SES found it would work for all types of hazards" (Walker & Bita, 2009, p. 1). Telecommunications became a significant issue in the aftermath to the Victorian bushfires where the then Premier John Brumby indicated his concern at the lack of progress that had halted the national alert system and efforts to renew telecommunications as a COAG agenda item (Dobbin, 2009, p. 6).

Through the course of the research, there was a strong sense that although it was recognised that 7 February was likely to represent a bad day – "In conjunction with the operational preparations for 7 February, there was also a heightened and concerted effort to inform and warn the community of the unprecedented and dangerous conditions" (Victorian Bushfires Royal Commission, 2010a, p. 4) – it was difficult to impress this on the general public. There was a disconnect in understanding how bad the events could potentially be and how to convey warnings to key political figures and the general public. This was highlighted by the difficulties conveying warning messages from the operational through to bureaucratic and political levels:

> No question that there are dilemmas there, goes back to my earlier observations and I think at the highest political level we hadn't been able to get Ministers, Premiers, Departmental Secretaries to appreciate just what it was that we were dealing with … . How do you articulate that to a politician who is used to comprehensive briefing notes and good numbers and lots of qualitative analysis, to go to the minister and say we have a really bad feeling about this boss.
>
> (Former Senior Emergency Management Officer).

It was noted that once the extent and scale of the crisis began to unfold that the institutional arrangements surrounding disaster response in Victoria were enacted and that most of the key protagonists believed that there was an appropriate response put in place:

> Once we realised what the situation was the extent of the crises that's when we really kicked in to the Central Government Response Committee (CGRC) and we got the agencies together … the Premier who'd been at the fires would come in and the relevant ministers would come in and we started immediately on the response.
>
> (Former Senior Bureaucrat)

There was also a strong theme that emerged from many respondents that there was something unique about whole of government in a crisis, which meant that in practice it worked best under this scenario due to the strong imperative. Indeed, there was a contrast to normal times, where whole of government is seen as more difficult to operationalise and subject to greater contestation:

While it was under crisis, I've always seen in this government because it so large, it works most effectively in crisis, because it has got the capacity and the resources you have got people that have very good experience who led correctly are able to order the decisions which are made and undertake the actions.

(Former Senior Bureaucrat)

Aside from the operational cooperation needed to make whole of government work, there was also an understanding of the political dimensions which underpinned this, particularly with regard to coordinating with the federal government:

There was a complex set of issues going on, you have the high level and immediate human dimension, the political level, there was the Prime Minister in the state roaming around areas and issues involved in that. There was a whole mix of issues but we were really able to focus resources correctly.

(Former Senior Bureaucrat)

One of the key acknowledgements was that in the wake of a large scale event, federal resources were needed in order to begin the immediate response task and move into recovery. In this way, there was an acknowledgement that state capacity was exhausted. Victoria required the assistance of the Commonwealth in the immediate response and into the recovery process in line with the national disaster management arrangements:

The size and nature needed strong Federal government support and involvement and people will critique the recovery but it's been a pretty strong mechanism put in place for recovery but the only way they would be that strong was if you have the Commonwealth in there as an equal partner and you needed them all over it.

(Former Chief Executive Officer VBRRA, Ben Hubbard)

Crisis management: The one in a generation event

One of the key themes which emerged from the research was the notion that this crisis was unique in terms of its size and scale and that it was an event of national significance that would remain in the national consciousness. Given the awareness which existed around this, there was an understanding that it needed a large scale response driven from the top of government. There was a clear sense that in a crisis there is a strong imperative to act in a whole of government way and urgency for doing so which may not exist in other domains:

Ours was always seen to be a very good and effective and fair and balanced response. So the key element is commitment from the leader so in that case me, so all of the early response was driven by the Premier.

(Former Premier, John Brumby)

There was an acknowledgement however that the scale of the events meant that this pushed the state beyond its capacity and this became one of the key narratives emanating after the crisis. Even shortly after the events there were serious questions being raised about how events had unfolded:

It seems everyone wants to know what went so wrong. Why were fire-fighters so powerless to stop the fires? Why were warnings issued too late to save people? Was it merely a freak act of God or was it also a failure of systems, leadership and policy?

(Stewart, 2009a, p. 9)

There was a sense that although CFA had attempted to put in place strategies to mitigate against risk, it had been unable to deal with the scale of the events on Black Saturday (Victorian Bushfires Royal Commission, 2010c, p. 3). This is consistent with the idea expressed in the literature which suggests that "even if a crisis is triggered by natural events, the human factors related to prevention and handling are still crucial" (Christensen, Johannessen, & Laegreid, 2012, p. 71). In Victoria, the latter viewpoint quickly gained momentum with a belief that there had been a failure in preparing for and responding to the events. This critique was demonstrated through an opinion piece published in *The Australian*:

At the heart of this tragedy, Australia's worst natural disaster is a clear failure of public policy, and official imagination. This generation of politicians and emergency services executives assumed, incorrectly, that every lesson from previous bushfires was sitting in their in-tray or inbox waiting to be applied.

(Megalogenis, 2009, p. 17)

As time passed and when the Royal Commission was established, this viewpoint continued to the point of recognising that the event represented a breakdown in disaster response systems and practices. In many respects this has become the dominant narrative around the Victorian bushfires, with the perception that it represents an instance of a 'failed' disaster management response. In reflecting on the nature and structures of the systems in place at the time of the fires, the former Victorian Emergency Services Commissioner Bruce Esplin indicated the scale of the events meant that the state of Victoria would need to reconsider whether its current legislation and governance arrangements would need change given that "the Black Saturday fires and the recommendations of the Royal Commission highlighted weaknesses in that space (coordination)". He further noted "I think they highlighted the small and the medium scale and even the large events are dealt with really well but that events that are of a catastrophic level have a whole set of additional requirements" (Esplin cited in ABC World Today, 2011). Through the inquiry process, it emerged that there was a general sense that there had been confusion and a lack of leadership on the day. As a result of Black Saturday significant changes to operational response strategies occurred including police officers being retrained in emergency management. In the wake of 7 February there was an overall perception that "the Black Saturday bushfires brought chaos and confusion to Victoria" (SBS, 2009a).

As the commission process continued, this view about chaos and confusion became one of the main narratives. The head of the Royal Commission into Victoria's bushfires indicated that the final report of the Royal Commission would be likely to contain stronger criticism of the Country Fire Authority and other agencies which was not deemed appropriate for the interim report (SBS, 2009b). Reports emanating from the Royal Commission placed a sharp focus on issues of horizontality and verticality in confronting the events. There was strong criticism of the response with the view that command and control elements were missing during Black Saturday. This was confirmed at the time of the release of the final report. In the report, the commission constructed 51 key recommendations for adoption in the state of Victoria. Recommendations aimed at addressing what was perceived to have been a lack of clear understanding from the public regarding the location and severity of fires, public response strategies and the management of emergency services (ABC, 2009).

Another of the themes that arose from the Royal Commission which has subsequently been addressed in the new emergency management arrangements in Victoria regards accountability and integration. The issue of accountability arose not so much in the immediate response to the disasters but through the Royal Commission process where information regarding the actions and whereabouts of key figures such as the Police Commissioner came to light and were heavily scrutinised:

> no excuse or 'spin' can justify this dereliction of responsibility at the very hour of crisis. It was said that emergency management coordination is a function; it is not a location. This, apparently, was put forward as some justification for those with the most important responsibility not being on 'location' at the height of the bushfire crisis.
> (Victorian Bushfires Royal Commission, 2010b, p. 8)

In many respects, there were serious differences between the commission and protagonists such as Christine Nixon in terms of the view of the type of leadership response required:

> I made a judgement call on the day and I had faith in the people who had worked for me that they would go about their work appropriately

and that others involved would continue to do that and made the decision to leave.

(Nixon, 2011, p. 323)

The criticisms that emanated from the Royal Commission were also mirrored from interview participants particularly at the operational level, who indicated that there were elements of the response which were less than optimal:

> There is a fairly significant list of issues there. Again my views, a view that I hold was that the government of the day didn't necessarily appreciate what we were facing. In 2008 the agencies, CFA and DSE in particular had prepared a report for government called 'Living with fire', it was a very strong advocacy for enhancing capability to deal with major events ... the message from agencies was that this was the norm and there was no way that our structures, systems and existing capability would enable us to cope with this every year.
>
> (Former Senior Emergency Management Officer)

> So I think it'd be really good if some of the handful of experts that exist around the world outside of Victoria could have a look at Victoria's arrangements and legislation and see if there's not a better way to do things that takes account of contemporary practice.
>
> (Esplin cited in ABC World Today, 2011)

It was suggested that in regards to the response to the crisis, significant questions arose regarding individual responsibility, community resilience and the degree to which the state or individuals share responsibility and how this became an issue around expectations and realities:

> I know that there are many people after the event who said nobody told us about that, yet in reality there was a huge amount of publicity. Those people working at the IECC who are immediately responsible were certainly getting caught up in the hype, so on the Thursday morning we both addressed the crew to try and settle the nerves a little bit and get them in the right headspace ... nothing we said could have prepared people for what they had to deal with.
>
> (Former Senior Emergency Management Officer)

A clear finding was that there is a unique response required to a crisis given the expectations that the public may hold of their leaders as a crisis emerges. This is particularly the case where there is an expectation from the public that leaders may be figures to which those affected can rally around. Part of this involved an active and on the ground leadership style described below:

So people felt that they were connecting immediately with government services, people who are highly traumatised, that we could get an assessment of what the real needs were, what the problems were and the Premier really encouraged all his ministers to get out to find out, they got into a mode of each day saying what are you seeing, given their role and it was an important level of intelligence, we also had the broader bureaucratic processes operating.

(Former Senior Bureaucrat)

There was a strongly political dimension to the crisis response which had the potential to impact on electoral outcomes. In the immediate period follow-ing on from 7 February it was seen as providing the incumbent Premier a political advantage: "like George W. Bush, John Howard and even Kevin Rudd at the moment, John Brumby seems to be the beneficiary of the voters' tendency to rally around a leader during a crisis" (Wallace, 2009a, p. 5). It was also noted that whilst the political response to the crisis may have started out "with an impressive spirit of bipartisanship forged between the Brumby Government and the Baillieu opposition" (Austin, 2009a), that this was indeed fragile and as time went on the bushfires became subject to political contestation. One of the first flashpoints to emerge surrounded the decision by the Victorian government to use one legal team to represent all departments, which was hotly contested by Opposition leader Ted Baillieu who opposed the government position. Baillieu argued "that all agencies and departments should have their own legal representation regardless of the cost, a view echoed by the Law Institute of Victoria" (Cooke, 2009). In fact, as the Royal Commission process continued and the state election drew nearer, the response to the bushfires became a significant political issue around the performance of the government and the adequacy of preparation and response to the events of 7 February. The political nature of the events was particularly apparent as many of the findings and recommendations were critical of the structures and procedures in place at the time.

Leadership: Accountability through the haze

One of the most contentious issues that emerged in the analysis and out-comes which arose from the Victorian bushfires relates to leadership and the degree to which there was a perception of a failure of leadership in the response to the events of 7 February. With regard to leadership there was a disconnect between views from Royal Commission process and the public and views from key people involved in the response to the disaster regarding the appropriateness of the leadership response. On one hand, there are strong views that emerged from the Royal Commission surrounding the lack of leadership shown on 7 February, including that "the state-level emergency management arrangements still faltered because of confusion about respon-sibilities and accountabilities and some important deficiencies of leadership"

(Victorian Bushfires Royal Commission, 2010d, p. 8). It was further noted that at key times "the war room was struggling to maintain control of the situation" (Stewart, 2009a).

The Commission process took quite a strong position in identifying individuals where it perceived there had been a failure of leadership, an example of whom being Russell Rees where it was suggested by lawyers in the Commission process that "Rees's activities were divorced from his statutory duties and there were calls for him to take on a greater role in predicting fire paths and issuing warnings" (SBS, 2009a). Strong critiques were echoed in the final report of the Royal Commission where there was clear reference to the role of senior operational leadership:

> On 7 February the leaders ultimately responsible for the operational response to the emergency were the Chief Officer of the CFA, Mr Russell Rees, and the Chief Fire Officer of DSE, Mr Ewan Waller, and the Chief Commissioner of Police, Ms Christine Nixon. Although many of the functions associated with each individual's role might have been delegated to subordinates, these people were still ultimately accountable.
> (Victorian Bushfires Royal Commission, 2010d, p. 8)

Beyond the interrogation of the activities which had taken place leading up to and around 7 February, the Royal Commission was also active in setting quite prescriptive view of leadership and what leadership in a crisis should look like:

> The Commission endorses this idea of an active leader: during a state wide disaster or an emergency it is this type of leadership that is needed. On 7 February strong leadership would have required not only the presence of the leaders at all crucial times but also the active oversight of those further down the chain of command. 'Active oversight' does not necessarily mean issuing directions to the incident management team or responding personnel: rather, it means monitoring the activities of those with direct control of response activities, informing oneself of the situation on the ground, and seeking information and feedback from subordinates.
> (Victorian Bushfires Royal Commission, 2010d, p. 78)

It also took a view of the kinds of personal characteristics that leaders should embody by citing the *CFA Red Book*, which was produced during the 1980s as an operational guide for CFA members, noting that "the leader is not a passive person" (Victorian Bushfires Royal Commission, 2010d, p. 39). The Commission strongly reiterated the view that leadership was very much embedded around the concept of an active figurehead coordinating the response to a crisis.

Views arising from the Royal Commission were also shared by members of the public who were directly affected by the crisis and who noted that "this lack of teamwork and leadership brought the State of Victoria to its knees in February or Black Saturday as it is known" (Householder cited in McLennan & Handmer, 2014, p. 117). Many members of the public were dismayed by the response: "I am shocked to think they were not organized as a team in communication and the lack of leadership. We saw local police take charge and save lives without the help of the echelon" (Householder cited in McLennan & Handmer, 2014, p. 117).

Perhaps the divergence between the Royal Commission, the public and those key protagonists in the response surrounding leadership is most starkly shown through the views of the Police Commissioner at the time Christine Nixon. Nixon was one of the most heavily scrutinised figures as a result of her perceived failure of leadership. In her biography, she reiterates her view that a delegation of authority surrounding emergency management matters was an appropriate part of the response. Indeed it was her belief that "the last thing any emergency team needs is the boss breathing down their necks second-guessing their decisions" (Nixon, 2011, p. 301). Further, she noted that there was a decentralised management approach which underpinned her views on these events:

> I had an expectation and understanding that I would be kept appraised of the situation and would participate in various briefings to satisfy myself that the responses were appropriate, but would not otherwise intervene in the processes they instituted unless specifically requested by them or deemed necessary by me.
>
> (Nixon, 2011, p. 297)

There is also an important distinction which needs to be made between the leadership exhibited from the operational level and at the political level. The suggested leadership vacuum described by the Royal Commission which became part of public perception was based on the operational level leadership rather than the political level. Indeed, the leadership and mandate provided from the level of the Premier down was cited as an important part of the overall response from the bureaucratic level:

> What was important was the Cabinet and the Premier of the day clearly really gave me as Secretary, a mandate to coordinate activities across the agencies and portfolios. I think it was one of the most important things to have a clear authority, to try and integrate a whole of government approach.
>
> (Former Secretary Department of Justice, Penny Armytage)

This contrast between the views of the leadership provided at the operational and political level also appears through the thinking of the then Premier, who noted the importance of connecting with the community "every day for the first three or four months, I was out in the field so that was important in breaking down the silos" (Former Premier, John Brumby). He also reflected his belief that his leadership at the time had been positively viewed:

> If you look at the commentary about my leadership around that period most of the commentary would say my leadership and the decision-making was crisp and timely and it was. When people go through that, they are looking for a way through, is there light at the end of the tunnel. They want to know that there is a way forward and things will happen.
>
> (Former Premier, John Brumby)

There was also a sense that the leadership task required at the time of the crisis necessitated strong leadership skills which encouraged cooperation, accountability and integration across government agencies and that this was paramount in terms of the public perception of being in command of the events:

> You've got it be attuned to what's happening, is that strong leadership or good communication, you're probably after both. I think there is a balance in that, I think you can be a really strong leader and a communicator and I think there is a balance about what we're trying to do in these times. With leadership in crisis, if the leaders are seen to be in crisis it all unravels.
>
> (Emergency Management Commissioner, Craig Lapsley)

Coordination under fire

Understanding key coordination mechanisms that impacted on the ability to respond to the events at the political, bureaucratic and operational levels was crucial to the response around Black Saturday. The emphasis on coordination was evident where "the State's approach to fighting ferocious fires is so highly dependent on cross-agency coordination it is unacceptable that effective coordination of information systems has not been achieved" (Victorian Bushfires Royal Commission, 2010d, p. 9). At the heart of understanding the perception of the response to the bushfires was the belief that there had been a breakdown in coordination that had negatively impacted on the response to the events themselves with claims of abandonment, inadequate warnings and isolation forming part of the narrative (Hughes & Davies, 2009, p. 7). Indeed, in early public hearings following on from the bushfires it was noted by residents that there had been "a lack of warning, poor mobile phone reception and little co-ordination between emergency services" (Cooke, 2009, p. 5). These views were also reflected through the final report of the Royal Commission which noted that:

> The experience of 7 February also highlighted several areas in which high-level state arrangements need reform. On Black Saturday the roles

of the most senior personnel were not clear, and there was no single agency or individual in charge of the emergency. The Commission notes changes made as part of the new coordination, command and control arrangements but considers that more should be done. It recommends that the roles be clarified, including through organisational change.

(Victorian Bushfires Royal Commission, 2010d, p. 8)

At a more specific level, key coordination mechanisms such as the Integrated Emergency Coordination Centre (IECC) were highlighted as being problematic. The IECC was intended as a means to bring together all emergency response agencies in a single command centre. It was noted however that this coordination mechanism had not had sufficient time to bed down given that it was the first season where the new model had been adopted. There was acknowledgement that this was a challenging activity given that it involved bringing together different response agencies under one roof and amalgamating different cultures, motivations and ways of working. The Commission identified a number of shortcomings in the logistical operation of the IECC including "location of various units, security procedures, deficiencies in systems and technology, and duplication in connection with weather forecasts and media releases and requests for resources" (Victorian Bushfires Royal Commission, 2010d, p. 94).

Similarly to the area of leadership, there was a disjuncture between the views expressed by the public and the key protagonists in the whole of government response around coordination. Although in this case whilst the political and bureaucratic level believed that coordination functioned well, the view was less than equivocal from the emergency services. The following outlines some of the views on the coordination mechanisms from the bureaucratic and political level:

> There was no doubt to me that the institutional structures embedded in the cabinet process where the Premier chairs and the Secretary of Premier's chairs and the senior people are sitting around the room is very important – to role model what happens when you're going to get into a crisis so you're constantly in regular meetings and that helps you do that.
>
> (Former Senior Bureaucrat)

> What we started to do, prior to Black Saturday, I think that it might have been the first year we had the Integrated Emergency Coordination Centre. It was where DSE and CFA had both of their control rooms in the same location. That subsequently has been developed further.
>
> (Former Police Minister, Bob Cameron)

These views can be juxtaposed against the views from the operational level where it was acknowledged that there were difficulties in coordination, particularly around the establishment of the IECC:

> I still believe it [the IECC] was the right decision and there is no question about it that it was the right thing to do. In August the team upped sticks and moved. It was fraught it was absolutely fraught the officers working for me and the officers working for DSE were at each other's throats, as well as trying to develop a facility that served the collective good, they were still trying to protect their own agencies needs and you needed to be bipolar to work in that environment.
>
> (Former Senior Emergency Management Officer)

There was also a sense that whilst coordination may have worked well across a strand of government, i.e. between departments at the bureaucratic level, coordination across the different strands of government was actually much more challenging. Coordinating across the three strands: political, bureaucratic and operational was one of the most serious threats to coordinating a response across the whole of government. At the political level the divide between the strands was seen as more of a necessary precondition to avoid political interference and confusion:

> So going back to talking about the divide, the relationships between agencies and government and about that interface, part of any job of any police and emergency services Minister was to try and keep the divide there. The emergency services deal with the emergency and the operational response and government deals with government response type matters ... . The Minister's job is to let you do your job and you let those people do their job, don't go annoying them for information all day, they've got things to organise and things to do, information has to be attained by this method.
>
> (Former Police Minister, Bob Cameron)

At the operational level, this divide was seen as more problematic and as a barrier to conveying the message about the potential seriousness of the events and being able to build relationships across the different strands of government:

> There was a separation between the bureaucrats who had a very close personal understanding of each other and the operational people who had a very close understanding but that crossover didn't work.
>
> (Former CEO CFA, Neil Bibby)

It was also evident that there were a number of key challenges that may have made the task of coordination across departments difficult, some of these involved technical aspects such as interoperability and the ability for organisations to share information, communicate and collaborate in real time using appropriate technological platforms:

My final comment is the need to focus on the one thing that every review talks about – interoperability. That is where the real challenge is. Make sure there remains a commitment from all agencies and not just the mainstream emergency services agencies, but across transport providers and others.
(Former Secretary Department of Justice, Penny Armytage)

Other respondents referred to more of the systematic and governance issues surrounding the management of crises, including shifting the focus from emergency services towards a more integrated emergency management structure. Under an emergency management doctrine, the task of coordination between the agencies themselves is seen as important as the individual tasks that the agencies may undertake:

The last five years have been about emergency service organisations the uniforms and the red lights coming together. The next step is the emergency management one, emergency services and emergency management are different. Emergency services are the cohort of different groups and emergency management is a broader process that's the next journey for us and we've done some good work on that.
(Emergency Management Commissioner, Craig Lapsley)

Organisational culture: Greater than the sum of its parts

One of the key areas that emerged throughout the conduct of the research was the importance of organisational culture and its impact on organisational and individual relationships. One of the key criticisms to arise from the Victorian bushfires relates to the degree in which there was a perception that there were different organisational cultures that did not meld well. It was also noted that some of the operational response agencies did not have a reflexive culture in terms of learning and knowledge transfer that could be harnessed from one disaster to the next. This is most succinctly indicated in the findings of the Royal Commission which noted:

If fire agencies are to lift their capability and performance and improve the response capacity of individuals and communities, they need to become true evidence-based learning organisations. The Commission proposes that the fire agencies adopt and fund a culture of reflective practice that routinely pursues current research, searches for best practice, and habitually evaluates policies, programs and procedures with a view to improving internal practice and that of the communities they serve.
(Victorian Bushfires Royal Commission, 2010d, p. 20)

It was also clear from within the emergency response agencies themselves, that there was an understanding that in many ways the different agencies had intrinsically different motivations and organisational cultures. Differences in organisational culture shaped the ability to interact and the outcomes of the interactions, particularly through mechanisms such as the IECC:

> There were still some substantive cultural differences between first responders CFA and DSE, which is inevitable because they've got very different charters, very different organisational cultures and it is difficult to bring agencies together and it's always sitting in the background.
>
> (Former Senior Emergency Management Officer)

Public views around the culture of collaboration which may or may not have existed between response agencies also suggested that organisational culture was a barrier to coordination. This is encapsulated in the sentiments of a householder directly affected by the bushfire events:

> There has been some suggestion that CFA and DSE compete for resources and compete for dominance; communication between the two agencies is inadequate. If this is so then the community should demand that fire danger is too important to tolerate bureaucratic egos.
>
> (Householder cited in McLennan & Handmer, 2014, p. 117)

With regard to the perception that organisational culture and relationships mediated the response to the bushfires, there was a sense that Victoria has been seen as a leader in terms of public management and the public sector as the 'state going places'. It was suggested as a result, that whole of government working was generally seen as part of the culture and fabric in the state. It was noted that whole of government as a means for connecting across different parts of government was very much seen as tied to the culture of the department and that this was easier for some areas than for others. The crisis event had however provided a means and an imperative to work collaboratively:

> In Victoria it is a quality public service, it's not uncomfortable with those models, my observation and I've got a lot of time across Australia because I was a long-term public servant and a very strong supporter, it is known for that and the reason for that is the long-term bipartisan support, as it hasn't been politicised.
>
> (Former Senior Bureaucrat)

> There will always be departments – and this is a relative thing – that are less responsive than others or more likely to engage than others, and over time they return to form. In the immediate aftermath of the fire everyone, whether here or in Sydney, who understood Victoria was shocked by the events and wanted to do something to help.
>
> (Former Chief Executive Officer VBRRA, Ben Hubbard)

An interesting issue to arise was the way in which the lessons and learnings from the 2009 bushfires could be integrated back into the culture of the public service to serve as preparation for future events. It was noted that there were useful mechanisms for knowledge to be retained as part of an organisation even if key individuals were to leave. In the first instance it was suggested that this would occur through record keeping protocols and through the Royal Commission process:

> Knowledge management is the key to making sure that knowledge is retained over time and it is shared. I think that's where in many ways having the Royal Commission provides that documentary record. Also having the monitor's reports tabled which contained the critiques about what needed to happen and monitoring of our progress helped to facilitate the knowledge transfer.
>
> (Former Secretary Department of Justice, Penny Armytage)

Secondly, it was suggested that organisational memory would largely be retained through the people to people links which endure from one crisis to the next. A prominent example which was cited was of Craig Lapsley who was involved in recovery efforts to the 2009 fires and who now holds the position of Emergency Management Commissioner:

> Within agencies there is a capacity to have through individual record management and presence of individuals who were involved at the time in different roles, a strong knowledge retained within a wide range of players who are still active in the state. There are also records within the agencies to make sure that knowledge is readily transferred.
>
> (Former Secretary Department of Justice, Penny Armytage)

Thirdly, there was the understanding that although, in the wake of the 2009, there had been a significant re-shuffle of staff at the top of the emergency response agencies much of the organisational memory was actually retained at the grass-roots level. In this respect, emergency response agencies were significantly different to the bureaucratic or the political level which were much more subject to the political cycle:

> The area where the corporate knowledge is retained is in the emergency services most of those people are career people, start as a baby fireman and become chief. In the bureaucracy they change rapidly. You don't have, I don't think any of the department heads who were there at that particular fire are there now.
>
> (Former CEO CFA, Neil Bibby)

Social capital: The bonds that define us

In terms of social capital, the importance of professional relationships across key actors and the ability to leverage these bonds and ties during the disaster itself was consistently raised as being important to the whole of government management of crisis. A crisis was not a point at which relationships could be built, but that relationships and rapport built in 'peace time' were critical so that they could be leveraged during the crisis itself. The disaster management community was a small and close knit one, where there were ample opportunities for engagement through both formal and informal mechanisms:

> That rapport and trust that you build with people is what is important, I suggest that the work which was being done over the preceding years to try and build relationships between individuals who had corresponding roles was one of the great strengths, I wouldn't say those relationships were perfect by any stretch of the imagination but say it was one of the strengths.
>
> (Former Senior Emergency Management Officer)

It was cited that in many ways, there was both a key need and ability for individuals to be able to connect with those in similar posts across different agencies and departments. This was seen to complement the broader systems and institutions that may have been in place to mediate interactions. In a fast moving and large scale crisis, it was important to be able to quickly make requests that would be actioned by counterparts without needing to move through the usual bureaucratic channels:

> Government is not about obfuscation, you can make decisions happen really easily or you can make it quite difficult, unfortunately often it's the latter sometimes things tend to get stuck. When you're in a crisis you need to make sure that when you tell the Head of the Department of Industry that I need X in two hours, that happens in two hours and they understand the importance of that and they do it. We had that type of relationship across the Secretaries and the Deputy Secretary levels. It was there before we didn't have to create it was already there.
>
> (Former Senior Bureaucrat)

There was though reflection on the nature of professional relationships in terms of the balance between systems and structures and individuals. There were some concerns about systems which were in place which were highly dependent on individuals given that these could potentially be subject to breakdown should the individuals be unavailable:

> The concern expressed by outside observers is that if those people aren't there it all falls apart, sure you have to have systems that allow this work but systems assume a degree of logical and rational thought. In my career I have noticed that logical and rational thought between human beings is a rare commodity on a good day, and certainly when people are under pressure.
>
> (Former Senior Emergency Management Officer)

The social capital manifested through professional relationships indicates that in an institutional sense there was fine balance between institutional structures and individual action. The professional relationships which existed occurred against an institutional backdrop as dictated through Victoria's emergency management arrangements.

Institutions: Putting together the jigsaw

The final thematic area to be examined through in the case study refers to institutions and formal government structures which existed leading up to and following on from the events of 7 February. The role of these structures and institutions were cited as being essential to the nature of the response, although there was some concern expressed at the way that these operated in the time up to and after the events of Black Saturday. At a general level integration between departments and agencies and overall governance structures were cited as areas of concern. This was reflected in the finding of the Royal Commission which recommended structural change to Victoria's emergency management structures given that "for many of the operational problems the Commission identified, previous attempts to improve coordination have failed. Typically, progress has been slow or incomplete or has not achieved the level of interoperability required" (Victorian Bushfires Royal Commission, 2010d, p. 18). It was noted that the Commission did not consider that the "shortcomings identified in connection with Black Saturday can be overcome simply by doing more of the same, even if it is done better" (Victorian Bushfires Royal Commission, 2010d, p. 18). A key part of this involved the role and function of the VEMC noting that "revitalising the Victorian Emergency Management Council (VEMC) (or its successor), so that it becomes: a more effective advisory body to the Minister for Police and Emergency Services" (State of Victoria, 2010, p. 7). Indeed, along with the structural reform which was recommended by the Royal Commission, there was also a sense that the fabric or underlying ethos of the system needed change in order to address "improvements to common operational policy and standards, stronger coordination and unambiguous command and control, greater interoperability, and a strengthened capacity to provide an integrated response" (Victorian Bushfires Royal Commission, 2010d, p. 18). As a result of the findings outlined by the Royal Commission, disaster management arrangements in Victoria have undergone radical change with the establishment of an operationally focussed Emergency Management Commissioner. This has been complemented by "new command, control and coordination arrangements as well as State Emergency Management Assurance Teams to review and report on emergency preparedness and response arrangements" (State of Victoria, 2010, p. 8).

Interview participants also had mixed views on the structure of the arrangements at the time of the bushfires, the then Premier John Brumby indicated that in his view he believed that Victoria had been at the forefront in terms of institutional arrangements around disaster management. In this way all of the necessary preconditions were in place for a successful response but which ultimately proved difficult:

> So the model was an interesting thing, if you look back at that time Victoria was probably seen as the leader in terms of the structural arrangements and the leadership arrangements with this model … Everything is in order, the cabinet subcommittee, whole of government, a premier who is across the issue or thinks he is, leadership structures down, the CFA on alert, no rostered days off on Friday, Saturday, Sunday everyone is on duty so it's textbook, tick tick tick all the boxes.
>
> (Former Premier, John Brumby)

Others indicated that perhaps the institutional structures which existed at the time did not allow for an adequate integration across the political, bureaucratic and operational divide. The lack of integration meant that at the time operational agencies needed access to the political level this was difficult and that there were problems in the way that the messages around what could potentially unfold on Black Saturday were able to be delivered:

> The State Emergency Response Committee was very informal at the time and we were still building that model and trying to make sure that it worked, perhaps that wasn't as effective as we would have liked it to being in terms of getting the message back, that's a group of senior agency personnel who you would hope would go away and say this is what I've just heard the fire-fighters are saying and hopefully those people are credible enough to say if George is saying this, there may be a need to sit up and have a look at what's going on.
>
> (Former Senior Emergency Management Officer)

> The Victorian Emergency Management Council was 30 people which met once or two times a year. It wasn't efficient. It was an information gathering and dissemination exercise for mainly the Minister to let him know what was going on.
>
> (Former CEO CFA, Neil Bibby)

As a result of the changes which have subsequently been made since Black Saturday, there is a belief that response capacity has been improved as there is now a clearer chain of command:

> In terms of the new arrangements and what's happened with the estab-lishment of EMV and responsibilities of the Commissioner, this has been an improvement on what we've had in the past. While we had that function and role I think it needed to be a step further than it was, I think that's been the benefit of having the new structure in place. If you

accept what I say about the importance of mandates, it is not just about relationships which are important and knowledge and expertise it is also about having authority and then being clear about what the responsibilities of each of the parties are.

(Former Secretary Department of Justice, Penny Armytage)

In the aftermath of the crisis, one of the most significant outcomes was the creation of the Bushfires Royal Commission. At the time Premier Brumby indicated that "Victorians rightly want and deserve to know all the details about how the bushfires occurred" and "that's why the royal commission will have the broadest possible terms of reference and capacity to inquire into every aspect of these fires ... no stone will be left unturned" (Stewart & Bita, 2009, p. 1). Although the Commission would be the primary mechanism in which institutional change may occur there was an acknowledgement that if immediate changes needed to be made that they could be enacted (Wallace, 2009b, p. 6).

In terms of the responses from the key actors involved in the Victorian bushfires, many respondents saw the setup of the Commission as an important step which was proportionate to the scale of the events that had occurred:

When the final report from the Royal Commission was released, generally speaking people felt that they had reached the heart of the issues. The recommendations they suggested, were with very few exceptions accepted by the government of the day and when the change of government happened all the recommendations were accepted. This was a testament to the validity of the Royal Commission process.

(Former Secretary Department of Justice, Penny Armytage)

The potential political consequences of a Royal Commission were acknowledged by the then Premier, who indicated awareness about the political ramifications that a Royal Commission may have leading into a state election:

To me in that case it was a no-brainer; I didn't take department advice which I would normally do. To be honest when I spoke to my department head about it, I spoke to the Minister Bob Cameron and the Attorney General Rob Hulls they were honest, they wanted me to be aware of all the risks 18 months down the road with a Royal Commission, Royal Commissions are very powerful, they can get out of hand.

(Former Premier, John Brumby)

There were however concerns about the Commission both in the initial setup and with the longer term outcomes. The then Police Commissioner Christine Nixon indicates in her biography that:

I was a bit ambivalent about enlisting a royal commission as a forum for the task. Of course it was imperative that there be a full, frank, penetrating investigation of the circumstances of that day … I just wasn't entirely persuaded a royal commission was the right track to go down.

(Nixon, 2011, p. 311)

Others more broadly identified that they saw the Royal Commission as a missed opportunity to create long-lasting change given that it took an adversarial role which was seen to have a negative impact on those involved:

I think in some parts of the Royal Commission that was too much time spent on looking for blame and not enough time looking for solutions. I'm very strong on those thoughts.

(Former CEO CFA, Neil Bibby)

Another of the significant outcomes was the creation the Victorian Bushfire Reconstruction and Recovery Authority. In the face of the large scale destruction that occurred on 7 February, there was an almost immediate response to create a reconstruction authority. The Authority was established on 10 February 2009, three days after Black Saturday, following agreement between the Premier of Victoria and the Prime Minister. The Authority was given responsibility to lead and coordinate the reconstruction and recovery of all areas affected by the bushfires – a task that became the largest rebuilding program in Victoria's history. Given the severe trauma as a result of the loss of life there was an understanding that the recovery which needed to occur referred to physical infrastructure as well as social reconstruction and psychological support needed (Victorian Bushfire Reconstruction and Recovery Authority, 2011).

The Reconstruction Authority was cited as a crucial vehicle in which to progress the recovery of the state. The Reconstruction Authority was established as "a high-powered reconstruction taskforce, similar to the reconstruction commission used to rebuild Darwin in the wake of Cyclone Tracey" (Hannan, 2009, p. 1). As part of the funding of disaster management arrangements between the state and Commonwealth, initial demolition and clean-up costs were jointly borne through the two governments (Austin, 2009b, p. 5). In the first instance this amounted to a figure of $193 million (Disaster Assist, 2014) in order to support the reconstruction taskforce which was involved in attempting reconstruction given that more than 4000 homes had been impacted in the fire events across 78 townships (Stewart, 2009b, p. 9). Christine Nixon who was appointed to head the recovery authority noted that community engagement and recovery was also a key objective of the authority predicated on community consultation: "It is a large task and we want to listen to the community as we go along, and allow them to make choices about the recovery process" (Stewart, 2009b, p. 9). A key emphasis was that not only would the "communities be rebuilt but also the sense of community in these towns" (Stewart, 2009b, p. 9) in this way taking a broader view of recovery beyond physical infrastructure but also encompassing social recovery.

There was a strong view that the creation of a special purpose reconstruction body was the most appropriate way in order to expedite the recovery process and this would send a strong message to the public regarding the intent of the state government following on from the disaster:

> I wasn't interested in politics I was just interested in what the right thing to do was. The reconstruction authority was part of that, it was also how I see the world, and I suppose again I see myself as a person who likes to do things, a doer.
>
> (Former Premier, John Brumby)

It was also highlighted that by creating a non-legislated special purpose body that there was more agility for this to move more quickly rather than may have been the case with standard government operating procedures. There was recognition that this was an extraordinary measure in the face of a severe crisis that could connect community, government and business:

> In terms of breaking down silos it reported directly to me with a substantial mandate in terms of responsibilities and funding and it really had the ability to break down silos that was the right way to go early on. The choice of who ran it was an interesting one, if you spoke to people in the building industry or others, they say Christine was too bureaucratic, and there is probably some truth in that. On the other hand if you look at the people side Christine was fantastic on supporting people and communities and moreover using this terrible tragedy as an opportunity to up skill and empower individuals and communities particularly women.
>
> (Former Premier, John Brumby)

> I think the biggest institutional thing was the non-government consultation group, where all the partners who weren't government were involved, there was a consultation group for them and then there, was a consultation group for government partners. When I first got there we were meeting on a weekly basis and sort of went back to every second and third week – that helped a lot in terms of having their regular discussion with the same people from the agencies.
>
> (Former Chief Executive Officer VBRRA, Ben Hubbard)

Conclusion

This chapter has provided a detailed overview of the 2009 Victorian bushfires, which as a result of a post-event inquiry has been considered a 'failed' crisis response. A number of key themes have emerged regarding the way in which the whole of government response shaped the outcomes of the crisis. Whole of government has been identified as being important in Victoria as a means to connecting departments and agencies in complex policy domains and has been seen as a potential solution in bringing together disparate departments and agencies. There were however serious barriers to its implementation which meant that in February 2009, there was not the organisational capacity to implement a successful whole of government response across Victoria. Whole of government as such was not a main focus of the Royal Commission process, although many issues which are intrinsically tied to whole of government such as leadership, coordination and institutional structures were cited in the Commission report.

A crisis has been cited as a unique opportunity for whole of government working given that there is a sense of urgency, motivation and commitment to work in more horizontal manner. This imperative may not be the case in more routine policy environments and as a result means whole of government may in fact best be implemented during a crisis period. The executive leadership in Victoria saw that the whole of government response needed to be strongly led from the top of government. The executive saw the need to provide a mandate for whole of government implementation and also believed that it was important for senior leadership to directly lead the immediate response. Significantly there was a disjuncture in the views of the management of the crisis between the key leadership and the narratives which would emerge particularly through the Royal Commission. Whilst senior leadership believed coordination mechanisms and the ability to connect across government functioned well, these were at odds with critiques which highlighted deficiencies, failures and inadequacies in the response.

In considering the institutional response, it is noteworthy that despite the acceptance that whole of government working was critical in a crisis situation and the efforts of the executive leadership to implement whole of government, there was a mixed evaluation of the mechanisms and ultimately success of these attempts. This meant that there was a disconnect between the political, bureaucratic and operational levels within government which made implementing whole of government difficult and was a confounding factor in the response. Indeed, as a result of events in 2009, there has been recognition of the challenge of crisis management in Victoria. Victoria has moved towards arrangements based on an emergency management doctrine which sees overall system integration as crucial to the task of government in responding.

Finally, it was noted that as the response moved from the immediate acute phase on 7 February into recovery and reconstruction that the VBRRA was seen as an important whole of government mechanism to coordinate the recovery process in the affected communities. The VBRRA was intended to cut across government and non-government partners. There was a strong understanding that given the size and magnitude of the events a special purpose body may have provided the best way to connect government in order to assist the communities impacted.

In conclusion, the review of the Victorian bushfires indicates whilst there was a strong will to connect government and work seamlessly in the response, a number of confounding factors such as the state's disaster management arrangements and institutional structures meant that there were serious challenges to the ability to implement a whole of government response. This meant that in the face of a severe crisis there were serious gaps in the overall response arrangements which have shaped the narrative of a 'failed' crisis management case.

References

ABC (2009, 29 May). Recommendation for national disaster plan delayed. Retrieved 31 March 2015 from http://www.abc.net.au/worldtoday/content/2008/s2584377.htm

ABC 7:30. (2015). GST row heats up as WA Premier Colin Barnett describes 'immature cat calling'. Retrieved from http://www.abc.net.au/7.30/content/2015/s4218030.htm

ABC World Today (2011). Former Victorian emergency chief backs call for reform. Retrieved 6 July 2014 from http://www.abc.net.au/worldtoday/content/2011/s3267463.htm

Armytage, P. (2014). Interview with George Carayannopoulos.

Attorney General's Department (2012). Disasters Database. Retrieved 8 March, 2012 from http://www.disasters.ema.gov.au/Browse%20Details/DisasterEventDetails.aspx?DisasterEventID=2894

Attorney General's Department: Emergency Management Australia (2008). *Australian Government Disaster Response Plan (COMDISPLAN)*. Canberra: Author.

Au, A. (2011). Analysis of command and control networks on Black Saturday. *Australian Journal of Emergency Management*, 26(3), 20–29.

Austin, P. (2009a, 19 February). How the bushfires bipartisanship almost came to grief. *The Age*, p. 17.

Austin, P. (2009b, 24 February). Rudd, Brumby to foot clean-up bill. *The Age*, p. 5.

Bibby, N. (2014). Interview with George Carayannopoulos.

Brumby, J. (2014). Interview with George Carayannopoulos.

Cameron, B. (2014). Interview with George Carayannopoulos.

Christensen, T., Johannessen, M., & Laegreid, P. (2012). A system under stress: The Icelandic volcano ash crisis. *Journal of Contingencies and Crisis Management*, 21(2), 71–81.

Collins, R. (2014). Interview with George Carayannopoulos.

Cooke, D. (2009, 19 March). Post-fires grievance finally aired. *The Age*, p. 5.

Council of Australian Governments (2002). *Natural Disasters in Australia: Reforming mitigation, relief and recovery arrangements*. Canberra: Commonwealth of Australia.

Council of Australian Governments (2011). *National Strategy for Disaster Resilience*. Canberra: Commonwealth of Australia.

Disaster Assist (2014). Victorian bushfires (January–February 2009). Retrieved 18 January 2014 from http://www.disasterassist.gov.au/PreviousDisasters/StateandTerritories/Pages/VIC/Victorianbushfires(JanuaryFebruary2009).aspx

Dobbin, M. (2009, 6 March). Ex-police chief attacks lack of alert system. *The Age*, p. 6.

Eccleston, R., Warren, N., & Woolley, T. (2013). Beyond the blame game: Political strategies for state funding reform. *Australian Journal of Public Administration*, 72(1), 14–30.

Emergency Management Australia (2004). *Emergency Management in Australia Concepts and Principles* (Vol. Manual 1). Canberra: Commonwealth of Australia.

Fenna, A. (2007). The malaise of federalism: Comparative reflections on commonwealth–state relations. *Australian Journal of Public Administration*, 66(3), 298–306.

Former Senior Bureaucrat (2014). Interview with George Carayannopoulos.

Former Senior Emergency Management Officer. (2014). Interview with George Carayannopoulos.

Government of Victoria (2010). *State Emergency Response Plan*. Melbourne: Government of Victoria.

Grattan, M. (2009). Rudd's plan for a new federalism is showing signs of strain. *The Sydney Morning Herald*. Retrieved 29 November 2014 from http://www.smh.com.au/federal-politics/political-opinion/rudds-plan-for-a-new-federalism-is-showing-signs-of-strain-20091113-ic9o.html

Hannan, E. (2009, 10 February). Murder hunt as toll tops 130 – Royal Commission on what went wrong. *The Australian*, p. 1.

Hubbard, B. (2014). Interview with George Carayannopoulos.

Hughes, G., & Davies, J. A. (2009, 21 March). We were abandoned: Fire survivors . *The Australian*, p. 7.

Kasper, W. (2007). Australia's hollow federalism: Can we revive competitive governance. *Review – Institute of Public Affairs*, 59(3), 35–38.

Lapsley, C. (2014). Interview with George Carayannopoulos.

Lecours, A., & Beland, D. (2013). The institutional politics of territorial redistribution: Federalism and equalization policy in Australia and Canada. *Canadian Journal of Political Science*, 46, 93–113.

Leonard, H. B., & Howitt, A. M. (2010). Organising response to extreme emergencies: The Victorian Bushfires of 2009. *Australian Journal of Public Administration*, 69(4), 372–386.

McLennan, B., & Handmer, J. (2014). *Sharing responsibility in Australian disaster management: Final Report for the Sharing Responsibility Project*. Melbourne: Bushfire Cooperative Research Centre.

Megalogenis, G. (2009, 14 February). On the edge – Hell and all its fury. *The Australian*, p. 17.

Nixon, C. (2011). *Fair Cop*. Melbourne: Melbourne University Publishing Ltd.

Office of the Emergency Services Commissioner (2003). *Report of the Inquiry into the 2002–2003 Victorian Bushfires*. Melbourne: State Government of Victoria.

Office of the Emergency Services Commissioner (2009). *Emergency Management Manual Victoria*. Melbourne: Office of the Emergency Services Commissioner.

Padula, M. (2011). *Case Program: The Victorian Bushfire Reconstruction and Recovery Authority (A): The Challenge*. Carlton, VIC: ANZSOG.

Parliament of NSW (2014). The Roles and Responsibilities of Federal, State and Local Governments. Sydney: NSW Government.

Parliament of Victoria (1986). Emergency Management Act.

SBS (2009a, 2 July 2009). SBS World News – Bushfire Commissioner slams Chief Fire Officer.

SBS (2009b, 30 September). SBS World News – Fire authorities not in the clear yet: Commissioner.

State Government of Victoria (2011). *Towards a More Disaster Resilient and Safer Victoria: Green Paper Options and Issues*. Melbourne: Victorian Government.

State of Victoria (2010). *Submission of the State of Victoria on Organisational Structure to Bushfires Royal Commission*.

Stewart, C. (2009a, 21 February). Blame is delicate question: Teague – Black Saturday Disaster. *The Australian*, p. 9.

Stewart, C. (2009b, 21 February). Bushfire Survivors rebuild their lives. *The Australian*, p. 9.

Stewart, C., & Bita, N. (2009, 14 February). Life or lifestyle, warns fire chief. *The Australian*, p.1.

Victorian Bushfire Reconstruction and Recovery Authority (2009). *100 Day Report*. Melbourne: Victorian Government.

Victorian Bushfires Royal Commission (2010a). *Hearing Block One*. Melbourne: Author.

Victorian Bushfires Royal Commission (2010b). *Hearing Block Seven – Counsel Assisting*. Melbourne: Author.

Victorian Bushfires Royal Commission (2010c). *Hearing Block Seven – Victorian Government Submission*. Melbourne: Author.

Victorian Bushfires Royal Commission (2010d). *Report of the Victorian Bushfires Royal Commission*. Melbourne: Author.

Victorian Emergency Management Council (2009). *Coordination Group –Meeting Summary Record*. Melbourne: Author.

Walker, J., & Bita, N. (2009, 13 February). Early alert cover-up exposed – Secret report reveals political argument over funding. *The Australian*, pp. 1–2.

Wallace, R. (2009a, 6 March). Crisis a positive for Premier. *The Australian*, p. 5.

Wallace, R. (2009b, 18 February). Informal public hearings within a fortnight. *The Australian*, p. 6.

Wanna, J., Phillimore, J., Fenna, A., & Harwood, J. (2009). *Common Cause: Strengthening Australia's Cooperative Federalism*. Canberra: Council for the Australian Federation.

4 Under water but spirits high – The Queensland Floods

Overview

This chapter presents the second of the case studies the 2011 Queensland floods, which is being used to analyse the intersection between whole of government and crisis management. The chapter builds upon the work undertaken in the earlier parts of the book by addressing how the key thematic areas outlined: leadership, coordination, organisational culture, social capital and institutions impact on the outcomes of the disaster. Similar to the previous chapter, it looks at the case study through the lens of key themes to understand what the case tells us about the way governments manage joined-up responses to crises. This is particularly relevant in a tropical state such as Queensland where events such as floods and cyclones are common and mean that in many ways it can be considered the 'disaster state'. It also reflects on the specific context and the disaster management arrangements in place in Queensland including how these were structured and implemented during the 2011 floods. The chapter provides insights into the way that whole of government functioned through the use of both primary and secondary sources including interviews across the political, bureaucratic and operational levels around the key themes of the book. The insights generated from this chapter will then be used as part of the comparison to the Victorian bushfires. Lessons from the case studies will also be considered in the final chapter to understand the bi-directional relationship with broader crisis management principles.

The Australian disaster management system in 2011: Integration and fragmentation

In the period between 2009 and 2011 there were very few changes in the federalist context that impacted on the response to disasters. In looking at the legislative context, there were no changes in the administrative arrangements which govern the management of crises. The principles that were in place through COMDISPLAN remained unchanged from 2009 to 2011.

In terms of the financial relationship, the NDRRA guidelines which were originally created through the Howard government in 2007, served as the main mechanism for the co-funding of recovery arrangements between the Commonwealth and the state during the 2011 floods. The NDRRA arrangements were unchanged in the intervening period from 2009 to 2011; however, the experience of the Victorian Bushfire Reconstruction and Recovery Authority did influence the way in which the Queensland Reconstruction Authority (QRA) was set up and the governance framework which was put in place. Figure 4.1 shows there was a strong emphasis on the coordination of funding programs and the management of acquittals as part of Queensland's reconstruction arrangements. To this end a new body, the Federal Government Reconstruction Inspectorate, was created in the wake of the Queensland floods to ensure the appropriate acquittal of funds.

Following on from the events in 2009, there was a strong emphasis on increased accountability that can be understood against the context of the global financial crisis where there was a heightened degree of scrutiny around the high value, complex contracts necessary for large scale reconstruction.

The framework below also indicates the interaction between local, state and federal government funding for reconstruction works. In Queensland,

Queensland reconstruction governance framework

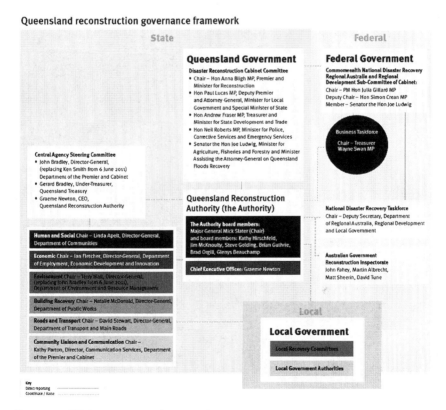

Figure 4.1 QRA governance framework
Source: Queensland Reconstruction Authority, 2012

reconstruction following the 2011 events was funded by the Commonwealth generally providing 75 per cent of funds and the Queensland Government 25 per cent, with several projects funded 50/50. Coordination of the program was driven by the Queensland Reconstruction Authority and delivery managed by local governments and state agencies.

In terms of the institutional context, the events of 2009 did prompt COAG to re-examine Australia's disaster management arrangements and the way in which these were to be positioned moving forward after the death and destruction caused by Black Saturday (ABC, 2009). Indeed, following on from Black Saturday there appeared to be an imperative to review and understand the lessons that could be adopted from the previous crisis and implemented into a disaster resilience framework. As a result, a working party was set up to produce a National Strategy for Disaster Resilience which was released in 2011. The timing of the report's release meant however that this did not have a substantive influence on the Queensland floods which occurred in early 2011. There was a strong awareness about the impact of the 2009 events both from an operational and political perspective that did impact on the key response agencies and government departments.

Finally, in terms of the political dimensions that impacted on the floods, Labor held power at the federal level and in Queensland. More broadly, however, there was a shift in the political mood meaning the renewed sense of optimism around Commonwealth and state relations was somewhat more subdued. The shift in mood occurred largely as a result of the election results, where at the federal level the ALP entered into minority government and changes in government in states such as Victoria, meant that negotiations between the Commonwealth and the states were a more contested space than they had been in 2009. There was a clear shift from the first term of the Rudd government, which started in 2007, and a decreased sense of optimism regarding the role of COAG was evident by 2011.

Queensland as the rain falls: Ready or not?

Queensland is by nature a state accustomed to frequent natural disaster events. Prior to the 2011 disaster, the state had experienced a number of other significant events such as floods and cyclones. This meant that ahead of 2011, the public rhetoric emanating from the state was that it was well practiced and well prepared to confront challenges occasioned by natural disasters. Queensland had in place a sophisticated emergency management system supported by a special purpose body – Emergency Management Queensland (EMQ). The emergency management system was supported by a decentralised structure which cascaded from local through to district and then finally state level.

Emergency management processes in Queensland in January 2011 were recognised as well positioned to face serious threats. The state had come through Cyclone Larry in 2006, which was a major tropical cyclone that brought about widespread destruction in far north Queensland. The state had also embarked on an ambitious capacity building program for disaster management amongst its regional councils that had been precipitated by council amalgamations in the preceding years. As a result, the rhetoric of a well-prepared state was supported by its emergency management arrangements, which meant that the ability to deal with serious disasters was supported by a capacity to do so.

In the immediate response to the unfolding disaster, the emergency agencies were strongly lauded for the efficacy of their response and the ability to galvanise against what was rightfully considered a worst case scenario. This was highlighted by the proportionate political response, which provided a strong rallying point for the state and demonstrated effective political leadership. It is clear that in the wake of the 2009 Victorian bushfires, lessons had been learned regarding the way the public response needed to be handled.

The response to the 2011 flood event is considered a highly successful intervention given an unprecedented scale of activity across the state. The emergency services were seen to have executed a highly proportionate response which justified the confidence in the prior experiences of the disaster state. Whilst there were regional differences in the response, with some regional areas being harder hit and less well-resourced to deal with events than their metropolitan counterparts, the overall perception was of a "successful" disaster response.

In the case of Queensland, whole of government was seen to represent a viable means in which to confront the crisis. Queensland had a sophisticated emergency management system in place that defined a clear set of responsibilities at each level. The commitment to whole of government working was supported by: strong leadership, effective collaboration structures and organisational values largely underpinned by a strong commitment to the state of Queensland. In contrast to Victoria where commitments to whole of government were notionally in place, in Queensland these were enacted. The selection below considers the specific disaster managements in place in the state in 2011. The remainder of the chapter considers the impact of the abovementioned thematic areas on the perception of a successful disaster response.

Queensland disaster arrangements in 2011: The disaster state ready for action

In order to frame the discussion of the crisis event, it is useful to provide an overview of the state disaster management arrangements that were enacted as part of the Queensland floods response. In the aftermath of the floods, disaster arrangements have subsequently changed as a result of the 2013 Police and Community Safety Review. The new disaster management arrangements which are in place have reduced the role played by Emergency Management Queensland and heightened the coordinating role of the emergency services.

It must be noted that it is universally accepted that these changes were not directly attributed as a result of the events in 2011 but rather based on the preferred approach of the Newman government.

At the time of 2011, disaster management arrangements in Queensland were governed by the Disaster Management Act (2003), which formed "the legislative basis for disaster management activities within all levels of government and the Queensland disaster management arrangements" (Queensland Government: State Disaster Management Group, 2010, p. 3). The implementation of the Act during the 2011 floods was strongly guided by the Disaster Management Strategic Policy Framework and State Disaster Management Plan, which guided "the development and implementation of disaster management policy and programs at state and local government level" (Queensland Government: State Disaster Management Group, 2010, p. 4). The model in place in Queensland in 2011 was intended to be an integrated one where disaster preparation and response cascaded from the local to district and ultimately to the state level (Parliament of Queensland, 2003).

Under the Disaster Management Act, the relationship between state, district and local government levels was set out as based on "whole of government disaster arrangements built upon partnerships between government, government owned corporations, NGOs, commerce, industry and the local community" (Queensland Government, 2012a). In Queensland, the disaster management arrangements were described as an all-agencies approach with a bottom-up ethos where "no single agency can prepare for and deal with the disruption to community life and infrastructure that can result from a disaster" (Queensland Government: State Disaster Management Group, 2011, p. 5). Figure 4.2 represents the structure of disaster management arrangements in Queensland at the time of the floods (Queensland Government, 2012a). In this model, there were three distinct layers involved in disaster response: local, district and state. This model was strongly predicated on a cascading approach where local response to disaster events is the first tier that is supported by district and state level responses when its capacity is exhausted.

Figure 4.2 Queensland Disaster Management Arrangements
Source: Adapted from Queensland Government

As part of this structure, the Queensland Government (2012a) defined the principal characteristics that made up Queensland's disaster management arrangements as being: disaster management groups operating at local, district and state levels responsible for mitigation and response; coordination centres at all levels that supported disaster management groups in coordinating resources and information and state government functional agencies which undertook the responsibilities of the state government with regard to disaster response.

A key part of the disaster management and response framework related to the central state government disaster management committee, the State Disaster Management Group (SDMG). The SDMG was the peak body that brought together senior members of the emergency response community, bureaucracy and political arm as a means of overseeing the state wide response to major disaster events. The SDMG comprised members of the emergency response services, the Premier, Deputy Premier, Minister for Health, Minister for Police, Corrective and Emergency Services as well as Director-General representation from the following government departments: Department of Premier and Cabinet, Department of Community Safety, Department of Communities, Department of Environment and Resource Management, Department of Infrastructure and Planning, Department of Justice and Attorney General, Department of Public Works, Department of Transport and Main Roads, Queensland Police, Emergency Management Queensland, Queensland Health and Treasury. Another key part of the system was the appointment of a State Disaster Coordinator to oversee operational coordination of the response. In 2011 Deputy Commissioner Ian Stewart of the Queensland Police Service was appointed to this role (Queensland Government, 2011).

One of the key characteristics of the SDMG was that it had a presence across the political, bureaucratic and operational levels which has been cited as one of the key factors related to the conduct of its business (Arklay, 2012). As a result, there was a single entity that brought together key agencies and provided information flows as well as an accountability mechanism. It also emerged from an examination of the minutes of the extraordinary meetings that there were close links which were formed across agencies and departments with a fluid movement of information and staff. The SDMG was seen as a central part of the emergency response, seen by comments from the then Premier in her submission to the Queensland Inquiry into the floods: "my understanding of the flood operations strategies used in the operation of Wivenhoe during this time was informed by the technical situation reports that were emailed to me by the Director-General and briefings provided at the SDMG meetings" (Queensland Floods Commission of Inquiry, 2011c, p. 2). The SDMG usually met on a quarterly basis, however during the Queensland flood crisis, the committee met on an almost daily basis under the guise of extraordinary meetings. The minutes of the SDMG, which have been obtained through the project, indicate that the committee

was highly engaged with regard to the crisis prior, during and in the inter-
mediate aftermath of the floods. Representation occurred at a very senior
level including the Premier, Ministers and Director's General.

Finally, in terms of the legislative context which existed in Queensland at
the time and underpinned the state disaster management arrangements, it is
critical to note that in mid-2010, significant changes were made to Queensland's disaster management legislation. The changes resulted in a shift of
operational command coordination from EMQ to Queensland Police in the
face of any future disaster. This change was largely predicated on the operational capacity of the police and their integration across state, district and
local levels. The shift towards a stronger coordination role for police was
based on the belief that expanding the operational capacity of EMQ may not
have been feasible at the time.

The Queensland floods: The tragic aftermath

The Queensland floods in January 2011 were a significant natural disaster
event and culminated with the flooding of a large section of the state
including Brisbane. During the floods; 37 people were killed and more than
3600 homes damaged (Attorney General's Department, 2012). Extensive
rainfall over large areas of Queensland, coupled with saturated catchments,
led to flooding of historic proportions in Queensland in December 2010,
stretching into January 2011. More than 78 per cent of the state was declared
a disaster zone; more than 2.5 million people were affected. The Queensland
floods also had a significant impact on the state economy as industries such
as agriculture and mining were heavily affected and estimates put the economic
losses in the agriculture and mining sectors at more than A$1 billion (Parnell
& Owens, 2011, p. 1). The nature and scale of the events meant that many
locations were deeply affected across the state of Queensland most notably
in areas such as the Brisbane metropolitan area, Rockhampton, Ipswich and
the Lockyer Valley. The argument has been made that the case represents a
'successful' crisis management response, "the publicized and largely effective
response to extensive state-wide flooding was not an accident, but rather that
were laid out over many years of prior experience in preparing for a diverse
range of disaster threats" (Arklay, 2012, p. 9).

As a state Queensland due to its diverse geography, climate and population base has a long history and experience around natural disaster events,
particularly flooding and cyclones which occur almost on a yearly basis.
Experience with natural disaster events is largely driven by the fact that
Queensland is situated at tropical latitude and has the most decentralised
population base in Australia with large and significant cities such as Cairns,
Townsville and Rockhampton susceptible to weather events. The trend
towards significant numbers of disaster events was no different in the years
prior to the floods with large scale events such as Cyclone Larry and frequent
flooding a regular feature. Due to its geographically distributed population

and large territory Queensland's disaster management system could only function in a decentralised manner. Given these characteristics, responsibility for planning and response is placed at the hands of local government and this has been cited as an important factor leading to a more coordinated response in disaster management (Arklay, 2012).

One of the most significant outcomes arising from the flood events of 2011 was the establishment of the Queensland Floods Commission of Inquiry. The Queensland Floods Commission of Inquiry was established as a result of the flooding event to look at future mitigation. The scope of the Inquiry was also driven by the loss of life which occurred in the Lockyer Valley and through the impact of the flooding of a large part of metropolitan Brisbane for the first time since the 1970s. In its final report, in excess of 50 recommendations were made from the Commission covering key areas such as floodplain management, state land planning, hydrology and the performance of private insurers in responding to the aftermath of the events (Queensland Floods Commission of Inquiry, 2012d).

The Queensland Floods Commission noted that "its approach across the terms of reference has not been one of seeking to attribute blame, its brief was not to seek out wrong-doers but … make recommendations for the improvement of preparation and planning for future floods" (Queensland Floods Commission of Inquiry, 2012, p. 30). This was further described in the following way "if it seems that our focus lingers on perceptions of failure and deficiency, it must always be remembered that the ultimate goal is to improve the system and not to reprove those who were administering it" (Queensland Floods Commission of Inquiry, 2011a, p. 1303). A very technical discussion emerged at the Commission where the release of water from the Wivenhoe dam was noted as crucial and the idea of "who knew what and when" being a strong theme: "It must be asked whether, as currently written, compliance with the Wivenhoe and Somerset manual allowed a situation to develop where certain areas were protected from flooding for such a period that much more widespread flooding became inevitable soon thereafter" (Queensland Floods Commission of Inquiry, 2011b, p. 21). The Commission's final report notes "an inertia" of government in regards to the possibility of early releases from the Wivenhoe dam (Queensland Floods Commission of Inquiry, 2012, p. 30). The list of recommendations arising from the reports can be considered highly technical with a strong emphasis on the preventative aspects or changes that could be made (often at local council level) in regards to land zoning and development on floodplains as opposed to the coordination arrangements that occurred in the disaster response itself.

Responding to the wall of water: The response and whole of government in action

Having established the context around the Queensland floods, the case was then examined through primary and secondary sources such as: the

Commission report, internal government documents, media reports and the conduct of interviews with key protagonists. Semi-structured interviews were conducted with key personnel involved in the lead up to, response and in the recovery arrangements to the Queensland floods. Broadly, respondents were asked for their views on the key areas of analysis in the book: whole of government, crisis management, leadership, coordination, organisational culture, social capital and role of institutions in the response to the crisis. The following section provides an overview of the outcomes arising from the research that can be used as a basis to support the comparative analysis between the case studies to be presented in Chapter 5.

Whole of government in action

Whole of government working was seen as something which was pervasive across government in Queensland at the time of the floods yet difficult to achieve: "whole of government has become a bit of a mantra in public sector administration in the last two decades, in my experience it is a highly desirable thing that is all but impossible to achieve" (Former Premier, Anna Bligh). The context of federalism was important in shaping the outcomes that occurred as a result of the flooding events in Queensland. The impact of federalism was particularly seen in the role of the defence force in the immediate clean-up which occurred particularly in metropolitan Brisbane and through the funding arrangements that were to follow through the NDRRA. There was a strong sense of collaboration and cooperation which existed at the time between the Commonwealth and state government and as a result a relaxation of some of the initial requirements set out through the NDRRA during the early response (Ryan, 2011, p. 6). As the response progressed and a decision to create a reconstruction entity was made, there was a strong degree of scrutiny around funding arrangements. The emphasis on appropriate governance arrangements in the reconstruction process was largely based on the Commonwealth's experience following on from the Victorian bushfires.

In many respects there appears to have been a strong perception from early on that the response to the Queensland floods was well handled: "the response from all levels of government – federal, state and local – has so far been exceptional. Everyone from the army to the State Emergency Service and thousands of police and emergency services workers has been involved in the operations" (Fagan, 2011b, p. 18). Minutes of the SDMG meetings obtained through the research indicate that members of the SDMG believed that the response to the floods was being handled in an efficient and integrated manner. The then Premier Anna Bligh often noted that the disaster was being well managed at the local level and that the interactions between key departments were working effectively and indeed that these could be seen to be of world standard (Queensland Government, 2011). The Prime Minister who also attended these meetings commented that the "Queensland flood event is being managed in exemplary fashion to date and thanked everyone for that past work, the work being undertaken now today and for the work that will be undertaken in the days to come" (Queensland Government, 2011, p. 65).

Within the context of what unfolded in Queensland in January 2011, the nature and structure of whole of government was generally seen as crucial and well-functioning by interview respondents. The key protagonists believed that whole of government working provided a solution to the difficulty of the immediate response as well as through the recovery and reconstruction process:

> Whole of government at the senior level does require that collegiate link between the Directors-General working at the operational level. It relies on good dialogue between heads of departments, if there are overlapping issues and challenging issues you need to be able to pick up the phone to the other person to allow cut-through in a time of crisis.
>
> (Former CEO QRA, Graeme Newton)

There was a pervading sense that the whole of government response was not only rhetoric but that it was accompanied by a deep commitment to this form of working. This commitment was supported by structures embedded through the disaster management arrangements which connected government during the crisis:

> I just need to say that we throw the words whole of government at random and most states use it. Most states will talk about whole of government but in Queensland we not only talked about it but the government in 2003, particularly with the state disaster management act encapsulated it in legislation and in all the procedures and all the guidelines strengthening the whole of government situation.
>
> (Former Assistant Director General EMQ, Warren Bridson)

It was noted that there was a uniqueness to whole of government working and that crises represented one of the few opportunities "when old animosities are cast aside and even the bureaucracy of business and government bends a little to ensure help is available where it is needed most" (Fagan, 2011b, p. 18). Indeed, it was suggested that the crisis represented a unique opportunity in which to implement whole of government given that there was an intrinsic motivation and urgency to do so whilst it was much harder to implement in "peace time":

> The only time I've genuinely experienced a whole of government process despite the rhetoric around whole government is during disasters.
>
> (Former Director General Department of Community Safety,
> Jim McGowan)

When you get into the hurly-burly of an event all that goes out the window, everyone has a mission, that mission is absolutely crystal clear, you have direct engagement with the political arm and executive government. You cut through all of those issues to get to a resolution very rapidly, it's an ability to be able to institutionalise that cultural construct, and it has proven to be impossible.

(Former Assistant Director General Department of
Community Safety, Bruce Grady)

The perception of a well-managed event at the state level was however juxtaposed against a belief that there were difficulties coordinating the entire response across Queensland, given the scale and extent of the disaster: "such was the magnitude of that which occurred in January, it might be thought unlikely that any system put in place prior to that time could have anticipated perfectly all of the problems which the floods created" (Queensland Floods Commission of Inquiry, 2011a, p. 1303).

Coordination difficulties across the state can be seen to be a result of the widespread nature of the events that unfolded. The structure of Queensland's disaster management system and its emphasis on local government was cited as an important consideration in understanding overall capacity. This was highlighted through the Commission of Inquiry which was critical of the level of preparation in some regional centres (ABC, 2011a). At a broad level, this points to the disparity that existed in capacity across the state and the variable capacities of organisational units such as small local government areas to manage events of the scale of 2011.

Crisis management: The dams are full

The 2011 Queensland floods were rightfully described as a "national disaster" (*Sydney Morning Herald*, 2011a, p. 14), given the severity and scale of the events which unfolded over a number of months and culminated in January 2011 affecting more than 78 per cent of Queensland (Queensland Floods Commission of Inquiry, 2012, p. 386). There was a strong sense that in wake of the 2009 bushfires in Victoria, there was a public awareness about these kinds of events which resonated and as such both these events occupied a place in the national consciousness (*Sydney Morning Herald*, 2011a, p. 14). There was also a uniqueness involved in the event given that large parts of an urban metropolitan centre, Brisbane, were inundated and cut-off which had not been experienced in 40 years (Murdoch & Lee, 2011, p. 19). The tone associated with the flood events and through the Commission of Inquiry report was very much one which acknowledged the events as perhaps an inevitable part of life requiring due diligence:

Contemporary society does not countenance a fatalistic approach to such inevitabilities, even if their occurrence is unpredictable. There is an expectation that government will act to protect its citizens from disaster, and that all available science should be applied so that the nature and extent of the risk is known and appropriate action taken to ameliorate it. (Queensland Floods Commission of Inquiry, 2012, p. 38)

Views and perceptions around the response to the crisis in Queensland are possibly a reflection of the disaster state mentality given that it is Australia's most disaster prone state: "no one is to blame for these terrible floods; they remain defined as an 'act of God'. But, for a state synonymous with a harsh climate and unforgiving environment, there is always room for improvement in how we deal with the inevitable" (Fagan, 2011a, p. 18). There is also a sense in Queensland that disaster events are inevitable in a tropical state "we've been through it before, we've been through a lot of floods. It's part of living here ... when they come, they come" (Resident cited in *The Australian*, 2011). This early tone around the events can be seen to be significant as it became the dominant narrative surrounding the nature of the flood crisis where the blame attributed was around dam management rather than the overall response.

The 2011 events provided a significant challenge for a state that was accustomed to frequent natural disasters. It was felt however that Queensland had strong vertical and horizontal structures in place to deal with what was considered a worst-case scenario:

> Nobody was caught unawares, what we are unaware of was the extent of the situation itself, in my wildest dreams I never thought I'd be dealing with a flood through the CBD of Brisbane, Ipswich washed away, the Lockyer Valley in turmoil, the Western Downs flooded and also traffic problems and people wanting to be rescued.
> (Former Assistant Director General EMQ, Warren Bridson)

It was also noteworthy that the length of the crisis also proved to be one of the more challenging aspects. Heavy rains had begun in Queensland in October 2010 and continued on into January 2011 with the culmination of events being the tragic flooding in the Lockyer Valley followed by widespread damage in Brisbane:

> I think the longevity of the disaster proved to be one of the challenges; disasters tend to happen over a period over 48 hours before they usually return to normal. In my diary it began on 24 December and ran through pretty continuously until 15 February.
> (Former Senior Emergency Management Officer)

It was clear than an important part of the response involved the level and degree of integration between the political arm and the emergency services which was deemed as highly desirable and as a way of reassuring the public about the integration and efficacy of the response that was occurring:

I think the other thing she [Anna Bligh] did exceedingly well which marks a strategy and risk communication that people take note of is that political leadership standing beside the experts, all the uniforms such as coppers or the military person beside her or the Bureau of Meteorology it reassures the public that there is no politics being played out here.

(Former Director General Department of Community
Safety, Jim McGowan)

Another significant issue which arose was that of resilience both at the state and the community level including the ability for the state and the community to be more resilient in the face of adversity. The ability for citizens and communities to be resilient in the face of a crisis was cited as being very important in a state such as Queensland which is extremely prone to natural disasters, has large territorial boundaries and has the most geographically distributed population of any state. Community needs were acknowledged by the Prime Minister during the immediate response to the floods where she noted: "this is a very, very severe set of floods, affecting communities that are very geographically dispersed and the Commonwealth government will be there" (Gillard cited in Parnell & Owens, 2011, p. 1). As a result discussions around community resilience were seen as important to understanding how to best support isolated or remote communities:

Cabinet had considered issues about that and how could the government instil that sense of self-reliance, self-reliance is predicated a number of things, understanding your hazard or risk profile and another thing is understanding what the hell do you want to do about this, what preparations do you need to make, there are a lot of social issues at play here, communities are a lot more disconnected than they used to be.

(Former Assistant Director General Department of
Community Safety, Bruce Grady)

It was also evident that at the government level there needed to be appropriate consideration of the way that disaster management infrastructure is integrated within other public resources and services in Queensland. There was a strong sense that the "all hazards" framework was an appropriate one in which to prepare for and respond to disasters given the synergies that exist between events:

Most disaster response is, in fact, generic – and that's why the Police are so good at dealing with them. You need a specific skill to, say, rescue people in flood waters, but: feeding them; sheltering them; distributing relief; organising evacuations; health; communication; infrastructure and supply restoration; emergency repairs etc. – they are pretty much common to all major disasters – and that's why it is those skill sets which are so critical.

(Former Deputy Premier, Paul Lucas)

There were also political consequences related to the flood events and in particular to the popularity of the incumbent government. In the lead up to the floods, the Labor government was trailing in the polls and there was an acknowledgement that the "Queensland floods possibly represent Anna Bligh's last chance of regaining electoral momentum". The news poll prior to the flood events at the end of 2010 indicated that the government was on track for a resounding defeat (Fraser, 2011, p. 4). There was a clear identification that the response of the government to the floods could potentially represent an important political issue and similarly to the Victorian case, the early sense of bi-partisanship dissipated with the Opposition questioning the Premier's response to the events (Parnell & Owens, 2011, p. 1). The response of the government and in particular the Premier Anna Bligh was however strongly lauded in the public domain in the aftermath to the crisis with a significant reverse in polling and popularity levels. The then Deputy Premier Paul Lucas noted that although in a political sense it may have been advisable to focus on the electoral outcomes, by trying to remove the politics from the situation the state may have achieved better outcomes than otherwise would have been the case:

> Anna didn't take the Machiavellian route of calling an election straight after, if she was merely interested in base politics she could have done that we might have had a chance of winning or at the least might not have had the result we did. When you're working in those disaster situations if you're worried about the political outcomes you will not have a good outcome.
>
> (Former Deputy Premier, Paul Lucas)

It is interesting however by the time of the state election the following year that the bounce in the polling that occurred following on from the crisis where the ALP increased to 38 per cent in March 2011 had all but dissipated by September 2011 to 27 per cent (Hawker Britton, 2012). In the following year the state government then went on to suffer a resounding defeat. This may also be as a result of the popularity of then Lord Mayor Campbell Newman, another key figure in the 2011 events who oversaw the response in the city of Brisbane. Newman would later become opposition leader and was at the time seen as highly competent and credible alternative to Premier Bligh. As a result any political advantage may have been neutralised by the fact that the opposition could also claim credibility in the disaster response through its leader. The then Premier Anna Bligh described this noting that with the passage of time any short term political advantage that may have been gained evaporated:

> Immediately after the floods news poll reported a turnaround in Labor's vote that was the biggest reverse in news poll's history, a week is a long time in politics and 12 months of going back through some of the other

issues from the disaster to things the electorate don't like such as what's happening at the hospital or whatever took its toll.

(Former Premier, Anna Bligh)

Leadership: We are 'Queenslanders'

The positive perception of the leadership response to the 2011 floods represents one of the most powerful and enduring legacies following on from the events themselves. It has often been noted that:

> Disasters can define a politician's leadership. Rudy Giuliani became a household hero as New York mayor on September 11, 2001. President George Bush's slide began when he took three days to properly respond to Hurricane Katrina. As Queensland is ravaged by floods, it is the Premier, Anna Bligh, who seems to have grown in stature.
>
> (Davies, 2011, p. 4)

Within this context, the narrative which emerged from early on in the disaster response from the media and the public was that there was strong leadership within the state "at a time for leadership, a time to pull together" where "it was reassuring to see the Premier back on the ground in central Queensland yesterday" (Fagan, 2011b, p. 18). The reflections on leadership picked up on many of the individual characteristics of the Premier in responding with "a combination of appearing to be in control but of caring deeply" (Davies, 2011, p. 4) and providing strong overall direction to the coordination of the response:

> Anna Bligh has proven to be sincere, articulate, objective and emotive in her regular media updates to the community regarding the Queensland flood catastrophe. Her diction has been clear, factual and sympathetic. Her demeanour reflects leadership, capability and empathy with the people affected. She's one of us, for us, and her handling of the crisis exemplary.
>
> (Keeley, 2011, p. 15)

> Disasters can define leaders, the classic history was in 1974 Cyclone Tracy, the headlines and I can still see them, Whitlam looks at the ruins of Rome while Darwin is in ruins. I mean visible leadership is where there are images of people on the ground. You've got to show empathy, you've got to show that you're there, you've got to show that you've personally seen it. If you look at all the images such as Anna Bligh sleeping in an evacuation centre and with her boots these are the most powerful.
>
> (Former Executive Director Red Cross, Greg Goebels)

Through the interview process with key participants, there were significant reflections on the type and level of leadership required with respect to the events and how the leadership response worked during the crisis. These confirmed that the view from within government was very similar to the public view that leadership emanating from the top of government was crucial and drove a successful response:

> The impression externally is how it was internally there wasn't any disconnect with that, the two strongest communicators were the Premier and the Assistant Police Commissioner and they both are gifted communicators anyway. What Anna would try and do is unlike many politicians she can be a details person as well, she would spend a lot of time and effort into distilling and understanding, not just communicating that we had a particular thing happening but why.
>
> (Former Deputy Premier, Paul Lucas)

> Within the operational side, people saw the Premier out there conveying to the public the information that the public needed to hear, they saw her providing moral support to the community, to the volunteers and our uniformed officers. That level of leadership was critically important.
>
> (Former Police Minister, Neil Roberts)

It was also noted that the task of leadership had been significantly helped by the experience in the broader SDMG group which had been obtained by working together through a number of other disasters in the preceding years. Experience in these previous events had built a sense of confidence in the Premier and vice-versa that could be harnessed at the time of the disaster itself:

> I think generally if you can't lead in a crisis you can't lead anywhere that would be my view and that is reflected elsewhere. I think there are two other factors that happened for us, we had had a series of disasters over the four years prior to 2010–11: The Gap storms in Brisbane, we had flooding in Ingham and a couple of cyclones in the years before. We had equine influenza, H1N1 influenza and we had an oil spill, the government and the key players had been meeting together through all of those events so there was an experience that we were basing decisions on … we had built leadership on experiences of a range of events.
>
> (Former Director General Department of Community Safety, Jim McGowan)

This was replicated at the local level through experience gained within the city of Brisbane. The Former Lord Mayor and subsequent Premier, Campbell Newman described it in this way:

> I had [disasters in] November 2004, November 2008 and May 2009 and these were progressively bigger events, I was being trained up, the staff

were being trained up. By the time of 2011 we had been practicing this for some time.

> (Former Lord Mayor Brisbane, Campbell Newman)

There was a strong sense that there was no panic in the face of such a large scale disaster and that the SDMG was well equipped to respond given that it had a strong core of politicians, bureaucrats and operational response agency people who had been in similar situations in the past:

> I think it's a feature of people who make it to the top, that they know how to stay calm under pressure, they don't panic, and they have a sense of urgency but never a sense of panic. That makes for much better decision-making having people whose temperature is low, yours stays low, and they were people who weren't escalating things that didn't need to be escalated.
>
> (Former Premier, Anna Bligh)

Another factor cited was the input from the political arm of government which mobilised resources, set priorities and coordinated the overall response. The emergency response agencies and government departments were appreciative of this input and saw it as a necessary given the scale and magnitude of the events:

> I think it was the fact that the Premier was very hands-on from the first sign of the crisis to pretty well until the crisis was over, very hands-on in the community, very hands-on with the leaders in local government and the state-wide recovery level in managing the crisis.
>
> (Former Director General Department of Community,
> Linda Apelt)

The strength of the leadership response has often been exemplified through the address of Anna Bligh usually referred to as "We are Queenslanders" an extract of which is included below. In many respects this address can be seen to typify the nature of the response to the crisis and the connection formed between the state's leadership and the public:

> We are Queenslanders; we're the people that they breed tough north of the border. We're the ones that they knock down and we get up again. I said earlier this week that this weather may break our hearts and it is doing that but it will not break our will and in the coming weeks and in the coming months we are going to prove that beyond any doubt. Together, we can pull through this and that's what I'm determined to do and with your help, we can achieve that.
>
> (Bligh, 2011)

In reflecting upon this address, the then Premier noted that in many ways she had a strong awareness that the task of leadership at the time required a strong sense of empathy and connection with the public. This connection was necessary in order to reassure the public that everything possible was being undertaken in the response to the events as they unfolded:

> My job was not only to make sure what needed to be done was being done as well as it could be but leaders have a responsibility beyond that to make sure that we uplift people and give them a sense they can do what needs to be done.
>
> (Bligh cited in ABC One Plus One, 2014)

Anna Bligh also reflected in an interview that the use of such strong language was not only geared as a means to calm public concern but also a rallying call to the government who were facing this large scale response. The speech was seen as a powerful symbol in the overall response to directly connect with the public and mobilise the internal response:

> I said that it will break our hearts but it will not break our will, as the words came out of my mouth I worried that I did not strike the right tone, I knew that it was a risk to get into that lofty kind of place, but it was clear that people responded well to it. I said it almost as a rallying call to myself, it was me saying the morning after the Toowoomba events it is not going to break us.
>
> (Former Premier, Anna Bligh)

Coordination: Across the sunshine state

The narrative surrounding coordination throughout the unfolding crisis was generally very positive with an acknowledgement that "as usual, the response of local government, police and Queensland State Emergency Service staff to the crisis has been outstanding" (*The Australian*, 2011, p. 13). Key coordination mechanisms which impacted on the ability to respond to the events at the political, bureaucratic and operational levels were cited as highly effective. The majority of participants agreed that coordination worked well across different layers of government through both vertical and horizontal means, noting however that in some areas there were complexities due to the sheer magnitude of the events and the complexity of the recovery process. Having representation from senior figures within departments and agencies meant that there was a sense of authority and mandate within the group which meant that things could move quickly in government as was required by the situation:

> A critical part of the success of that group was that the DGs were there, so when decisions were made, directions could be given to their

departments or agencies for action. That was one of the major strengths. It's not just the decision-making: it's their experience, capacity and knowledge which can be fed into a discussion around critically important decisions in terms of the response to a disaster.

(Former Police Minister, Neil Roberts)

There was a strong sense that emerged throughout the research that in order to provide an adequate response, there needed to be a degree of hierarchy within the horizontal approach being undertaken through the SDMG. By maintaining control of the overall direction, the Premier could direct processes around prioritisation of tasks and ensure effective dialogue between the state, district and local levels:

> What it demonstrated to me was that people sat through these coordination meetings at levels of seniority that you would otherwise not expect and here was me Head of the Queensland Civil Service chairing these meetings involving much more senior people than me who were incredibly engaged; this meant that we were able to get an understanding of issues on the ground and had the authority of political and other leaders.
>
> (Former Director General Department of Premier and
> Cabinet, Ken Smith)

A strong theme to emerge was that coordination between the different levels of whole of government: political, bureaucratic and operational functioned very well and that this represented a strongly integrated approach between departments and agencies. As a result, it was suggested that this integration led to a higher degree of precision and meant that many of the potential risks of fragmentation were mitigated:

> The political level and awareness of political people was of the highest level, the Premier and her Ministers and through the local networks were able to get information from many and varied sources.
>
> (Former Assistant Director General EMQ, Warren Bridson)

There was recognition that there were difficulties in coordinating across the different layers of the emergency response arrangements particularly at the local level where the capacity of local governments differed, both in terms of size and scope as well as individual orientations towards managing disasters:

> I thought that in a sense it went from the SDMG straight to a very local level and bypassed a lot of the structures, when it got to the local government level the quality of the people and their experience in some senses meant that things just came in over the top.
>
> (Former Executive Director Red Cross, Greg Goebels)

Large and well-resourced councils such as Brisbane City Council were also able to have an effective machinery in place in order to respond to the events which were unfolding: "at that time as the Mayor of Brisbane, I had the power to direct, that's the way it should be if you want to effectively manage disasters" (Former Lord Mayor Brisbane, Campbell Newman). Brisbane was very much seen as a focal for the strength of the response: "the very concept of disaster management derives from the need to confront such situations and some of the experiences in metropolitan Brisbane provide a prism through which the effectiveness of the state's disaster management system can be examined" (Queensland Floods Commission of Inquiry, 2011a, p. 1303).The importance of having a clear set of arrangements in place was emphasised by the independent review of Brisbane City Council which found that:

> Council has developed a very effective set of arrangements to enable it to deal with a major flood event. These arrangements reflect and follow the various Commonwealth and Queensland Government Acts, policies and best practice guidelines pertaining to disaster management.
> (Independent Review Board – Brisbane City Council, 2011, p. 2)

Organisational culture: The embedded ethos

The impact of the cultures of different organisations and how these shaped the response, as well as the strengths and challenges of operating in a whole of government framework were seen as central to the outcome. With regard to organisational culture it was almost universally accepted that Queensland, due to being frequently hit by natural disasters, had built a culture of accountability across agencies and departments which could be leveraged in times of crisis:

> For me relationships are important in understanding how the system works; the relationships that develop between the people sitting around the table and the different levels of the committees are really important. They can actually achieve where a system or structure can fail and even with a bad structure when something needs to happen people get it done.
> (Former Police Minister, Neil Roberts)

> As Premier by the time we were sitting there in 2011 there was not a single person at the table I didn't know or who I hadn't sat around a table with through a lesser scale disaster. It wasn't just true from me as a politician it was true for the public servants in the room. That's a really an important thing, as a major scale disaster is not the time to start to get to know each other.
> (Former Premier, Anna Bligh)

The view was expressed that a culture of collaboration was built as part of the ethos of the disaster management system and that this spirit of collaboration was one of the most pervasive elements of the system. It represented an intangible binding quality rather than a concrete or formal mechanism:

> We can talk about the culture of collaboration and the culture of cooperation and I think personally it's very strong within the system … The culture however is often embedded in the structure, and we've always had some continuity and recognition that this is the system we have and that it works.
>
> (Former Police Minister, Neil Roberts)

Another key feature of the nature of the organisational culture and the relationships between members of the SDMG related to the sense of accountability which existed amongst its members. There was a strong sense that senior figures within government not only saw the response as a state-wide responsibility but as a personal responsibility. This was exemplified by then Lord Mayor of Brisbane Campbell Newman who said "for me, that moment when I looked at the reading, it was the incredible feeling of a burden on my shoulders" (Newman cited in *The Courier Mail*, 2011). It may be the case that Queensland due to its history and geography as a frontier state may have developed a unique sense of identity and solidarity that could be harnessed during a crisis as a rallying point:

> When you eyeball people the heads nod and you expect that the rest of the actions follow, so you don't get that passive resistance or whatever the right word if you meet on a daily basis. The more frequently you meet, the closer the personal accountabilities are, I think that is what happened.
>
> (Former Director General Department of Community
> Safety, Jim McGowan)

Another highly significant issue which impacted around coordination and organisational culture was the changes to the Queensland disaster management arrangements that occurred immediately prior to the crisis. The argument was made that the review of emergency management arrangements in 2010 which assigned operational command to the Police had the potential to cause clashes in culture "everyone was very twitchy about that, the culture of the police and the culture of the emergency services was entirely different" (Former Executive Director Red Cross, Greg Goebels). Concerns around the increased role for police were largely ameliorated by the nature of the relationships and the leveraging of social capital which had been built both at the institutional and individual levels:

> He (Ian Stewart) made sure the police who were going to work with EMQ had a history of working with EMQ and understood EMQ and

were appreciative of what we did and made sure their attitude never was stand aside we will now take over. And your question, the reason it worked was because Ian Stewart handpicked his team and he knew full well the issues and problems, all those petty things that can happen in operations and brings things undone pretty quickly.

(Former Assistant Director General EMQ, Warren Bridson)

The changes made around the operational command during major crises exemplified debates around command and control versus horizontality in disaster management. There was the possibility that by giving the police an increased role in the disaster management system, this could be seen as a further step towards command and control. Any of these concerns were largely ameliorated by the police who were able to work in a cooperative manner across government:

One of the issues and debates which took place and this is a critical issue in my view is whether disaster management should be managed through command and control or through collaboration ... . You can't have an effective response from someone sitting in Brisbane giving directions to someone in Mt Isa ... . The experience I had with police over five years was that the people who moved into disaster management were committed to collaboration.

(Former Police Minister, Neil Roberts)

Social capital: The personal connection

In terms of social capital, the importance of professional relationships across the key actors and the ability to leverage these bonds and ties during the crisis itself was cited as crucial to the overall response. There was however the need to be aware of the important balance between personal relationships and institutional structures:

The Keelty review talked in quite disparaging terms about the reliance on relationships to achieve outcomes, I happen to hold a different view, it wasn't just relationships, it was relationships that operated within a very structured framework, it wasn't just about who you like and all that stuff which goes on but there was a very strong structured approach to disaster management and then within that, the ability to have relationships.

(Former Assistant Director General Department of
Community Safety, Bruce Grady)

As the response moved into recovery, leveraging relationships was critical in the reconstruction phase. In this respect the Head of the Queensland Reconstruction Authority acknowledged the important role that professional relationships would play through interactions with stakeholders at the local government level:

> Very early in the piece I gave a speech at the local government con-
> ference in May 2011 and spelt out the approach that we were going to
> take in the recovery and reconstruction. In this forum of several hundred
> council CEOs, mayors, councillors in the audience, I gave out my
> mobile phone and said you must call me if you need assistance ... It was
> a doctrine of working together in partnership with them to deliver a
> mutual outcome rather than adopting an adversarial relationship.
>
> (Former CEO QRA, Graeme Newton)

It was clear that there was a social capital that existed across government (political, bureaucratic and operational streams) which had been forged through previous shared experiences in responding to major disasters. The strength of relationships can also be seen to be predicated on the unique sense of identity which exists in Queensland, where there is a strong affilia-tion to the state. In this way professional relationships where supported by a culture which pointed to a collective good in doing the best for the state in its time of need.

Institutions: United we stand

Following on from events in January 2011, the governance and disaster management arrangements in Queensland were not placed under the same degree of scrutiny and pressure as what occurred in Victoria. The general perception was that the disaster management arrangements operated well and there were no significant structural concerns related to the way in which the system operated. Institutions mandated as part of the Queensland disaster management arrangements played a pivotal role. It also emerged that the agency and actions of individuals were complementary to institutional structures and provided an integrated response system:

> I can start with the experience of the SDMG, which had clarity in
> statute that meant that as Director General of Premier and Cabinet, I
> was clearly responsible for the coordination of the response and in
> bringing that whole of government focus together. I could not have done
> that job unless I was the most senior public servant in the state. The posi-
> tion had statutory backing, it had clarity of purpose and the group
> had met outside of disaster situations on a regular basis to discuss
> and prepare for the inevitable disaster that would occur and we'd
> already been through situations in sometimes the same or different
> formal roles.
>
> (Former Director General Department of Premier and
> Cabinet, Ken Smith)

Within the Queensland system, there was a clear delineation of roles and responsibilities. This meant that there was clarity around the role of the response agencies, government departments and the political arm:

> It's best described as a series of roles, similar to the UK Bronze, Silver and Gold systems. If you imagine those three systems; at the Gold level it is about what needs to be done, the Silver level is about how to do it and the Bronze level is just do it. To an extent the first is dictated by how the top-level works, what should be done, at the second it is how should it be done, it's not the priorities, it is how do we implement that.
>
> (Former Senior Emergency Management Officer)

There were also significant reflections on the legislative changes which occurred in 2010 that gave police control of operational control structures. Whilst there had been some trepidation prior to their enactment, these had worked well during the event and indeed strengthened response arrangements:

> You have to be very pragmatic, in no circumstances can a government legitimately go to its community and say we want to build a greater standing capacity for an event that might occur every half a dozen years or so, it's very expensive if it is not practised regularly then how effective and efficient is it going to be. So I think governments legitimately have to work around that and see what is the latent or available capability and capacity that we have.
>
> (Former Assistant Director General Department of Community Safety, Bruce Grady)

It was noted that the success in adopting this new model so close to what was to be the 2011 Queensland floods was based on an understanding that operating exclusively within a command and control model would not work. Implementation of the new coordination arrangements required a spirit of collaboration and coordination in order to work horizontally with the myriad of agencies involved in the response to the crisis:

> If you simply overlay command and control over a disaster management system it is chaos because people will rail against the way that command and control operates relative to management, it will be an anathema to one group and the other group won't understand why what I'm direct-ing isn't getting done, why are people questioning this. It's not as though we have a single system to deal with this, we have an amalgamation of all sorts of different cultures, you have to come together and be effective. If everything was management by committee it wouldn't work, if every-thing was command and control it wouldn't work. What we had in

2010–2011 was a pretty good collection of all of those things; people understood one versus the other.

(Former Assistant Director General Department of
Community Safety, Bruce Grady)

Whilst in general terms there was little criticism of the overall response to the crisis, there were some clear issues identified by the Royal Commission around the way in which matters such as dam releases were handled and where discrepancies were cited (Queensland Floods Commission of Inquiry, 2012, p. 515). Other major recommendations surrounded land management and planning regulations and how these were applied in floodplains and the effect that these may have had in exacerbating what unfolded throughout the course of January 2011.

Another important critique which was noted by the Commission referred to planning. As a result of the bottom-up ethos in disaster preparation and response in Queensland, there was a disparity in the quality of planning. Disparities in preparation and planning were consistent with the notion that there was variable capacity amongst councils. A key finding of the commission was to charge EMQ with reviewing and reducing variability amongst operational plans at the local level:

> The Commission observed in its interim report that Emergency Management Queensland had not had a consistent approach to how it conducted the review of disaster management plans. Accordingly, the Commission recommended that Emergency Management Queensland take steps to improve the overall review process, and that it assess the effectiveness of the review system before the end of 2011.
>
> (Queensland Floods Commission of Inquiry, 2012, p. 400)

Similarly to the Victorian bushfires, one of the significant outcomes arising from the Queensland floods was the decision to undertake a Commission of Inquiry into the events. Through discussion with the participants many noted that they believed that the process was not optimal in terms of ensuring improved outcomes. Indeed, there was a perception that the Commission did not represent the strength of the response which had occurred:

> I felt that the Commission of Inquiry didn't pick up on the strength of our response and I suppose a person in the public looking at the media coverage on the nature of the Commission's report would think it was a bad response to the Queensland floods. I actually believe we had an exceptionally good response, obviously some terrible situations occurred and when you look back we might now address some things differently in the future.
>
> (Former Police Minister, Neil Roberts)

Upon release of the final report in 2012, the Queensland government indicated that it would move to strongly implement the recommendations arising from the Commission particularly around land use, planning and management. The Commission process had served to highlight that it is "vitally important that, as a state, we also act decisively and proactively to improve our response and recovery capacity" and "engage in better planning and flood mitigation to protect Queensland families and communities from the impacts of major floods" (Queensland Government, 2012b, p. 4). Whilst a Commission of Inquiry was a useful process to review what may have happened in a particular event, it could not be used to try and understand what may happen in the future. Ian Stewart noted this during the unfolding of the crisis where he stated that whilst parallels could be drawn to previous flood events there were significant changes which had occurred in the urban landscape "the challenge for everyone in this is that, whilst there are great flood maps for the 1974 event and a lot of modelling has been done since then, Brisbane is a far different town to what it was" (Stewart cited in ABC, 2011b). Particularly with regard to flood events it was noted that there is a high degree of variability and one event may differ significantly to the next:

> My criticism of Commissions of Inquiry which are set up under a legal framework is that their reports are designed to be the absolute best response to the event that occurred, it doesn't matter if the event happens in the same place it won't be the same … . We need to create structures and systems that provide people with good training with the ability to make decisions to respond to that stimulus and respond as best as they possibly can.
>
> (Former Assistant Director General Department of
> Community Safety, Bruce Grady)

The final key institutional mechanism that was reviewed as part of the research related to the Queensland Reconstruction Authority. The Queensland Reconstruction Authority was established under the Queensland Reconstruction Authority Act 2011 following the unprecedented natural disasters that struck Queensland over the summer months of 2010–11. The authority was created as a special purpose entity in order to address the large scale reconstruction activity required as a result of the 2011 floods across not only Brisbane but throughout regional Queensland. It sought to create a systematic mechanism in which to address the large scale infrastructure projects which were required and create an accountability mechanism for the reconstruction funding which had been allocated following on from the flood events. The Authority's role was to work within the context of government particularly at the interface between state and local government in order to deliver value for money and best practice expenditure and acquittal of public reconstruction funds (Queensland Government, 2011).

The Reconstruction Authority can be seen to be a highly significant outcome of the events in 2011, given that it has remained in place and has been cited as a highly effective means to take on large scale reconstruction activities. Indeed, the World Bank has acknowledged the response to the Queensland flood events and the establishment of the Authority as "meeting international good practice standards in many ways and building on a wealth of experience" (World Bank, 2011, p. 3).

The establishment of the QRA was recognition that in extraordinary circumstances a business as usual approach would not be sufficient given the estimated $5.8billion worth of damage (*Brisbane Times*, 2011). The then Premier described it as "a reconstruction task ahead of us that is of post-war proportions and I said it because I believed it. It was like the place had been bombed" (Former Premier, Anna Bligh). There was a strong feeling that the events required a special purpose entity to work across government in order to ensure that the reconstruction task could be completed and acquitted appropriately:

> Obviously because of the scale of the disaster it was felt that agencies and councils could go about their normal business, make applications for funds and start the work etc. Given the scale of the destruction, the road works, the community infrastructure, the public infrastructure you needed a more coordinated response to make sure that the resources would be put to where they were needed and prioritised ... the clear thinking from the Premier and in the Cabinet was that we needed to have a more focused coordinated response, so the reconstruction authority was the vehicle which is going to achieve that.
>
> (Former Police Minister, Neil Roberts)

The QRA was cited as an effective example of a reconstruction body given that in many ways it had looked at events in Victoria two years earlier and had been able to learn from the experiences of the VBRRA. Specifically, it was noted that having the mechanisms to control finances were of utmost importance and that having this enshrined through legislation gave the QRA much more mandate and authority than otherwise may have been the case:

> I think given the extent of damage that there was in the state it was pretty much needed; the federal government was particularly interested in finding out where its money was going through the disaster recovery funding arrangements. For those reasons an independent authority gives you something to get things going and which is powered by legislation. Giving you the legislative clout and the ability to look after finances in a much more robust fashion than ever before has been a useful vehicle since then.
>
> (Former Senior Emergency Management Officer)

The QRA Act draws powers from a range of different pieces of other legislation, which meant it could be rapidly drafted and was unanimously adopted by the Queensland Parliament. It is worth noting that you can have legislated power and authority and you don't necessarily have to use it. We have used elements of the QRA Act, but on the whole we haven't had to use it much, but by having it we have that scope to intervene if necessary.

(Former CEO QRA, Graeme Newton)

The creation of such an authority is a strong political symbol. Some commentators noted that this may have been the result of a political imperative and the need to be seen to getting on with the task of reconstruction:

No doubt Bligh is genuine in her desire to help flood victims. But she is also motivated by an ugly political imperative. With her popularity floating downstream, she needs to be seen to be doing something. She must create a perception that she has taken charge.

(Houghton, 2011, p. 56)

From the inside of the QRA, it was noted that the decision to pursue a reconstruction authority was a quick one and the Head of the QRA Graeme Newton reflected "it was like a ship sliding down the slipway and we were still hammering planks on the sides". There was a strong imperative to implement a reconstruction authority in a timely manner and "there was a very narrow window after a major crisis to establish the framework for a successful recovery" (Former CEO QRA, Graeme Newton). The impetus for the establishment of the QRA had been driven from the level of the Premier who was keen to ensure that reconstruction activities began in earnest in order to return the state to a sense or normality:

The Reconstruction Authority was very much Anna's idea, she was very emphatic about that ... we knew that people needed the infrastructure restored quickly and business will go out the door unless you have contracts out quickly and spending money on reconstruction had a positive effect in those communities, with the quick approval processes that related to things, that was deemed to be the one stop shop in having approval processes happening.

(Former Deputy Premier, Paul Lucas)

It has also been suggested that the QRA understood the imperative to work on the reconstruction of the most badly affected towns. Prioritising the worst hit locations ensured that there was not a sense of desperation or abandonment which built up in the public as a result of the damage which had been caused. This was a difficult task given that 51 of the state's 73 councils were affected by flooding and the then Federal Treasurer described this as "very big ... . It's not just something which is going to occupy our time for the next few months. It will be a question of years as we go through the rebuilding process" (Swan cited in *Sydney Morning Herald*, 2011b). The then

Head of the Reconstruction Authority Graeme Newton outlined the importance of the symbolic value of addressing the most badly affected localities in the first instance:

> Tully Heads (impacted by TC Yasi) and Grantham (impacted by flash flooding) were two towns we realised that would be seen as the barometer for the success of the disaster recovery. While we had to get the program delivered across the whole state, we knew we had to get it right in these two towns. We had to act quickly and work with the local councils to have a plan for the recovery of these towns. The success in these areas would rebuild confidence across the state, where the recovery of these towns would be a demonstration that the rest of the recovery would all happen as a matter of course. We needed to have a particular vigilance in those areas, and while there were plenty of other areas which were destroyed, these were the two towns everyone know about.
>
> (Former CEO QRA, Graeme Newton)

Conclusion

This Chapter has provided a detailed overview of the 2011 Queensland floods. There is a general that the whole of government response was highly effective and 'successful' in the face of an unprecedented crisis. From the research which has been conducted, a number of key themes have emerged regarding the way in which the whole of government response shaped the overall outcome to the crisis. In the first instance, there was a strong acceptance around the value of whole of government working. The acceptance of whole of government working was underpinned by the understanding that it represents an important but difficult to achieve concept within the public service. It was noted that in the Queensland context, crisis situations actually provide the best means in which to operationalise whole of government. In these situations tensions between objectives, targets and goals of individual agencies or departments may be put aside for the collective good. Mobilising government in a crisis is particularly relevant to a state such as Queensland, where there is a strong identity amongst its residents despite regional rivalries which exist. In this way, it was noted that if a similar spirit of cooperation could be harnessed from these crisis times into peace time, this would represent an extremely valuable means to create value in the public sector and address other complex policy problems.

As a result of being a disaster prone state, Queensland was in a strong position to respond to the flooding events in 2011. This was based on experience of similar events in the past, albeit at a lesser scale. There was a strongly established structure as well as individual linkages which drove the whole of government response. Indeed, it was noted that given the size and scale of the events, the floods were in fact a unique event which strongly pushed the state to the brink and at times exhausted its capacity, however did not break its spirits.

One of the crucial elements emanating from the response was the role of senior leadership in terms of providing authority and mandate for horizontal working during the response. There was a strong intersection between the political, bureaucratic and operational response agency levels and through the institutional structures in place such as the SDMG. Through the SDMG there was a regular means to connect the different strands of government. Disaster management arrangements and the relationships between key actors were long standing and as a result could be leveraged effectively during the acute crisis phase in order to respond to the unfolding disaster. It was felt that the political intervention which occurred in the acute response phase was highly proportionate and improved the quality of the response rather than being seen as interference.

The Commission of Inquiry created as a result of the events was also identified as being a pivotal part of the overall response. It was noteworthy that there was very little emphasis on the whole of government response in the Commission's final report. Given the focus on more technocratic issues, there was recognition that the system worked appropriately in the face of the crisis. Instead, the Commission took a more detailed technical approach to its findings particularly based on land use planning and the release of water from key dams during the flooding event. Similarly to the Victorian case study, the creation of a special purpose reconstruction body, the QRA was highly significant and there was a strong understanding that operating in a business as usual manner would not have helped to resolve the large scale reconstruction task. The QRA was recognised as a world class authority which continues to exist today and serves as a benchmark for reconstruction practice.

In conclusion, there was a strong commitment to whole of government working in Queensland. Commitments to collaborative working were embedded as a cultural construct throughout the disaster management system. There was also a strong individual commitment to work across government from those within the political, bureaucratic and operational response agencies. As a result of its risk profile and the frequency of natural disaster events, there was a highly evolved structure which brought together political, bureaucratic and operational agencies in a strongly integrated response network. As a result, the Queensland floods response demonstrates the effective implementation of a whole of government response

References

ABC (2009, 29 May). Recommendation for national disaster plan delayed. Retrieved 31 March 2015 from http://www.abc.net.au/worldtoday/content/2008/s2584377.htm

ABC (2011a, 1 August). 7:30-Grantham residents remember flood. Retrieved 31 March 2015 from http://www.abc.net.au/7.30/content/2011/s3283019.htm

ABC (2011b). 7:30 Report-QLD Police on the Latest. Retrieved 31 March 2015 from http://www.abc.net.au/7.30/content/2011/s3110842.htm

ABC One Plus One (2014). Interview with Anna Bligh. Retrieved 12 August 2014 from http://www.abc.net.au/news/2014-03-28/one-plus-one-anna-bligh/5353616

Apelt, L. (2014). Interview with George Carayannopoulos.

Arklay, T. (2012). Queensland's State Disaster Management Group: An all agency response to an unprecedented natural disaster. *Australian Journal of Emergency Management,* 27(3), 9–19.

Attorney General's Department (2012). Disasters Database. Retrieved 8 March 2012 from http://www.disasters.ema.gov.au/Browse%20Details/DisasterEventDetails.asp x?DisasterEventID=2894

Bligh, A. (2011). Press Conference 13 January 2011. Retrieved 14 August 2014 from http://statements.qld.gov.au/Statement/Id/73282

BlighA.(2014). Interview with George Carayannopoulos.

Bridson, W. (2014). Interview with George Carayannopoulos.

Brisbane Times (2011). Reconstruction buck stops with Newton. Retrieved 31 March 2015 from http://www.brisbanetimes.com.au/queensland/reconstruction-buck-stop s-with-newton-20110316-1bx54.html

Davies, A. (2011, 13 January). Captain Bligh steers the ship in the face of adversity. *The Sydney Morning Herald,* p. 4.

Fagan, D. (2011a, 3 January). Always room to improve in our preparedness. *The Courier-Mail,* p. 18.

Fagan, D. (2011b, 4 January). Time to wash away red tape for flood victims. *The Courier Mail,* p. 18.

Fraser, A. (2011, 8 January). Calamity may be the Premier's only chance. *The Australian,* p. 4.

Goebels, G. (2014). Interview with George Carayannopoulos.

Grady, B. (2014). Interview with George Carayannopoulos.

Hawker Britton (2012). Queensland Election Brief. Retrieved 31 March 2015 from http://www.hawkerbritton.com/images/data/QLD%20Election%20Brief%2012.pdf

Houghton, D. (2011, 8 January). Floods great for some. *The Courier-Mail,* p. 56.

Independent Review Board – Brisbane City Council (2011). *Independent Review of Brisbane City Council's Response to the 2011 Floods.* Brisbane.

Keeley, G. (2011, 13 January). Letters to the Editor. *The Australian,* p. 15.

Lucas, P. (2014). Interview with George Carayannopoulos.

McGowan, J. (2014). Interview with George Carayannopoulos.

Murdoch, S., & Lee, T. (2011, 13 January). Interest rates likely to be on hold for a year – Floods to slash $13bn from economy. *The Australian,* p. 19.

Newman, C. (2014). Interview with George Carayannopoulos.

Newton, G. (2014). Interview with George Carayannopoulos.

Parliament of Queensland (2003). Disaster Management Act.

Parnell, S., & Owens, J. (2011, 4 January). PM turns funding tap on to help flood-hit state weather the storm. *The Australian,* p. 1.

Queensland Floods Commission of Inquiry (2011a). *Day Fifteen Transcript.* Brisbane: Queensland Government.

Queensland Floods Commission of Inquiry (2011b). *Day Two Transcript.* Brisbane: Queensland Government.

Queensland Floods Commission of Inquiry (2011c). *State Representation: Statement of the Honourable Anna Bligh.* Brisbane: Queensland Government.

Queensland Floods Commission of Inquiry (2012). *Final Report of the Queensland Floods Commission of Inquiry*. Brisbane: Queensland Government.

Queensland Government (2011). *State Disaster Management Group Extraordinary Minutes*. Brisbane: Queensland Government.

Queensland Government (2012a). Disaster Management Arrangements. Retrieved 22 September 2012 from http://www.disaster.qld.gov.au/

Queensland Government (2012b). *Queensland Government Response to Queensland Floods Commission of Inquiry Final Report*. Brisbane.

Queensland Government: State Disaster Management Group (2010). *Disaster Management Strategic Policy Framework*. Brisbane: Emergency Management Queensland.

Queensland Government: State Disaster Management Group (2011). *Queensland State Disaster Management Plan*. Brisbane: Emergency Management Queensland.

Queensland Reconstruction Authority (2012). Overview. Retrieved 18 January 2014 from http://www.qldreconstruction.org.au/u/lib/cms/annual-overview.pdf

Roberts, N. (2014). Interview with George Carayannopoulos.

Ryan, S. (2011). Canberra relaxes rules on publicity for aid handouts. *The Australian*, p. 6.

Smith, K. (2014). Interview with George Carayannopoulos.

Sydney Morning Herald (2011a, 12 January). Fire and water we face together. *The Sydney Morning Herald*, p. 14.

Sydney Morning Herald (2011b). People may be dead in their homes: Lord Mayor. Retrieved 31 March 2015 from http://www.smh.com.au/environment/weather/peop le-may-be-dead-in-their-homes-lord-mayor-20110116-19syb.html

The Australian (2011, 3 January). Resilience in facing catastrophe. *The Australian*, p. 13.

The Courier Mail (2011). Lord Mayor Campbell Newman sees prediction of devastating Brisbane floods come true. Retrieved 31 March 2015 from http://www.couriermail. com.au/news/queensland/lord-mayor-campbell-newman-sees-prediction-of-devastating-brisbane-floods-come-true/story-e6freoof-1225988047498

World Bank (2011). *Recovery and Reconstruction in the Aftermath of the 2010–2011 Flood and Cyclone Yasi*. Washington, DC: Author.

5 Not all crises are created equal

Overview

Chapters 3 and 4 analysed the immediate responses to the Victorian bushfires and Queensland floods, as well as the dynamic interactions between key people, institutions and organisational culture as the disasters progressed. A strong narrative emerged regarding the perception of the Victorian bushfires as a 'failed' crisis response, and the Queensland floods as a 'successful' response – both consistent with the notion that understanding the scope, severity and causes of a crisis involves a strong element of subjectivity. A comparison of the two cases provides original insights into why two large scale events were dealt with in substantively different ways. The comparison also raises deeper issues about perceptions of 'success' or 'failure', even in the face of tangible differences.

This chapter provides in-depth analysis of the similarities and contrasts between the cases, acting as a primer for a deeper analysis (in Chapter 6) of crisis management. The chapter uses comparative methods to integrate findings with the thematic framework which has been adopted throughout the book. Specifically, it focuses on understanding political, bureaucratic and operational level responses examined via the themes of whole of government, crisis management, leadership, coordination, organisational culture, social capital and institutions.

Given the case study methodology used in this research which provides an "in-depth explanation of particular cases" (Vennesson, 2008, p. 227), the comparative method is an appropriate means to undertake cross-case analysis. It has been noted that the comparative method is a "preferred strategy for political and social scientists when they investigate institutions or other macro-political phenomena" (Della Porta, 2008, p. 202). Given the stark differences between the two cases, the comparative method provides the means to understand how various factors shaped the whole of government response and overall outcomes. Comparison between the two cases allows the ability to uncover the specific meaning in each case whilst "extracting generalizable knowledge actually or potentially related to other cases" (Vennesson, 2008, p. 226). In order to provide a reference point for the more detailed analysis of similarities and differences to follow, Table 5.1 below provides a

Table 5.1 Overview of key similarities and differences

Category	Similarities	Differences	Link to overarching level (Chapter 6)
Whole of government	• Given risk features these states are accustomed to connected responses to disasters • Whole of government viewed as a practice imperative in disasters	• Variations in risk profile mediated the whole of government structures in place • Strong differences in the implementation ethos of whole of government	• Trust in public sector management of crisis events and inter-organisational trust between agencies • Public sector context in each jurisdiction i.e. Victoria and Queensland • Federalism including impact of local, state and federal levels of coordination
Crisis management	• Large scale natural disasters which had a significant impact on communities • Events of national significance and resonance	• Different types of natural disaster events • The impact and outcomes differed in the aftermath	• The 'all hazards' approach • Short vs long term outcomes
Leadership	• Leadership from the executive central in the immediate response • Long term political consequences for both governments similar	• Form and nature of leadership roles varied significantly • The nature and scope of relationships between key leaders differed	• Political consequences • Perception of 'successful' or 'failed' political leadership
Coordination	• Both states had mechanisms in place to coordinate the crisis response • Responses drew in non-legislated elements	• The level of integration between political, bureaucratic and operational agencies varied significantly • Role of local government varied	• Political vs bureaucratic vs operational response • Command and control or networks
Organisational culture	• Existing whole of government arrangements leveraged to respond • Trust and accountability critical mediator	• Variations in nature and form of organisational culture • Different structures for information flow and sharing	• Trust and accountability • Knowledge transfer across agencies
Social capital	• Existing relationships leveraged as part of response • Variability in community preparedness	• Centralised vs decentralised ethos in role of community • Frequency of events and impact on community engagement	• Disaster resilience
Institutions	• Large and highly publicised commissions of inquiry	• Structure of institutional arrangements	• Recovery and Reconstruction arrangements • Inquiries as a mechanism to review organisational responses

Source: Author

comparison for each case based on the thematic areas. Similarities and differences between the cases are then discussed in more detail in the remainder of the chapter to better understand underlying reasons and implications.

The perception of a 'failed' and a 'successful' response: Understanding lessons from the Victorian bushfires and Queensland floods

In analysing the way that whole of government was implemented during the crisis situations, there were both synergies and differences between the events which shaped the responses. A comparative analysis of key features of each disaster allows us to better understand the implementation of whole of government management of crises in Australia. Understanding state level disaster responses is crucial given that there are limited overarching national frameworks and the management of these events is the domain of state governments. If we consider the dimensions in which crisis policy can be considered a 'failure' or a 'success', both cases provide important insights into the management of disasters. If we reflect on McConnell's (2011) typology of success or failure, we can see that there is an underlying tension between the perception of those involved in the government response and the public appraisal. In the Victorian bushfires, there is a sense of procedural success which can be juxtaposed against decision making and political failure which led to a major revamp of the disaster management system. In the Queensland floods, there is an acknowledgement that the process of disaster mitigation and recovery was supported by appropriate decision making. Despite the strength of the response to the floods, the short term political success did not translate into electoral outcomes.

We can also consider the nature of each state's disaster management arrangements within a historical perspective. Victoria and Queensland are states with a long history of natural disasters. The type of natural disasters, i.e. bushfires and floods, are typical of the risk profiles within each of the jurisdictions. In the immediate lead up to the crisis episodes the states experienced other significant disasters in the preceding years. As a result, there were disaster management frameworks in place in Victoria and Queensland that outlined policy actions and procedures through the crisis management cycle – that is, preparation, response and recovery. Given previous recent experience, disaster management structures had been tested but the severity of the 2009 bushfires and 2011 floods were of a more significant scale compared to earlier events.

Prior to the crisis episodes, the disaster management arrangements that were in place meant that the states were at least 'on paper' ready to respond. In many respects, the combination of events and meteorological activities meant that they were challenged in a way beyond what they may have imagined. This is also consistent with the idea that has been cited in the literature by Lee Clarke (1999) that planning for crises and emergencies is indeed "fantasy" as the true scope and scale of these events cannot be envisaged beforehand. There was an acknowledgement that each event required an unprecedented response: "the scale certainly drove an extraordinary whole of government response largely because there was no choice, it was such a big event, had to be all hands on deck if people had have stayed in their silos people would have died" (Former Queensland Premier, Anna Bligh). Large scale events also pose serious questions regarding the national disaster management framework which has led many disaster management practitioners to ponder: "I wonder how Australia would deal with a truly catastrophic event; the Federal government has great people and all the best intentions but they don't have a lot of capacity in this space, what happens if the Victorian bushfires had happened at the same time as the Queensland floods" (Former Assistant Director General Department of Community Safety, Bruce Grady). The unpredictability of these events was in line with the nature of crises where high degrees of uncertainty compromise the ability of an organisation to respond appropriately and push organisational capacity to its limits (Coombs, 2007, p. 3).

One of the key similarities to arise was the understanding from key actors that the response to the disasters had been handled well given their scale and severity. There was a belief that those involved in the response to the crisis showed a willingness and ability to divert all of their resources and energies into the crisis response. Whole of government was seen as being central in the response period as a pathway to the effective management of the unfolding events. There was a strong acknowledgement that no one agency or department would be able to coordinate these events but that they needed a collective response across the political, bureaucratic and operational levels. Collective responses are also consistent with what has been described as a change in emphasis in the management of natural disasters moving from "emergency services which are the cohort of different groups and emergency management which is a broader process" surrounding the integration required in order to respond to crises (Emergency Management Commissioner, Craig Lapsley).

In this sense, whole of government working particularly in a disaster was seen as representing a possible solution to the management of crisis situations given that coordination and communication flows are critical. Whole of government working and structures allow agencies to connect across government in a horizontal manner. Connecting government provides a potential answer to the complexity and chaos that can often be caused by crisis and as a means to improving coordination outcomes. The value of whole of government implementation in the practice examples supports the academic literature which has posited that hierarchical forms of command and control cannot adequately account for the volatile nature of crises. Indeed, traditional government agencies are simply not able to deal with crises (Boin, 2009). As such, there is a need to look at more horizontal forms of working based on the failures of hierarchy in large scale disasters (Comfort, 2007). The information emanating from practitioners in the research working in the area of crisis management corroborates the importance of collaboration in managing disaster responses.

The key protagonists in the events also expressed views that there is something unique about a crisis, which means that whole of government often works at these times where it may not work in other policy areas: "every time an event occurs, culturally we go there, but then we put so many blockages and impediments to actually getting there in peace time" (Former Assistant Director General Department of Community Safety, Bruce Grady). This is an interesting point to note given that it is suggested that whole of government is more routinely applied to other policy formulation and service delivery areas and that whole of government may be difficult to implement during a crisis. As a result, the narratives suggested by participants in the research indicate that the inverse may be true and a crisis represents the ideal time to implement whole of government. In a crisis, traditional barriers such as: turf wars, targets, objectives and other metrics may be put aside for a collective response. There was also a strong sense through the research that there was a power and efficacy to whole of government arrangements, that if harnessed during 'peace time', i.e. a period of non-crisis, would provide an important ability to counter-act fragmentation across government. The potential of whole of government was thus noted as highly consistent with the third wave of public sector reintegration cited in the literature, which focuses on reintegrating government as a whole (Halligan, 2007).

In terms of differences between the disaster responses, there were a number of key factors which meant that the implementation and application of whole of government were different in each of the states. The nature of the geography in Queensland as well as the spread of its population meant that whole of government arrangements were very strongly influenced by a bottom up ethos. Arrangements in Queensland were underpinned by a notion of decentralisation. Decentralisation approaches place importance on the ability to collaborate horizontally as part of disaster responses (Kapucu, 2008; Moynihan, 2009). In Queensland, the primary responsibility for preparation and response was at the local level. This then cascaded up to a district level and then finally to the state level. As a result, the local government tier of the emergency management response system retained a high degree of responsibility in terms of being the first line of the response. A sophisticated system of training and engagement particularly driven through Emergency Management Queensland was central in facilitating support to build capacity at the local level. It is also important to note that there are large council areas in Queensland that had in many cases undergone amalgamation prior to the events. As a result, many councils were well-resourced, most notably Brisbane City Council, which is one of the largest councils of its type. There were however differences in the capacity of local areas to coordinate whole of government and provide meaningful responses, mainly driven by their size, scope and orientation: "there was different capacity across the state.

Some local governments were really good they had very effective plans in place ... . It demonstrated to me the importance of prior planning and readiness capacity" (Former Director-General Department of Premier and Cabinet, Ken Smith). It was noted that this had a strong impact in mediating the outcomes in places which were less resourced and unable to cope with the demands occasioned by the disaster that required greater support from state level mechanisms.

The role of local government in Queensland contrasts with Victoria where generally it was seen that many of the local councils in areas affected were unable to provide adequate or appropriate responses. At a broad level coordination of the whole of government response was primarily left at the state level. In this way, it was more difficult for the Victorian government to harness local resources and collect information from the local level during the crisis. In some instances, there were differences in state agency disaster boundaries and generally these linkages do not seem to have flowed as well as Queensland. The differences which occurred in the whole of government response also seem to be driven by the geographical and population base. In Victoria the population base is much more centralised than in Queensland, meaning that mechanisms for connecting across different parts of the state had not developed as effectively. As a result, when the disasters occurred and Victoria needed to harness information and a response from the local level, it was not able to do this.

Finally, perhaps the most striking point of contrast between the responses to the events was the way that whole of government was implemented in the response to the crisis and the underlying ethos of connecting government. If we reflect upon key tenets of connecting government in Australia as outlined by the APS Connecting Government Report (Management Advisory Committee, 2004), it is evident that the management of programmes across agencies and implementation of whole of government requires integrated institutional structures. If we look at Victoria in 2009, the institutional emergency management arrangements delineated a clear divide between policy, political and operational responses to crises. The delineation was cited as being problematic by the emergency response agencies who noted the difficulties in being "arm's length from government" (Former Senior Emergency Management Officer). The divide between operational agencies and the political arm meant that intrinsic motivations between agencies and government departments varied significantly: "the cultures of a government department and a statutory authority are very different" (Former Senior Emergency Management Officer). In Victoria, the intention of the emergency management system was to decouple the operational response from the political tier in order to avoid interference. The analysis conducted indicates however that there was a disconnect between the political, bureaucratic and operational response levels driven as a result of this approach. This may be largely attributed to the structure of the arrangements which existed at the time; for example, having an Emergency

Management Commissioner who was in a policy and information position rather than being involved in the operational response.

In essence, the Victorian whole of government arrangements meant that there was not an appropriate mechanism to connect the different layers of the disaster response system. This is a strong point of contrast with the Queensland response arrangements, which consciously attempted to integrate the political, bureaucratic and operational response levels. Integration between services in Queensland was actively driven by the political level in the 'disaster state'. High level political input was cited a way of making things happen efficiently and to create a set of coherent priorities. Emergency response agencies saw the involvement of the political tier as important and highly appropriate. In Victoria there was more scepticism about the involvement of the political level in the operational response with the perception that "an emergency is good for politics, but it can cause harm because you can't tell them [politicians] what to say or do to coordinate" (Former State Emergency Response Officer, Rod Collins). As a result in Victoria, there was a conscious decision to decouple the political and operational parts of the whole of government response. Whilst in Queensland integration between strands was described as one of the most important mechanisms in the overall response: "we had quite an advanced process in place for coordination between a range of state, federal and local government agencies" (Former Director-General Department of Premier and Cabinet, Ken Smith).

In the lead up to the flood events in 2011, significant changes were made to Queensland's disaster management arrangements which gave the police a clear lead in the operational response. The legislative changes were a strong attempt to assist with integration across response bodies. The emended legislative framework aimed to have a clear connection point between the agencies. Police were cited as the most appropriate group to undertake this coordination role given they had a presence across local, district and state levels. It was noted that the coordinating role of police was a highly effective mechanism, given the operational reach of the Queensland Police Service (QPS) and its ability to mediate communication flows. As a postscript to the events which occurred in Victoria and in Queensland, both states have now changed their disaster management arrangements. In the case of Victoria, this can be seen as a direct consequence of the 2009 fires and an attempt to provide clearer leadership and coordination through an Emergency Management Commissioner who now has an operational role in overseeing events. There is also a clearer structure of relationships between the political and operational level, a direct result of criticisms which arose after Black Saturday. In the case of Queensland, this has involved reducing the role of EMQ and vesting further responsibility and coordination control with the emergency services. There is an acknowledgement that changes in Queensland were driven by the underlying ethos and position that the Newman government took rather than as a direct consequence of the events which occurred in 2011.

Crisis and disaster management: Beyond imagination

Crisis management has been noted as being strongly linked to the management of perceptions and the ability to frame a response to a crisis in an effective way. At the political level, the perceived success or failure of the management of a crisis event can have significant repercussions both in the short and long term. This is largely based on public perception, where the public retain a high level of expectations regarding what government is able to do in a time of crisis. Indeed, if we reflect on the definition of policy success or failure in crises presented by McConnell (2011), it is apparent that consideration needs to be given to the type of success or failure that occurs. Where the design of policy and the implementation of programs may be procedurally successful, they may fail in the political realm if not supported by appropriate decision making (McConnell, 2010, p. 351). Success or failure is acutely part of the response to crises where these are low probability but high consequence events with high levels of public expectation. There is also recognition that politicians and bureaucrats need to be accountable for responses that occur. It has been noted that where "there is a big gap between what citizens expect the government to do … and what government executives think they are able to do" a legitimacy problem may arise to challenge the perception of a successful crisis response (Christensen, Fimreite, & Laegreid, 2011, p. 562). Within this context, the section below considers the synergies and differences that existed between the two cases with a view to understanding why the perception of the outcomes differed.

The most natural synergy between the two case studies was the size and scale of the disaster events which took place. Both of the cases resonate with the public because they had significant impact on human life and property as events of national significance. The loss of human life which occurred was particularly difficult in the Victorian context given that many communities such as Marysville or Kinglake were not fully prepared. Whilst there were strong warnings in the immediate lead up to 7 February, there had not been adequate time to respond to this threat. In this sense, it was considered "a monster – whilst you can prepare and train to minimise, you could never and will never stop it, we will do it better but this was a monster" (Former State Emergency Response Officer, Rod Collins). In Queensland, while different in some respects due to the nature of the event, a flood rather than a fire, events also moved quickly and in a deadly way in places such as Grantham and the Lockyer Valley.

In the aftermath to these events, there was close scrutiny of arrangements which could have been put in place to mitigate the loss of life. This extends to whether there could have been any preventative actions that could have avoided the outcomes experienced. This is consistent with the literature which suggests that once where natural disasters were seen as an 'act of God' (Seeger et al., 2003), there is now an understanding that although governments may not be responsible for natural disasters, they may in fact be central in creating the human factors which may either mitigate or perpetuate the crises (Mitroff,, 2001). To this end, there were similarities in the way that issues such as land use, planning and management were examined in the aftermath. An example relates to the scrutiny that was given to issues such as the release of dam water in Queensland and land management practices in Victoria. The review of these mechanisms indicates the expectation that more could have been done to mitigate the events. There was a sense however that although there were different risk profiles and the events played out in different ways, that an 'all hazards approach' was appropriate given that "most disaster response is, in fact, generic … feeding them; sheltering them; distributing relief; organising evacuations; health; communication; infrastructure and supply restoration; emergency repairs etc. – they are pretty much common to all major disasters" (Former Deputy Premier, Paul Lucas). In this way, the task of crisis response is seen as based on the preconditions needed in order to respond to the crisis rather than the specific type of crisis itself.

Apart from the large scale of the events, both also share the human and social dimensions given the communities involved were profoundly impacted by the disasters. Eight years on from the Victorian bushfires and six years on from the Queensland floods there remains significant work to be done on the human recovery within the affected sites. The human recovery can be juxtaposed against infrastructure reconstruction which is now largely concluded. The Red Cross noted this on the fifth anniversary of the events in Victoria in 2014, suggesting there was a need to "continue to support communities to this day" and that the psycho-social recovery remains in progress (Red Cross, 2015). In Queensland, communities such as Grantham also still seek to understand what can be done to avoid further tragedy and further examination of events are still occurring. In the immediate aftermath, it was also apparent that there were significant requirements to work with those communities impacted in order to help rebuild the social capital as well as assisting them to be more resilient in the face of future disasters.

In looking at the infrastructure reconstruction which was required this was unprecedented in both states. To this end, special purpose bodies of recovery and reconstruction were created as a means to try and streamline the dealings of those impacted by the disasters. The creation of these bodies was recognition of the difficulty of the task involved as well as creating a means for an organisation to have the task of reconstruction as its sole purpose, rather than in addition to other departmental responsibilities. In the case of Victoria, the Victorian Bushfire Reconstruction and Recovery Authority took on the role of recovery at both the social and infrastructure level, whilst in Queensland the reconstruction efforts of the Queensland Reconstruction Authority were heavily focused around the physical infrastructure which had been damaged or destroyed.

Whilst there are similarities given that both events were large scale and significantly impacted on the relevant communities, the different type of natural disaster is a significant point given what occurred. In Victoria, there was complete destruction in the area which had been impacted by the disaster.

The nature of the fires also meant that the events were highly traumatic for those involved and often meant that housing and infrastructure had been completely destroyed albeit in a smaller geographical area. In many cases, although victims knew that the 7th of February was likely to be a bad day, people may have had little or no warning about the impending fire front, given the speed and ferocity at which the fire moved. The nature of the fire event meant that there was little choice around the ability to leave once the fire had encroached upon regions such as Kinglake. This contrasts with the nature of the flood event and reconstruction within Queensland. The events in Queensland were extremely wide spread and also impacted upon a major urban centre in Brisbane; this added a layer of complexity to the response required. Floods by their nature also have a different pattern of awareness and lead up, with the exception of the flash flooding events which occurred in places such as Grantham and the Lockyer Valley. In the rest of Queensland, there was often a significant lead in for the floods to reach their peak levels. Where the destruction caused by the events in Victoria was complete, it occurred in a more geographically limited area and with less of an impact on more general infrastructure such as highways, bridges and the like. In Queensland the reverse is true with widespread damage of key infrastructure and assets an outcome of the flooding events. Where fire may have meant that houses were completely destroyed in Victoria, in Queensland there was a large clean-up effort required in order to clear the streets and houses of mud as well as the removal of possessions. This occurred against a backdrop where both the defence force and famously an army of community volunteers – the "mud army" – were mobilised in order to assist with the large scale clean-up effort and as part of the sense of the community spirit engendered as part of the response (Haertel & Latemore, 2011, p. 864). Due to the sheer terror of the fire event, the psychological and social recovery in Victoria has proven to be extremely challenging and many years on there is an acknowledgement that there is still further work which needs to be done with the impacted communities. On the other hand the emphasis in Queensland has been on the reconstruction of physical infrastructure and it has been noted that these tasks are now largely complete.

Finally, there were significant differences in terms of the aftermath of the events in Victoria as opposed to Queensland with regard to the perception whether they were indicative of failed or successful crisis response. If we reflect on the literature related to crises, a crisis can be seen as difficult for political leadership given that breakdowns or failures can be seen to cause adverse political consequences (Seeger et al., 2003). In the aftermath to both events and in the years to follow, the Labor governments which were in place at the time and who oversaw the crisis responses were not elected at subsequent elections. In Victoria, the loss of the election was by a narrow margin whilst in Queensland the election loss was a resounding one. The election results seem counter-intuitive to the way that public perception seems to have been around these events described in more detail below.

In Victoria, through the Royal Commission process there was a significant degree of scrutiny over the leadership within government and more particularly within the operational agencies at the time. This contrasted with views from within government which indicated that Victoria through its structural arrangements and predisposition of leadership was ready to confront a large scale disaster: "if you look back at the time Victoria was probably seen as the leader in terms of the structural arrangements and the leadership arrangements with this model" (Former Premier, John Brumby). The disjuncture was clearly highlighted at the Royal Commission where it was noted there were serious deficiencies with the operational leadership shown as part of the response. Following on from this, there was significant public backlash which arose as details of the inner workings during the crisis response became known. Criticism particularly through the media was largely directed towards individuals and in particular senior figures in the operational response agencies, who were blamed for the outcomes.

When we look at Queensland, however, it is clear that there was not the same degree of scrutiny around senior leadership or the public backlash surrounding the overall response. Indeed, from within government it was noted that in "2010–2011 the level of cross agency collaboration was much greater than for previous ones. I never saw whole of government work anywhere else despite the rhetoric" (Former Director-General Department of Community Safety, Jim McGowan). Within this context, it is interesting to consider that although the management of a crisis may be politically important, any outcomes from this may be short term. In the long term, management of crises may not be seen as critical as other key policy portfolio areas at the state level such as education, transport and health which dominate the electoral agenda. This is apparent through the election results in each state where although the incumbent government was defeated in both instances, the Queensland election defeat of the Bligh government was a resounding one and the Brumby government lost in a much narrower defeat.

Here we have considered the public perception of the crisis episodes in trying to understand the synergies between the two cases. The case studies represent significant and large scale events which had a deep impact on the affected communities; however, the perception of the events did not have a direct impact on the political outcomes through election results. In terms of the impact on affected communities, fires and floods represent different types of risk, trauma and recovery. Although important consideration needs to be given to the particular type of response that each of these events requires, the all hazards framework provides a common set of response considerations which can be implemented.

Leadership: accountability the 'public face'

With regard to the research, one of the key thematic areas to emerge is the importance of leadership in driving whole of government responses. In both case studies, leadership was cited as being central in the immediate response phase although with different perceptions around the long term aftermath of the leadership response. There were also different views around the relationships between key leaders from within the political, bureaucratic and operational spheres.

Leadership was cited by all participants as being pivotal in the response to the disasters. There was strong recognition that to have a whole of government response work effectively, mandate and authority is required from the top-down through the executive. In both the Victorian bushfires and the Queensland floods, participants noted that leadership needed to be shown from the Premier, Ministers and key figures in the bureaucracy as well as from operational agencies. The executive leadership were very much seen as the figureheads for the response. There was a strong sense that it was necessary for leaders to have a highly visible presence in terms of the public as part of the immediate response and then moving towards longer term recovery. The leaders in many ways became a rallying point around which the public could express its concerns and to directly connect with government. Consequently, the executive leadership spent significant time on the ground of the affected sites in the aftermath to the crises. The desire to have an on the ground presence was in order to have direct contact with those who were affected but also as a means of directly collecting information about the scale and the severity of the disaster which could then be fed back into recovery efforts. There was recognition that having leadership on the ground could also help the whole of government response. Leaders were hearing first hand concerns which may have existed about evacuation centres, distribution of emergency funds and plans for the long term recovery of the affected sites. It was therefore important for leaders to be connected to the reality of the response, particularly in many regional areas which were hit hard by the disasters.

At a political level, it has been noted that there is a strong imperative for political elites to be seen to be adequately handling crises to avoid a potential backlash (Drennan & McConnell, 2007, p. 160). The senior leadership in both cases identified the importance of their personal intervention. The Former Premier of Victoria John Brumby described the importance of these visits in terms of "giving me and my staff a level of knowledge to break down silos and bureaucratic red tape". The Former Premier of Queensland Anna Bligh described it similarly "every single person feels the public expectation that we will deal with it and we will look after their best interests and everybody will give their best". There was a strong acknowledgement that senior leadership figures needed to be visible and connect directly with those impacted by the disasters.

The perception around the leadership shown in both case studies was positive in the initial aftermath to the crises. The presence of the Premiers, Prime Ministers, Ministers, and Police Commissioners on the ground was well received from a public perspective. Following on from the crises, both

Premiers received a bounce in popularity, consistent with the idea that a crisis helps an incumbent government. A number of strong and clear decisions were made with strong support from the top of government during this period such as the creation of commissions of inquiry and recovery authorities. In both cases, the decision to move quickly was very much driven from the level of Premier with the belief that the scale and magnitude of these events necessitated a strong and comprehensive response. In this sense, there was clear decision making around the immediate response. These decisions were made within a political context, given that in both states elections were to be held relatively shortly thereafter. In the longer term and through details which were released through the inquiry process, there did emerge different narra-tives about the leadership and accountability shown by senior office holders within operational agencies which contrasts to the initial positive perception of leadership.

A normative picture of leadership emerged in line with how leaders are expected to act. This was closely aligned to the perception of the performance of leaders. The importance of perception is consistent with the notion that crises are a construction rather than statements of fact (Dunleavy, 1995; Brandstrom & Kuipers, 2003). There was an acknowledgement that with "leadership in crisis, if the leaders are seen to be in crisis it all unravels, there can be a lot happening behind us but it can't be seen that the leaders are rattled" (Emergency Management Commissioner, Craig Lapsley). The narrative which emerged as a result was of a 'failed' leadership response in Victoria and a 'successful' response in Queensland largely based on the actions of key leaders including their movements, availability and public response as the events unfolded. Despite the difference in outcomes, electoral results in the following election remained the same and that "leadership does not translate into long-term popular outcomes, but people expect their leaders to lead in a disaster and if you don't you're dead" (Former Executive Director Red Cross, Greg Goebels). Long term political outcomes in the cases indicate that what happens in the immediate period following on from a crisis does not always lead to long term political success. It can be seen that whilst a successful response does not lead to improved electoral fortunes a failed response may irrevocably damage a leader in the eyes of the public.

With regard to the longer term perception of leadership which occurred, details that arose through the Commission of Inquiry process became pivotal to the way that the overall leadership response was perceived. This is most starkly the case with the Victorian bushfires where there was a significant amount of scrutiny placed on the responses from senior emergency response agency figures such as Christine Nixon and Russell Rees. There was a sig-nificant prolonged criticism of Christine Nixon for departing the emergency operations centre on the evening of the bushfires. There is a strong contrast with the Queensland floods where there was not the same level of scrutiny over key leaders and indeed the Victorian experience was very much in the awareness of those involved with the response to the Queensland floods. Indeed, many of the key leaders in Queensland spent nights at the emergency operations centre in Kedron and many reported not having a day off during the entire time of the flood events. There was an acknowledgement that it was important for leaders to have an on the ground experience of events as they were unfolding "every event I've been in no matter who you are, everyone is in denial. What I've learned is that you need to force yourself to fight for the information, you need to go down there, inform yourself, see it with your own eyes" (Former Lord Mayor Brisbane, Campbell Newman). In the longer term in Queensland, decision making at the more technical level by those involved in running key dams became a key focal point and questions were raised over who knew what and when in terms of water releases. In Queensland, whilst there was a scrutiny placed over leadership it was at much more of a technocratic level. On the other hand in Victoria, leaders of the key emergency services such as the Police and CFA were placed under the highest level of criticism. In many ways, this pointed to the importance of accountability and the ability of leaders to retain a control of the details which may have been unfolding at the operational level. As a result, accountability was recognised as an important characteristic of leadership alongside empathy and the ability to listen. There was a strong perception that some of the leadership in Victoria may not have been accountable for their responses in the immediate aftermath to the crisis. On the other hand it was noted that accountability was a key theme of the response in Queensland. Accountability in Queensland was underpinned by the ability to answer key questions, direct actions and essentially be in the operations area for a sustained period.

Another area of difference between the two responses was the nature of the relationships between key leaders at the different levels of the response i.e. political, bureaucratic and operational. One of the consistent messages to emanate from the Queensland floods was that although in many ways the political level did not have a legislated role in the response to crises and disasters, having escalation and intervention from the top political level was crucial in order to positively impact the response. It was noted in particular that the State Disaster Management Group was a focal point for this engagement. The work of the SDMG was supported by the fact that many of the key figures such as Ministers and Directors-General had close links and established histories of working with each other on previous disasters. There was also a reflection that particular traits or characteristics from people, such as the ability to communicate effectively and passionately in the case of Anna Bligh was a strong way of maintaining cohesion through the different levels involved in the response. To this end, the characteristics of the State Disaster Coordinator Ian Stewart (now Police Commissioner) were also cited as important given that he was able to instil a culture of collaboration into QPS. Stewart's leadership style meant that there was less of a command and control structure in place which may not have otherwise been the case. This differs to the Victorian case study where there was a disconnect between some of the key leaders involved in the response to the disaster. Whilst the leadership of the Premier of the time was positively evaluated, the relationships between political and operational leadership were cited as more difficult. There was a strong belief from the operational level that more input was required from the political side in order to assist with an event of this magnitude in Victoria. The operational agencies felt that many of the warnings emanating from the operational level did not reach the political sphere and as a result impacted on the operational response.

As a result of the leadership shown at the time, there was a belief that in both events the senior leadership from the level of the Premier down were engaged with the immediate crisis response. Senior leadership were keen to maintain a close interface with the public as part of the leadership task but also as an important means in which to collect data firsthand about the experiences of those who had been impacted by the disasters. In this sense, the immediate response to each crisis maintains similar characteristics. Through the forensic analysis which occurred at the commissions of inquiry there was greater scrutiny placed on the operational leadership in the Victorian bushfires. There was strong recognition that the Victorian leadership response has not been perceived as well as the more acclaimed Queensland response, a key factor in driving the perception of 'success' or 'failure'.

Coordination: Different strokes

Coordination across government through both vertical and horizontal means is one of the core elements in understanding how whole of government works in a crisis. It has been noted that "the presence of multiple agencies, jurisdictions and levels of government ... in managing emergency response and recovery necessitates some form of integrated authority" (Leonard & Howitt, 2010, p. 381). As a result, it is necessary to review the variety of coordination mechanisms (formal and informal) that existed in order to understand how integration occurred. The following section considers the synergies and differences which existed with regard to coordination and how these mechanisms impacted on the outcomes to the disasters.

It is clear from the literature that working in a horizontally coordinated manner has been cited as a key element of whole of government working and that horizontal structures are considered more effective than traditional hierarchy (Moynihan, 2008). Victoria and Queensland both had formal and informal mechanisms in place to coordinate the crisis responses and connect across government. Coordination mechanisms were strongly geared around bringing the key people from the different levels of government together as a means to try and address the difficulties arising through the crisis situations. Coordination mechanisms relied upon a combination of horizontal as well as vertical means in order to integrate key players involved in the responses. They were also influenced by the structural arrangements as well as being informed by more informal aspects such as relationships between key actors. In terms of the Victorian case, the existence at the time of the Victorian Emergency Management Council was cited as a mechanism that formally brought together different elements of government for the preparation and response to the bushfires and provided a forum for the vertical and horizontal flow of information.

The cabinet and expanded cabinet arrangements were also cited as a key means of bringing the relevant actors together throughout the immediate response to the events of 7 February and as a way of sharing information which had been gathered from the field. The relationships which had been formed by key people in the bureaucracy and within government in the Victorian Public Service meant that there was a store of goodwill and intellectual capacity which could be leveraged in a time of crisis. This collective goodwill was less about the structure of the system as such but more about the quality of relationships which could be harnessed. In many ways, the experience of the importance of formal coordination mechanisms was also replicated in Queensland with the SDMG being cited as a central means to bring together key departments and agencies as a single reference point "when the floods came along SDMG was the central point for us ... we were meeting so regularly in the lead up to and during the crisis" (Former Head of Queensland Reconstruction Authority, Graeme Newton). The SDMG was seen to have a high degree of authority and that accountability was emphasised as one of the key aspects that facilitated the flow of information across government. Similarly to Victoria, in Queensland it was also acknowledged that there were strong informal coordination mechanisms driven through personal contacts and linkages. As a result the disaster management arrangements and system had been embedded within the state as part of its ethos and values and through people links.

It is also important to note that in both states, there were elements which were cited as highly critical to the set-up of the recovery phase which were not formally part of the legislative disaster arrangements. These elements the VBRRA and QRA although different in their focus and nature were both created as special purpose bodies in the immediate aftermath of the crises in order to speed up and coordinate the process of recovery and reconstruction. The decision to create these special purpose entities was consistent with the idea that there needed to be an overarching framework or direction from the top to oversee coordination and provide a clear governance model which has been cited as helping government to interconnect (Hood, 2005). There was an understanding that "business as usual was not going to cut it" (Former Premier, Anna Bligh) and that there was a need to create structures to support reconstruction given the scale of the events. There was a strong sense that these structures were essential to overcome red tape where "you have silos in agencies and across government who get obsessed that it has got to be X or Y" and where "the reconstruction authority takes the view broadly what are the key things to stop silly local rules" (Former Deputy Premier, Paul Lucas).

There was a realisation that the task of coordinating across government in the response to crises is difficult. Whilst whole of government may be facilitated in a crisis due to the emergency measures which are put in place; it may be more difficult to sustain this as part of the recovery and reconstruction effort. Within this context, it is interesting to note that the work of the VBRRA was largely completed in the year following the event, whilst the QRA continues to exist. It is also noteworthy that the VBRRA seems to have merged elements of the social and physical reconstruction, whilst the QRA seems to have more heavily focussed on physical reconstruction. It is possible that the nature of the disasters, i.e. fire vs flood, may have played a role in this, given that the trauma exacted by a fire may be more severe and where the destruction caused by a flood may be more widespread.

One of the key differences between the responses and coordination mechanisms between Victoria and Queensland was the degree to which different strands of the whole of government response e.g. political, bureaucratic and operational levels felt integrated within formal coordination mechanisms. In the Victorian case study, many respondents felt that the coordination structures in place at the time (particularly the VEMC) did not allow for adequate information sharing. Indeed they cited that groups such as the VEMC were mainly a vehicle for reporting up rather than a more horizontal forum. It was noted that ideally a group such as the VEMC would have served a dual purpose at both the vertical and horizontal levels. Institutional structures in Victoria did not facilitate links across the different tiers involved in the whole of government response. There was a strong sense that there may not have been a good mutual awareness across the different groups. This contrasts to the Queensland arrangements and in particular the SDMG where it was felt that the very structure and nature of the representation within this group meant that it was a very good and useful coordination mechanism across the strands of government. As a result, a clear contrast emerges between the two case studies around the coordination of the broader whole of government effort.

It is also important to note that there were differences in the ability of authorities at local government level to coordinate activities and feed information back to the relevant state government forums. Given the scale and magnitude of the disasters one of the key outcomes related to the perception of local government and the role it played. In Victoria, the response which emerged was impacted by the belief that many local councils did not have the capacity or ability to manage and as result the state level took over many of these functions. This may be in part to the nature of structural arrangements in Victoria where structures around district level arrangements between some agencies e.g. Police, CFA and DSE did not align and meant that a local level response was often complicated by difficult bureaucratic arrangements. This can be contrasted against the Queensland case, where local government was very much seen as the first line of response to the crisis. In Queensland, this was consistent with the bottom-up ethos which escalates matters up from the local to district and then finally the state level. As suggested earlier, it may be the case that these differences are in large part a response to the geographic features and risk profiles of the states. Queensland by necessity needs to have a more decentralised approach than may be the case in Victoria. There is uniqueness around the local government system in Queensland, particularly Brisbane City Council which retains significant bureaucratic machinery and scale which means in the areas impacted in the metropolitan parts of Brisbane, there was a large existing capacity that could be leveraged during the crisis itself.

This section has presented an overview of the different coordination mechanisms which were cited as being crucial to the overall whole of government responses which occurred. In both cases formal and informal structures were seen as essential and special purpose bodies were created to assist with the coordination of recovery and reconstruction given the scale and severity of the events. There were differences in the way that these mechanisms may have integrated different tiers of government and hence shaped interactions between local and state government as well as operational and political strands.

Organisational culture: Together we are one

In both cases, the cultures of the particular organisations and agencies as well relationships were seen as pivotal to the overall response. It is also clear however, that there were differences in the way that the organisational cultures of agencies in Victoria and Queensland impacted upon the responses and also the way in which relationships were leveraged.

The key similarity between the two cases was the belief that having strong existing cultures and relationships between departments and agencies involved in the response phase was a primary consideration. In both states, there were governments who had been in place for many years and also senior figures in the public service such as Directors-General who were well established in their positions. In this way, it was suggested that across both states there was a culture of working in whole of government not only in the crisis realm but also in other key policy areas such as law and order, industrial relations and through the yearly budget cycle. Ling (2002) suggests that in order to connect government, organisations should be joined by culture, values and the appropriate institutional structures. In these cases, both states met the necessary preconditions to be described as whole of government. In reflecting on the reasons why they thought coordination worked in a crisis situation, senior members of the bureaucracy suggested that in government you have got "the capacity of the resources, you have got people that have very good experience who led correctly are able to order the decisions which are made and undertake the actions" (Former Senior Bureaucrat). A key part of implementing a whole of government response was based on a collective rather than individual response: "acting in the state's interest rather than their own individual agency responsibility. That was what was decided and ultimately what we achieved in terms of those structures" (Former Secretary Department of Justice, Penny Armytage). As a result, many protagonists noted that there was an organisational culture which provided support for connected working, consistent with concepts identified in the academic literature such as shared meaning, understanding and sense making (Kloot & Martin, 2007).

Given the prior history of working horizontally in other policy areas, there was a store of goodwill and depth to the relationships which was important at the time that the events occurred. The depth of positive prior history was crucial given the view that in the immediate unfolding of a crisis it was important to have relationships already established as opposed to trying to set these up on the run. The community of people involved in responding to the crises were aware of who the key players were in the disaster management space and these relationships had developed in the responses to earlier disaster events. Personal links could then be called upon during the crisis which aided coordination at the time when it was most needed.

With regard to the nature of the organisations and relationships between key people, trust and accountability were two of the essential factors that benefited from the close nature of the personal relationships. An important by-product of the links between people was the level of trust that existed which had formed through established working relationships. As a result those involved in the response had the ability to trust counterparts and leverage support in the response process. If one department or agency needed assistance or further capacity, this could be called upon through the existing network of relationships. The sense of goodwill and cooperation which pervaded throughout government at the time of disasters meant that there was a culture where departments were willing to put aside what may be considered the traditional turf wars in order to prioritise high order collective goals. Another important part of the organisational culture which was consistently cited involved the culture of accountability which was in existence throughout the crisis response. Having a culture of accountability where departments and individuals needed to take responsibility for actions and to report back on these or answer questions created a stronger sense of urgency. The culture of accountability assisted in order to coordinate the sharing of information. The emphasis on accountability also reiterated the importance of the tasks being undertaken in response to the crises and the role that departments, agencies and individuals needed to play within this. As such, it was noted that a culture of accountability emerged where "it is about accountability and leadership and these going hand in hand" (Emergency Management Commissioner Craig Lapsley). In the Queensland case study, this was described by the Head of the Reconstruction Authority Graeme Newton in the following way: "in the room at the time there was a personal responsibility felt by everybody ... . It was for Queensland's sake and that was the really strong feeling, almost parochialism to say we needed to help Queensland get back on its feet".

Organisational culture was at the crux of understanding the outcomes in each of the cases. Victoria had a very strong core group at the senior levels of government and the bureaucracy who were accustomed to working together in diverse complex policy areas and implementing solutions. This occurred within a context around the longevity of the Labor government and meant that there was a network of relationships that underpinned the business of government. Links at the emergency response agency level were far more tenuous and there were differences in the cultures and motivations of groups which provided a strong barrier to connected forms of working. Cultural differences were acknowledged by senior leadership as a chasm between agencies which were only partially resolved by the time of February 2009. This is exemplified through the IECC which was set up in 2008 to bring response agencies together under one roof. The intention of the IECC process was to create a common fabric of coordination to transcend problems around interoperability. At the time of the events however this new structure was in its infancy and the scale and severity meant that there had not been adequate time to bed these arrangements down. These issues epitomised the confusion which arose around command and the role of individuals within the disaster management framework. Issues related to coordination and integration would later emerge as a focal point for reforms to the Victorian disaster management system. This is best summed up by the State Emergency Response Officer Rod Collins who described it in the following way:

> The problem (with the IECC) was the concept was great, the preparation wasn't correct and we had different people in different areas. One piece of information which caused problems at the Royal Commission was that the fire prediction expert was on a different level ... doing it was right but it was far from efficient.
> (Former State Emergency Response Officer, Rod Collins)

In the Queensland context, there was also a very strong core group within cabinet and at the senior levels of bureaucracy as well as relationships between Queensland Police and Emergency Management Queensland. Before the 2011 floods, amendments were made to the disaster management arrangements which gave the police responsibility for overall coordination. Whilst there were initially some concerns about the role of police and the prospect of a command and control ethos being implemented, it was felt that this functioned well. The QPS were able to leverage personal relationships and also use staff from their own ranks whom were skilled in collaborative working arrangements to ensure that the integration of activities with EMQ ran smoothly. In this way, there is a contrast which emerges to the Victorian arrangements where the immediate changes in the lead up to the crisis may have complicated matters in spite of efforts from leadership to overcome these.

Finally, one of the key differences which occurred in the aftermath of the crises was the ability to retain information and institutional memory following on from the events. The outcomes of the Victorian bushfires led to a significant change and revamp of disaster management arrangements in the state. As a result, there were also a number of high level casualties from within the emergency services whose positions may have been made untenable as a result of Royal Commission and its findings. To this extent, it can be argued that much of the experience and intellectual capital gained from the response to the crisis may have been lost. The most notable link between the events of 2009 and the present is through Emergency Management Victoria and its Commissioner Craig Lapsley who was involved in the 2009 recovery coordination effort. This is significant given that the place where organisational knowledge is best retained is through the emergency response agencies, keeping in mind the fragility of political and bureaucratic level appointments as a result of the electoral cycle.

With regard to Queensland, the move to make amendments to the disaster management arrangements were not so much driven as a response to the events but rather as a change in ethos driven by the new Newman government which was elected after 2011. As such, it has been noted that many of key individuals within the emergency response agencies remain in place, albeit in a different form given the change in focus for EMQ. This is perhaps best highlighted and exemplified by Police Commissioner Ian Stewart who in the aftermath of his role as State Disaster Coordinator was appointed as the Commissioner of Police in Queensland. Given this, there is a very real and tangible link and retention of organisational memory which has occurred in Queensland. The retention of organisational memory has been cited as pivotal but complex "after three or four days of an event, you get into it. Things are happening all the time, a few days feels like a lifetime. People don't really keep those skills unless they are practising them all the time, I was a big believer in practice" (Former Lord Mayor Brisbane, Campbell Newman). In the Queensland context, where disaster events occur on a frequent basis, there are greater opportunities to be able to transfer knowledge between events. It also points to broader questions such as how institutional knowledge is retained where events may be spread out over a number of years such as the case in Victoria, which generally experiences less events but where these have highly damaging consequences.

This section has reviewed the synergies and differences which existed in regards to how organisational culture shaped whole of government responses to the case studies. Organisational culture was seen as central to the overall response including; the nature and fabric of an organisation as well as the relationships between individuals which were leveraged during the response to the crises. On the other hand, there were differences in the way that the organisational cultures may have played out and in the nature of the relationships and bonds that existed. Ultimately these were important in shaping the outcomes which occurred as a result of the disasters.

Social capital: Linking government and the community

Social capital represents a multidimensional concept with dual applicability in the context of the Victorian bushfires and the Queensland floods. At one level, it can be used to understand the network of professional relationships which existed between individuals and across agencies involved in disaster response. At a second level, it provides explanatory power with regard to disaster resilience and the way in which shared responsibility for disasters lies across government and the community. The below section considers both of these dimensions to better understand the synergies and differences which existed across jurisdictions during the disaster events.

If we look at the degree to which social capital impacted on both events, it is clear that professional relationships across the emergency response agencies were well established. These institutional relationships were often predicated on the basis of individual ones where the network of responders to disaster events is small and well-defined. It was noted that having built relationships over previous events allowed for this to be leveraged during the event itself "it is about trust and relationships" (Former Assistant Director General Department of Community Safety, Bruce Grady). In the Queensland context, the ability to leverage existing social capital was cited as one of the important factors in the success of the overall response. The degree to which pre-existing relationships were harnessed emerged as much more problematic in Victoria. There was an acknowledgement that despite the links which existed, the overall design of the disaster management system did not provide the opportunity for relationships to overcome structural deficiencies.

If we look at the second dimension of social capital, the degree of inter-connectedness between government and the community in terms of preparation and response to crises, there was substantial variability in community preparedness to confront large scale events. Whilst the 2002 COAG Report highlighted the need to "build community resilience" (Council of Australian Governments, 2002, p. viii) against major disasters, there was a substantial disjuncture between the rhetoric and practice in place at the times of the events. If we look at Victoria, there was a strong view that communities were vulnerable to the potential impact of a major fire event. There was not however appropriate consideration of the risk or personal responsibility that existed in living in a bushland setting. In the wake of the event and as a result of the destruction caused, it has been acknowledged that there has been "a change in people's risk barometer" (Former Senior Bureaucrat) in line with shared accountability principles. In the Queensland context, a disparity was highlighted between the resilience of citizens in the city of Brisbane as opposed to those in regional areas. Whilst Brisbane is a large well-resourced urban centre with a significant bureaucratic council infrastructure, it was noted that many citizens who lived near flood prone areas of the Brisbane River were not well prepared and did not grasp the fundamentals of disaster resilience. This was exemplified by the then Premier Anna Bligh who indicated that in her discussions with wholesale suppliers, frozen food was the item which sold out most quickly, indicating that potential loss of electricity had not registered with a wide section of the community.

A fundamental difference between the two case studies relates to the degree of centralisation and decentralisation which underpins the response to disasters. Concepts of centralisation also impacted on the degree to which local communities were empowered to prepare and respond to disaster events. In Queensland, it was acknowledged that because of its geography "it's got less reason to have a centralised command control model, we have a wide geographical stretch, which in disasters means that it is best done locally because that's what people understand" (Former Senior Emergency Management Officer). Through the disaster management arrangements and the decentralised ethos, there was a strong emphasis on local capacity to resolve local problems based on local knowledge. On the other hand in Victoria, there was no sense that local communities should be empowered to deal with major events but that these required direction from the centrally located Melbourne authorities.

Finally, in considering the role of social capital and its impact on the events which transpired in both case studies, there is a need to be cognisant of the frequency and severity of events and how this impacts on community resilience. If we look at Queensland, the state due to its tropical latitude experiences major flood events or cyclones on an almost yearly basis. Victoria on the hand experiences severe fire conditions on a more sporadic basis. The result is that it is easier to maintain a stronger sense of community memory around how to confront and deal with events when they occur on a more regular basis. This is more difficult in Victoria which experiences more sporadic events where "long-term recognition of the risk environment that we live in (is important) and (a there is a need) to maintain a strong emphasis around that" (Former Secretary Department of Justice, Penny Armytage).

This section has considered the role that social capital played in the preparation and response to the disaster events. Social capital can be understood as impacting on the case studies through both the relationships that existed within and across response agencies as well as through the concept of community engagement in building disaster resilience. Resilience in the case studies was strongly influenced by the relationships which existed in the emergency response context, the degree of interconnection between government and the community, the philosophical approaches to centralisation and decentralisation and the retention of community knowledge based on the frequency and severity of disaster events.

Institutions: Underpinning our actions

In examining the responses which occurred in both cases, an important point of analysis occurs around institutional arrangements and the institutional response to each of the events. Both crises pushed institutional arrangements to their limits and at times exhausted the capacity of the state in order to respond. Within this context, the below considers how both states approached the immediate recovery and reconstruction efforts in a similar way before considering how the different arrangements may have shaped longer term outcomes.

One of the key areas of similarity between the cases was the degree to which early decisions around the creation of an inquiry can be seen to be part of the broader institutional response and as part of a trend around the growing use of royal commissions as a policy response mechanism (Prasser, 2006). In both cases, one of the clear narratives to emerge was that in the face of such a large scale event there was a need to establish a commission which would be independent and seek to review the events. The decision to create a commission was deemed important as a vehicle both to share lessons and prepare for future disasters. In both disasters, it was felt that other mechanisms such as parliamentary committees or reports from the emergency management agencies would not provide the necessary scope or analytic scrutiny to assess disaster management arrangements including preparation, response and recovery. There was also a sense that the community may have viewed anything less than an inquiry as not being transparent which was a key consideration given the importance of public perception around crisis responses. As a result, both the Royal Commission and Floods Inquiry were announced in the immediate aftermath to the events.

With the benefit of hindsight, the commissions have also been central in shaping the longer term narratives that have emerged regarding the crisis responses including the perception of a 'failed' or 'successful' response. Indeed, the commissions took a key role in the forensic examination of procedural arrangements and the broader policy programs which underpinned disaster mitigation and response. There have also been questions raised regarding the nature of such commissions and whether the adversarial and legalistic struc-tures which are inherently part of inquiries best facilitate learning from these events. In both crisis episodes, it was felt that there may have been an over-emphasis on individual blame and exposing individual failures in what where highly charged and difficult circumstances. This is consistent with the literature on blame attribution in crises and presenting failures of leadership in a public way to seek admissions of inadequacy from key leaders. In terms of the Vic-torian Bushfires Royal Commission, there was concern about the impact of this on reconstruction and recovery and this was described in the following way:

> in relation to the Royal Commission, I actually think that Rush as the lead counsel had a broader obligation to the community and that was

not an obvious consideration in their tactics, they were just tactics which effectively undermined our work in terms of working with communities on recovery.

(Former CEO VBRRA, Ben Hubbard)

Another of the significant moves was the quick decision in both instances to create special purpose recovery and reconstruction entities. This was also acknowledged as an important step in the aftermath given the scale of destruction which had occurred both at the human and infrastructure levels. In each of the case studies, the decisions were strongly guided from the top of government with a sense that there needed to be a structure put in place to cut through the usual bureaucracy that could achieve its outcomes quickly and efficiently. To this end as part of the strategy for both groups, a number of secondments were made from government departments in order to tap into existing networks and relationships and to circumvent any blockages that may have been experienced as a result of navigating through the bureaucratic systems. One of the significant differences between the cases relates to the way in which funding and accountability mechanisms from the recovery and reconstruction authorities were set up. It has been noted that the control of funding and the ability to monitor and audit spending has been seen as one of the strengths of the Queensland Reconstruction Authority. Audit processes which were put in place at the state and federal level following on from the experience in Victoria meant that the QRA was operating under a different paradigm that than the VBRRA in terms of funding allocations and acquittals. On the other hand it has been noted that part of the difficulties experienced by the VBRRA related to the way in which the control of funding operated, where it was more difficult to retain a centralised overview of the funds being distributed and the means under which objectives were being achieved.

There were a number of ways in which institutional arrangements were different between Victoria and Queensland. Most notably this appears to have been with respect to the more decentralised and bottom-up ethos embedded as part of the Queensland system and the more centralised nature of the Victorian disaster management arrangements. These differences impacted upon the ability to respond to the crisis at the time of the events as well as into the longer term recovery and reconstruction. If we look at the Queensland disaster management arrangements as a starting point, these were strongly predicated on an approach which builds from local council level through to district level and finally to the peak state government body the SDMG. Across the levels of government and vertically there is a degree of integration which happens based on the membership of the groups Primarily charged with the responses. At the local level, these groups were chaired by the Mayor of the local government area with representation from police and relevant agencies. At the district level, these groups were chaired by police and at the state level this group brought together politicians, senior bureaucrats and police. Given the nature of arrangements in Queensland, there was both a vertical and horizontal integration across the different strands of the whole of government response and through the political, bureaucratic and operational levels. This can be juxtaposed against the disaster management arrangements which were in place in Victoria at the time. The model in place in Victoria strongly delineated between the policy role of the Emergency Management Commissioner and the operational response coordinated by Victoria Police and in the case of bushfires through the CFA and DSE. The primary coordination mechanism in place at the time was the VEMC; however, generally, there has been a mixed response to the efficacy of this in bringing together political, bureaucratic and operational levels in order to share information. The committees of cabinet which were set up may have functioned well at that level of government although there may have been a disconnect particularly with the operational agencies, who themselves were restructuring their own internal relationships due to the creation of the IECC in the months leading up to February 2009.

As a result of the more fragmented nature of institutional arrangements in Victoria, these arrangements were placed under greater scrutiny than the more integrated model in Queensland. One of the most relevant criticisms was at the operational response level. With regard to the operational response there was a lack of clear direction as to who was ultimately in charge of it. At times the number of actors involved meant that the messages that needed to be given may have a lacked a crispness. In the aftermath to the events, the Victorian government undertook a significant review of its disaster management arrangements culminating in the appointment of an Emergency Management Commissioner charged with overall coordination responsibilities as opposed to purely operating on a policy level. There has been a clear shift towards an emergency management rather than an emergency services doctrine. Under this new doctrine management and coordination of the entire system is seen as being as important as the emergency response. In Victoria, the scrutiny and review of institutional arrangements which has occurred has led to a significant change in the management of crisis situations. Ultimately the new disaster management arrangements in Victoria may only be able to be evaluated in the face of a large and significant event, which to date has not occurred. With regard to the events in Queensland, the disaster management arrangements themselves were put under far less scrutiny with the general perception being that the system in place functioned well in the face of extreme pressure. What did become clear however was that there was a level of scrutiny around the actions of individuals involved in highly technical roles related to the release of water from the key dams. Given this a different type of critique emerged, in Queensland based more on the technocratic level rather than the political or bureaucratic levels.

This section has considered the way in which institutional arrangements between the case studies may have been similar, with particular reference to two significant institutional responses; the decisions to create commissions of inquiry and the decisions to move towards special purpose reconstruction bodies. It has also considered differences between the two cases highlighted by the structure and nature of the institutional arrangements which show that the Victorian system was placed under greater scrutiny in the long term aftermath to the events.

Conclusion

This chapter has analysed and contrasted the cases to understand why the outcomes were so different despite being underpinned by a whole of government approach. The chapter has provided a rich narrative and identified the importance of: leadership, organisational culture, social capital and institutions in shaping the perceptions of 'failed' or 'successful' outcomes. Each of the factors or preconditions listed above have strong explanatory power and provide an important framework to better understand crisis management. The chapter has shown that these issues go the heart of understanding how the political, bureaucratic and operational agencies within government respond to the complexity of crises. The contrast arising from the analysis can also be seen to exemplify debates about verticality and horizontality in public policy and whether policy making and decision taking is best made by a small centralised group or through more plural and engaged processes. There is also a clear mandate that arises which shows that crises provide a unique if unexpected opportunity to test the working of whole of government and put this into action. As a result, there is a broader and novel contribution around understanding how goodwill created in a crisis can be leveraged in other policy areas. The comparative method has also emphasised that for such a translation of practice to occur it is necessary to have a strong overall direction for whole of government, a mandate from senior figures in the executive, mechanisms which can enable coordination and an alignment of culture and values between agencies.

Given the detailed accounts and comparisons of the cases, it is appropriate to then understand what may be the implications of these findings within the broader panorama of crisis management. The final chapter will consider a two way analysis between the cases and crisis management principles. The chapter will also reflect on how the cases can be integrated with the academic literature presented in earlier chapters before concluding by providing a future research agenda which seeks to advance work on collaborative responses to crisis management.

References

Armytage, P. (2014). Interview with George Carayannopoulos.
Bligh, A. (2014). Interview with George Carayannopoulos.
Boin, A. (2009). The new world of crises and crisis management: Implications for policymaking and research. *Review of Policy Research*, 26(4), 367–377.

Brandstrom, A., & Kuipers, S. (2003). From normal incidents to political crises: Understanding the selective politicization of policy failures. *Government and Opposition*, 38(3), 279–305.

Brumby, J. (2014). Interview with George Carayannopoulos.

Christensen, T., Fimreite, A. L., & Laegreid, P. (2011). Crisis management: The perceptions of citizens and civil servants in Norway. *Administration & Society*, 43(5), 561–594.

Clarke, L. (1999). *Mission Improbable: Using Fantasy Documents to Tame Disaster*. Chicago, IL: University of Chicago Press.

Collins, R. (2014). Interview with George Carayannopoulos.

Comfort, L. K. (2007). Crisis management in hindsight: Cognition, communication, coordination, and control. *Public Administration Review*, 67, 189–197.

Coombs, T. (2007). *Ongoing Crisis Communication, Planning, Managing and Responding*. California, CA: Sage Publications.

Council of Australian Governments (2002). *Natural Disasters in Australia: Reforming mitigation, relief and recovery arrangements*. Canberra: Commonwealth of Australia.

Della Porta, D. (2008). Comparative analysis: Case oriented versus variable oriented research. In D. Della Porta & M. Keating (Eds.), *Approaches and Methodologies in the Social Sciences* (pp. 198–223). Cambridge: Cambridge University Press.

Drennan, L., & McConnell, A. (2007). *Risk and Crisis Management in the Public Sector*. London: Routledge.

Dunleavy, P. (1995). Policy disasters: Explaining the UK's record. *Public Policy and Administration*, 10, 52–70.

Former Senior Bureaucrat. (2014). Interview with George Carayannopoulos.

Former Senior Emergency Management Officer. (2014). Interview with George Carayannopoulos.

Goebels, G. (2014). Interview with George Carayannopoulos.

Grady, B. (2014). Interview with George Carayannopoulos.

Haertel, C. E. J., & Latemore, G. M. (2011). Mud and tears: The human face of disaster – A case study of the Queensland floods, January 2011. *Journal of Management & Organization*, 17(6), 864–872.

Halligan, J. (2007). Reintegrating government in third generation reforms of Australia and New Zealand. *Public Policy and Administration*, 22(2), 217–238.

Hood, C. (2005). The idea of joined-up government: A historical perspective. In V. Bogdanor (Ed.), *Joined-Up Government* (pp. 19–42). Oxford: Oxford University Press.

Hubbard, B. (2014). Interview with George Carayannopoulos.

Kapucu, N. (2008). Collaborative emergency management: Better community organising, better public preparedness and response. *Disasters*, 32(2), 239–262.

Kloot, L., & Martin, J. (2007). Public sector change, organisational culture and financial information: A study of local government. *Australian Journal of Public Administration*, 66(4), 485–497.

Lapsley, C. (2014). Interview with George Carayannopoulos.

Leonard, H. B., & Howitt, A. M. (2010). Organising response to extreme emergencies: The Victorian bushfires of 2009. *Australian Journal of Public Administration*, 69(4), 372–386.

Ling, T. (2002). Delivering joined-up government in the UK: Dimensions, issues and problems. *Public Administration*, 80(4), 615–642.

Lucas, P. (2014). Interview with George Carayannopoulos.

McConnell, A. (2010). Policy success, policy failure and grey areas in-between. *Journal of Public Policy*, 30(3), 345–362.

McConnell, A. (2011). Success? Failure? Something in-between? A framework for evaluating crisis management. *Policy and Society*, 30(2), 63–76.

McGowan, J. (2014). Interview with George Carayannopoulos.

Management Advisory Committee (2004). *Connecting Government: Whole of Government Responses to Australia's Priority Challenges Summary of Findings*. Canberra: Commonwealth of Australia.

Mitroff, I. (2001). *Managing Crises Before They Happen*. New York: American Management Association Press.

Moynihan, D. P. (2008). Combining structural forms in the search for policy tools: Incident command systems in US crisis management. *Governance – An International Journal of Policy Administration and Institutions*, 21(2), 205–229.

Moynihan, D. P. (2009). The network governance of crisis response: Case studies of incident command systems. *Journal of Public Administration Research and Theory*, 19(4), 895–915.

Newman, C. (2014). Interview with George Carayannopoulos.

Newton, G. (2014). Interview with George Carayannopoulos.

Prasser, S. (2006). *Royal Commissions and Public Inquiries in Australia*. Sydney: Lexis Nexis Butterworths.

Red Cross (2015). Victorian Bushfires 2009 – 5 years on. Retrieved 17 July 2015 from http://www.redcross.org.au/victorian-bushfires-2009.aspx

Seeger, M., Sellnow, T., & Ulmer, R. (2003). *Communication and Organisational Crisis*. Westport, CT: Greenwood Publishers.

Smith, K. (2014). Interview with George Carayannopoulos.

Vennesson, P. (2008). Case studies and process tracing: Theories and practices. In D. Della Porta & M. Keating (Eds.), *Approaches and Methodologies in the Social Sciences* (pp. 223–240). Cambridge: Cambridge University Press.

6 The flames and water are gone – crisis management in Australia

Overview

This chapter builds on insights from the case studies and the academic literature in order to enhance our understanding of crisis management. In doing so, it turns these insights back on the case studies to provide an even deeper understanding of bureaucratic coordination in the Victorian bushfires and Queensland floods. The chapter draws together empirical, theoretical and institutional analysis that illustrates the bi-directional relationship between the cases and disaster management principles. This allows for an explanation of how the crisis management principles impact the cases and how the cases have broader implications for crisis management. Firstly, the chapter will revisit the research model to determine whether commitments to whole of government working in crisis were 'rhetoric' or 'reality'? Secondly, it will consider whether the chaos and complexity during crises ultimately make whole of government responses implausible. In doing so, it draws together the findings of the research to consider their contribution to the literature on whole of government crisis management. Thirdly, the significant outcomes of the case studies are understood against the backdrop of crisis management to obtain a deeper understanding of their implications. The chapter also provides further insights by considering high level enablers and constraints from the disaster management field which impact on the case studies. This includes the institutions and processes related to federalism which influence disaster management, as well as the 'all hazards' framework and how both address the research themes. The comparative analysis demonstrates that the cases are not 'outliers' but are strongly shaped by and epitomise the challenges of managing disasters. The symbiotic relationship between the cases and disaster management principles provides the basis for a concluding reflection on whether idealised crisis management can ever be achieved. Finally, important future research questions are suggested in order to continue the development of research in the nexus between crisis management and whole of government.

Revisiting key themes in the face of disaster: Whole of government an imperative

In order to understand the broader implications of the case studies, it is important to consider the aims and objectives of the book. The research themes sought to understand whether the public commitments to whole of government working, a pervasive concept in the public sector, can be seen to be 'rhetoric' or 'reality'.

A number of key findings arise regarding the application of whole of government strategies in response to crises including: strong commitments towards whole of government at the political-bureaucratic level, recognition that a crisis provides a unique mechanism in which to engender whole of government working and understanding the necessary preconditions to implement a whole of government response. All of the above factors have a clear impact on the response to a crisis and crucially shape the perception of a 'failed' or 'successful' response across procedural, programmatic and political grounds.

At the political and bureaucratic levels, whole of government working is seen as pervasive idea which provides an important contribution to the business of government during and beyond crises (6 et al., 2002). There is significant untapped potential that can be achieved by better connecting government as a whole rather than through the sum of its parts. Although strong commitments have been expressed around whole of government working, it is often a difficult construct to operationalise across departments and agencies. The difficulties in operationalising connected government comes against a backdrop of individual performance measurement regimes and pressures on public sector agencies to reach targets (Hood, 2005). As a result of the emphasis on individual performance, there may be few if any incentives for departments and agencies to work in a whole of government way. The lack of incentive or motivation around connecting across agencies thus represents a crucial hurdle to collaborative working.

Whilst whole of government is a highly desired form of coordination, there are other very real and tangible barriers which can impede its implementation notably; organisational structures, culture and institutional arrangements (Page, 2005). A key outcome which emerges from the research is the understanding that whole of government can be difficult to implement across different strands of government; for example, political, bureaucratic and operational. Whilst strong linkages may exist within groups such as Directors-General of government departments, there are difficulties in bringing government together across the three strands. Difficulties in implementing a whole of government approach are predicated on the challenges of drawing together disparate agencies, given that each brings a different world view and emphasis on collaboration. This was succinctly described by one of the research participants who noted "the cultures between of a government department and a statutory authority are very different" (Former Senior

Emergency Management Officer). Cultural differences represent real challenges to operationalising whole of government during crisis situations and prompt the need for further thought on the nature of inter-organisational coordination.

Despite the barriers to implementation, a crisis represents a unique opportunity to connect government. Crises provide the necessary imperative and sense of urgency in which to engender connected forms of working. The ability to implement horizontal working is based on leveraging long standing relationships rather than requiring a set of introductions during a crisis itself. During a crisis, there is recognition of a store of collective goodwill where 'turf wars' are put aside for the greater common good. In this way, a crisis can be contrasted to other policy areas and there is a strong belief that obtaining a deeper understanding of why whole of government works in crisis could be usefully applied to other complex policy problems.

A crisis is seen as the ideal moment to connect across government, when institutional structures are supported by a network of personal relationships. In reflecting on the research themes, each state did show a commitment to implementing whole of government responses in the face of crisis. Commitments to whole of government did not necessarily lead to a successful response but provide an important recognition of the importance of horizontal working in responding to complex problems. Crises in fact provide a catalyst for enhanced cooperation "every time an event occurs, culturally we go there [whole of government], but then we put so many blockages and impediments to actually getting there in peace time" (Former Assistant Director General Department of Community Safety, Bruce Grady).

If we consider the enablers around whole of government implementation, there are a number of factors which are crucial including: the nature of the crisis, leadership, coordination mechanisms, organisational culture, social capital and institutions. In the case studies, there is recognition that the scale and dimension of the events meant they could not be handled through command and control. The literature suggests that command and control models do not represent an adequate means to respond to complex crisis events, given the need to connect strategic decision making with events at the coalface in real time (Mitroff, 2001). Indeed, crisis responses need the collective resources and efforts of the entire government, strong leadership, relationships and institutional arrangements. If we analyse some of the individual elements in further detail, leadership and authority emanating from the highest level of government is seen as a driving factor. The ability of Premiers, Senior Ministers and Director-Generals to set the tone is crucial in achieving the necessary 'buy in' for a whole of government response. There is a strong sense of consciousness and awareness from the executive leadership about the need to have responses which are driven from the highest levels. Direct responses from the executive leadership are important to provide authority and mandate but also to meet public expectations around leadership 'on the ground' as events are unfolding. The direct leadership shown in the cases was described in the following way "the Premier and the selected inner circle of her Cabinet, the ministers drove what happened in Queensland so the leadership came from the very top and it was direct and it was about whole of government and was non-political" (Former Assistant Director General EMQ, Warren Bridson).

Coordination mechanisms are also at the heart of whole of government responses, with recognition of the need to have coordination mechanisms which are in place during 'peace time' and leveraged during a crisis. Appropriate coordination mechanisms can also assist the integration between political, bureaucratic and operational agency levels before, during and after an event. Having structures in place which facilitate consistent and informative dialogue between all parties is seen as a pre-condition to improve integration. The establishment of appropriate communication mechanisms is acknowledged as a highly complex undertaking given the diversity of the public sector, its departments and operational agencies.

The nature of organisational culture within response agencies and the social capital built between organisations, individuals and the community is a strong pre-condition to implementing a successful whole of government response. In many respects, whilst relationships existed across strands of government in the case studies, these may not have been close i.e. operational level relationships with the political level. The gap between groups is a strong factor that shapes the ability to respond as events unfold. There is recognition that there needs to be closer collaboration between operational agencies to improve integration. As a result, the development of closer links and bonds between agencies remains a point for ongoing development for disaster management practitioners. There is strong advocacy for an emergency management doctrine which recognises that overall system coordination is as important as the response of individual agencies. The current Emergency Management Commissioner in Victoria who was involved in the response to Black Saturday (in a different capacity) described this in the following way:

> Culturally at the time, it was very much seen as the uniforms are in control and those who didn't wear uniforms were there to get information. Now ... it is not just sharing, it's the interaction, it is fundamentally different so there is a whole of government approach.
> (Emergency Management Commissioner Craig Lapsley)

Finally, institutional structures and disaster management arrangements in place in each of the jurisdictions were pivotal in mediating and framing the whole of government responses. Legislative frameworks around disaster management provide the tangible structure around coordination mechanisms in each of the states. There is a strong requirement however to juxtapose legislative frameworks against the need to act flexibly in the face of emerging crises. Decisions taken in a crisis, outside legislative frameworks, also need to be considered against the ethos of the disaster management system and the nature of unfolding events.

From academia to practice: Reintegrating the literature in the management of crises

The intersection between whole of government and crisis management remains underdeveloped, given the synergies in the literature which exist around issues of coordination, governance, command and control and horizontality. There is potential to better understand how disaster events play out by further examining the link between crisis management and whole of government. If we look at whole of government, it has high relevance to the management of disasters but remains difficult to operationalise. Perceptions of 'failure' or 'success' are also a paramount consideration within public policy during a crisis. Perception remains crucial in measuring both the short term and long term outcomes of an event. These issues are considered at further length below as a means of integrating the work in the book to the broader literature.

With regard to whole of government being a new mode of working as suggested by the APS (2007), there is a general understanding that it represents a paradigm shift. Connected forms of working are a move away from silo based thinking towards more collaborative approaches based on reintegrating government (Halligan, 2007). In many ways, whole of government moves in parallel with changes towards governance and more pluralised forms of working in the public sector. There is an understanding that traditional command and verticality in public policy is not appropriate to confront 'wicked' policy and service delivery challenges (Rittel & Webber, 1973). Across a number of policy domains there is an understanding that no single agency or department can adequately respond to complex needs and input from multiple angles is required to improve outcomes. Whole of government implementation does require a number of preconditions to be met as suggested in the literature (Ling, 2002), meaning it is still seen as highly desirable in public administration. The analysis undertaken through the research indicates that there is a contribution to the literature based on crisis being the ideal time to implement whole of government.

The notion of a crisis being a catalyst towards whole of government implementation is consistent with the literature. The literature suggests that rather than being organic and self-organised, whole of government requires extrinsic factors such as leadership from the highest levels of the executive (Management Advisory Committee, 2004). As such, moves towards institutionalising whole of government are a higher order ideal rather than being organic. In order to connect government there is a need for a clear vision and direction, authority and mandate from the highest level of government (Humpage, 2005). There is also a need for institutional structures which encourage collaboration and for financial mechanisms to be in place that engender cooperation rather than foster competition. Driving the move towards horizontal working requires a strong mandate and authority provided from the very top of government, be this Premier, Ministers or senior figures in the bureaucracy. Without the authority or mandate provided by key figures, it is difficult to operationalise connected forms of working and move beyond business as usual. Institutional structures that support and encourage whole of government working are also cited in the literature (Australian Public Service Commission, 2007). The importance of institutions has been validated through the research where institutional structures underpinned by strong networks were pivotal to the responses. Indeed, strong institutional structures and networks are central at all stages in the crisis management cycle from planning to response and reconstruction.

With respect to the perception of crisis, being as important as the events themselves, crises are deeply contested and subject to contextualisation (Rosenthal et al., 2001). The research undertaken indicates that the perception and understanding of an event plays a powerful role in shaping the outcome. The political management and response to the initial acute response phase was pivotal along with the need to be 'seen' to take a proactive stance on leading the response and recovery efforts. As time passes other parts of the institutional response such as commissions of inquiry have a key part in shaping the legacy of an event. If we look at the Victorian bushfires, the information which arose from the Commission of Inquiry was pivotal in influencing the longer term narrative of the event. The institutional response to create a Commission of Inquiry and its outcomes resulted in a change of perception from what was originally a more positive outlook to a more negative appraisal.

An examination of how the two case studies unfolded provides an insightful review and reflection on the literature at the nexus of whole of government crisis responses. Crisis management principles strongly impact on the responses and provide an extra layer to analyse the case studies and input into the success or failure of responses. The section below provides insights on how crisis management principles impact on the cases and the broader implications for disaster management in Australia.

Beyond the ashes and through the mud: A deeper understanding of Australian disaster management

Beyond the comparative analysis which has been provided in the research, the cases also epitomise a number of high level issues around disaster management practices. The section below provides a summary of higher level issues which address the research themes including: the importance of trust in the public service, the impact of federalism on disaster management and the 'all hazards approach'. Further, the section below also considers short and long term outcomes to crises, political consequences, perceptions of leadership, the nature of interactions between levels of government, knowledge transfer and resilience, recovery/reconstruction and commissions of inquiry. Consideration of the above issues and their contribution to the original aims of the research allows for further insights to be generated and reflection on the future of the Australian crisis management literature.

Whole of government: The Holy Grail

Underpinning whole of government responses to crises are concepts regarding citizen's trust in government. In general, the public have high expectations that governments will be able to plan, prepare and resolve crises in an effective manner. Expectations from the public are often based on the desire to quickly return to normality after an event given "people who have planned for emergencies are usually the first to recover" (Lentini, 2014, p. 52). There is a unique level of expectation around the role of government in protecting its citizens from harm. Former Lord Mayor of Brisbane and subsequently Premier of Queensland Campbell Newman described it as such "community expectations are very high, they think it is like CSI with amazing technology, there is a disconnect between what is achievable and what the community expects (in relation to disasters)". Public expectations provide a significant test for government given that in a crisis situation the "public's trust in governing institutions is tested and it is in these situations where the exercise of power is needed and fundamental values are at stake" (Svedin, 2012, p. 166). There is also a strong link between trust and legitimacy "the legitimacy of political and administrative institutions and actors is based largely on trust" (Christensen & Laegreid, 2005, p. 487). Hence, where there are breakdowns or failures in the response to crisis events, governments are placed under heavy scrutiny and their legitimacy is challenged. From a public perspective there is a strong need to reach an understanding of how events unfolded, what improvements can be made and how they can be better prepared for future crises.

The degree of trust around government agencies comes against a backdrop where in many countries trust in the public service has dropped to all time low levels and citizens are feeling increasingly disengaged from the processes of government (Organisation for Economic Co-operation and Development, 2015). As such, a perfect storm arises where citizen expectations are heightened against a backdrop where there is an increased scepticism in the ability of government to meet societal needs. The result is an even greater imperative for governments to perform well through a period of crisis where the results of a failure are seen as even more damning. There is strong explanatory power in the trust paradigm when we reflect on the case studies. A high level of public scrutiny is acutely evident in the cases where in Victoria there was a significant media and public backlash based on disappointment and the perceived lack of accountability from key leaders. On the other hand, in Queensland, despite a string of policy and service delivery problems in other areas leading up to the 2011 events, there is recognition of the excellent performance of government in responding. The perception of responses to natural disasters shows that citizens view crises as different to other policy areas. The public also retain high expectations of government which are difficult to meet, a key part of the political challenge in managing disaster events.

The trust paradigm also has a second stream which relates to the degree of trust between agencies and how trust between key parties may serve as a mediator of organisational performance. Arguably in the era of NPM, trust between agencies or individuals is more complex given the disaggregation which has occurred and the focus on objectives and performance metrics. The level of inter-organisational trust between individuals and agencies represents a key factor underpinning whole of government endeavours during peace time or in a crisis. In a crisis however, the ability to leverage "well-established and trusting relationships is crucial" (Arklay, 2015, p. 188), given the inherent chaos and complexity means there is a lack of time to establish new relationships. In this way inter-organisational trust represents a crucial consideration in responding to crises.

Although there is a general perception that whole of government working is important and needs to be leveraged in order to improve policy and service delivery outcomes there is not a unitary model for implementation. One of the most important factors relates to the nature of the public service and its ethos. Factors that shape public service ethos can be seen to be part of historical legacy issues where each state has developed its own public service culture (Wanna, 2007). An example of differences between states can be seen in Victoria, which has generally been seen as a strong leader in terms of public sector reform and innovation ahead of other states. Where government in Victoria tends to be more Melbourne centric, the large spread of population and regional cities in Queensland means there has been a need to use devolved mechanisms in public policy and service delivery. Whilst it would appear logical that whole of government may have been easier to implement in a smaller centralised state like Victoria, the inverse is true as there is a greater imperative of working in a horizontal way in Queensland.

It is important to recognise that there are a wide range of factors which influence state level approaches to disasters. States have developed their own policies and operating procedures which vary and arguably lead to inconsistency across the national disaster management arrangements. An example was succinctly described by a senior operational response agency figure in the following way with regard to the classification of fire warnings:

We have categories of emergency warnings for fires; in the rest of Australia the highest level is called catastrophic, the Premier at the time John

Brumby for political reasons said catastrophic is an outcome, which is correct. It does however mean we are the only state with code red, which is ridiculous. That's where federation gets in the way of emergency management in a big way.

(Former State Emergency Response Officer, Rod Collins)

Another important debate regarding whole of government responses to crises, relates to the role of federalism and its associated structures. There are very real questions which arise regarding the interaction of the three levels of government: federal, state and local in dealing with large scale events. In Australia's federal system planning, response and recovery around disasters is the domain of the states. Most states proscribe a key role for local government given it is at the coalface. If responsibility for the initial response to a crisis is predominantly left at the local level, there is a need for serious consideration of support mechanisms to resource councils. Differences in the support of local government in managing crises are acutely evident in the case studies where there is a decentralised approach in Queensland and a more centralised view in Victoria. Differences in the ethos of each state also impact the implementation of its disaster management arrangements. As a result, there should also be consideration of how broader changes which are happening within the public sector influence crisis responses. At the local government level, if we consider processes of council amalgamations, restructures and staff cuts which have occurred in states such as Queensland and New South Wales, questions arise whether changes have boosted or weakened emergency response capacity.

Finally, it is also worthwhile reflecting on the ability to handle multiple events that may occur at the same time. If we were to imagine as a worst case scenario events of similar magnitude to the 2009 Victorian bushfires, 2011 Queensland floods and 2013 NSW bushfires, occurring simultaneously capacity at the national level may quickly be exhausted. Considerations of overall system capacity are relevant when we look at discussions around the resourcing of fire, emergency services and the defence force. Resourcing is largely based on reciprocal relationships across the states which mean that states would be under extreme pressure should large scale simultaneous events occur. The lack of federal overarching machinery could also have negative effects in such a scenario. As a result, it has been argued that "COAG and the Attorney-General's Department could take a more active role in providing guidance and assistance in defining national aims and objectives" (Jones, 2013, p. 19) and an overarching national framework may assist with disaster coordination.

Crisis and disaster management: When scenarios become real

With regard to the management and response to crises, another key consideration is the 'all hazards' framework and whether different types of events such as fire, floods, cyclones and even terrorism can be considered in a similar way. In Australia, the variations in risk profiles across states raises an issue of whether the 'all hazards' approach can be seen to be an appropriate way to plan, prepare and respond to crises across a geographically variable continent (Cornall, 2005). What emerges however is the understanding that key characteristics and features of disaster management such as leadership, organisational culture and social capital are more important than having specific provisos for each threat. There are also serious debates around the role of personal responsibility for "safety and property protection in order to minimise the impacts of future events on communities" (McLennan, Elliott & Wright, 2014, p. 11). In the cases, although different i.e. fire vs flood, it is the generic characteristics or attributes of the disaster management systems which are more important e.g. the shared experiences within a group of responders and their capacity to respond. There does need to be recognition of the differences that may exist between the risk profiles but the overarching characteristics of responses remain similar. There is also a strong need to differentiate between smaller events and large scale catastrophic disasters where "due to their rarity and complexity ... knowledge is limited" and where there is an underlying lack of capacity to manage effectively (Crosweller, 2015, p. 50). As such deeper considerations around the 'all hazards' framework strongly shape the outcomes in each of the individual cases, which were once in a generation events.

Another important consideration in understanding responses to crises are differences that exist between short and long term outcomes. The actual crisis response is a small part of an overall panorama related to preparation for and long-term recovery from large scale disasters. Indeed, much attention is often placed in the immediate lead up to and response period and considerably less on the long term outcomes. Long term outcomes refer to both emergency management arrangements and the experiences of survivors. There is a need to take a long term view of crises to understand their impact on the affected communities as the psycho-social recovery from an event may not have the same discrete end point as physical reconstruction (State Government of Victoria, 2010). As a result "recognition of the wellbeing of a community, beyond its disaster experience, affords the potential for empowerment and self-reflection through a strengths-based lens" (Gibbs et al., 2015, p. 23). The consideration of community well-being is particularly relevant where there is a threat of ongoing risk for impacted areas and to improve community resilience. Taking a long term view to crises is also relevant with regard to the organisational learning that occurs as a result of an event and the retention of organisational memory. If we reflect on the cases, there are very different narratives between the immediate aftermath and the longer term recovery. Long term outcomes also need to be considered relevant to the frequency of events, where Queensland as the 'disaster state' deals with large scale flooding and cyclones on a more regular basis than severe fire events in Victoria.

Leadership: Leading from the front

The political consequences arising from crisis events and reflections on the types of leadership required are an ongoing consideration in the current political landscape and 24 hour news cycle. Traditional wisdom had held that leaders who perform well in a crisis situation may often see a bounce in polling and popularity with the electorate. Conversely, those leaders who are viewed as performing badly may experience adverse outcomes at the ballot box. The case studies examined have indicated something different that is worth further exploration. If we look at the outcomes in Queensland, we may see an example where the perception of a successful leadership response did not lead to electoral success. Although a failed response may have the possibility of irrevocably damaging a leader, a successful leadership response may not have a long term benefit in terms of the electoral cycle. The observation noted above is an interesting discussion point, particularly where it is argued that personality politics and the presidentialisation of Australian politics has occurred (Kefford, 2013). It may also indicate that in the wake of a crisis, the public themselves may want to move on from the events. The public may choose to return to a discussion of issues which more commonly shape the electoral agenda such as law and order, health, education and the economy. That is to say as part of the process of recovery there is an emphasis on returning to normality. Although the management of a crisis is never forgotten it does not buy a longstanding political capital.

With regard to leadership, another interesting observation which arises refers to the degree in which the perception of a leader meeting public expectations becomes a critical part of the leadership task (Heifetz & Laurie, 1997). In pressure situations "leaders might find themselves isolated from each other and unable to communicate in the usual ways…with the loss of data, tools, structure, relationships and communication, can come the ultimate losses – those of role and identity" (Cherry, 2014, p. 33). The sense of identity and perception of leadership is pivotal in the immediate response phase given strong public expectations around the role of government. Expectations are particularly heightened in times of crisis. At these times government, more so than any other group, is seen as the reference point of the public, as part of the social contract that may exist between leaders and government (Svedin, 2012). We then see a particular type of relationship that emerges, where the public may have expectations not only about the performance of their leaders on technical matters but expect leaders to be empathetic and accountable. Therefore, more profound considerations of leadership can be seen to have strong explanatory power with regard to the case studies as well as crisis management more broadly.

Coordination: Putting the pieces together

Whole of government coordination refers to horizontal coordination across a level of government or vertical coordination across levels of government e.g. federal, state and local (Management Advisory Committee, 2004). In terms of disaster management organisations, community groups, councils and others can be:

> represented as both independent and interdependent systems within a whole system. On one hand, some parts of the system are connected to one another in a hierarchical way ... other parts of the system operate in an autonomous way and collaborate informally.
>
> (Cavallo, 2014, p. 47)

Understanding the diversity of disaster management systems allows us to reflect and delineate the type of coordinating body within these systems; for example, political, bureaucratic or operational. An important inclusion in the discussion of coordination is to add this layer of coordinating body and embed it as a further parameter of analysis. As a result, networks can be analysed both within and across levels of government. An example occurs at the operational level where we may look at police at the local level. We may also look at police at the state level through state disaster command structures and finally at the Commonwealth level by understanding the relationship between police and the defence force. An analysis of whole of government coordination takes on a form which we can analyse at the local, state and federal level. The analysis can then also further be extended through the type of coordinating group – that is, political, bureaucratic or operational. By adding a layer of analytic capacity, a matrix is created which combines both horizontal and vertical dimensions and provides a richer research tool to understand crisis responses. If we look at the case studies, understanding this layer of coordination is at the heart of some of the key differences in the outcomes, given the higher degree of integration in the Queensland system.

The study and review of coordination mechanisms within the crisis episodes analysed also reveals debates about the merits of vertical command and horizontal networks in responding to crises. Increasingly, command and control has been cited as not meeting requirements for the management of crises given its inability to coordinate complex communication flows (Au, 2011). Increasingly decentralised network approaches where information from multiple sources is used to create an operational picture is more appropriate to these situations (Robinson et al., 2013). Strong horizontal networks can be juxtaposed against the need for a strong centralised coordination presence and high visibility from executive leadership. Issues of coordination are related to the literature on hierarchy, governance and meta-governance which seek to understand the way in which changes in the state impact on bureaucracy and underpin moves to more horizontal means of working (Bell & Park, 2006). There is a strong link to understanding whether vertical forms of policy making and service delivery have been supplanted by horizontal forms or whether the central executive still retains power in setting policy directions.

Organisational culture: Public service values

Organisational culture heavily shapes the interactions of public sector organisations. The concept of trust in the public sector can be viewed from two
angles. The first refers to the extent in which citizens maintain confidence
that the public sector can deliver on its promises. In a crisis period, public
anxiety is more acutely felt where there may be physical dislocation and fear
compounded by the loss of life and infrastructure. On the second front,
trust is also important in terms of the relationships between key people and
agencies involved in the response to crises. The ability to leverage off existing
relationships through trust in other departments and agencies within the
public sector is pivotal through the disaster response cycle. The network of
relationships that exist, allows for a crisis response to function even where
there may not be optimal institutional structures. Consideration must also
be given to the way that performance management, managerialism and NPM
have helped define relationships in the public sector and whether sufficient
incentives to collaborate exist. The balance between institutional structures
and personal relationships is at the crux of the differences in outcomes
between the two cases. Based on the frequency of disaster events, there is an
obligation for a state such as Queensland to have its disaster management
arrangements ready for implementation at all times and be embedded as part
of its public service culture.

Another crucial element which relates to the culture around a disaster
response is the way that institutional memory is captured and transferred
from one disaster to the next. The ability to retain organisational memory
and knowledge is difficult, particularly at the political and bureaucratic levels
which are subject to the electoral cycle. In many respects, knowledge transfer
and the retention of memory occurs through the emergency services. There
are however intrinsic differences between agencies, their motivations and
modus operandi. As such, it is appropriate to consider each of the response
agencies e.g. police, fire separately and understand their internal context.
Also worth consideration is that in major events, senior operational figures are
under immense pressure and scrutiny. The high degree of pressure was particularly the case in Victoria where operational figures were at the front line of
criticism. Ultimately a number of senior figures lost their positions with
significant restructuring of the emergency response agencies in the aftermath
to Black Saturday.

Social capital: Resilient communities

Community resilience is an integral part of the planning, response to and
recovery from natural disasters (Council of Australian Governments, 2011).
Community resilience can take on a number of forms including resilience of
the general population and resilience that occurs through the social capital
formed between members of the community, it "recognises that enhancing

resilience involves multiple stakeholders and activities across the socio-ecological system" (Goode et al., 2011). The argument has been made that general resilience of the population has declined given moves towards urbanisation and changes in population demographics. The length of time between major disaster events also means that lessons learned may not be transmitted from one generation to the next, causing a loss of community memory. There is a general belief that "Australians are not very resilient these days, they are becoming increasingly reliant on the state to provide for them[during crises]" (Campbell Newman). Further, broader social trends such as community bonds, social capital and the ties between members of a community are pivotal where there has been large and widespread destruction. A pertinent example lies in the creation of the 'mud army' in Queensland which mobilised large numbers of people to assist with clean-up of the flood events in the metropolitan Brisbane area. The narrative of "community resilience has emerged as part of this dynamic ... it has been favourably compared against a state-centric view of crisis management" (Stark & George, 2015, p. 592). Given the importance of community resilience, it may be useful to reflect upon whether crisis outcomes might be related to other social phenomena i.e. the balance between individual and collective action and overall sense of community.

Institutions: Structuring success

The role of institutions is central in the lead up to a crisis, through the immediate response and into the recovery phase. Special purpose recovery and reconstruction bodies have been recognised as the mechanism in which to embed the recovery and reconstruction efforts given their ability to cut through bureaucratic red tape. The creation of reconstruction bodies indicates that standard operations and government procedures may be inadequate to provide a large scale recovery effort. Reconstruction bodies have increasingly been seen as part of the initial political response during the acute crisis phase and provide a powerful symbol. They serve a means to be proactive at the political level in order to meet the expectations that the public may have in the face of a disaster, a fact strongly acknowledged in both case studies. The use of reconstruction bodies remains highly political given that the public retains high expectations about the ability of recovery and reconstruction authorities to quickly and expeditiously return life to normal. At the broader level, the creation of reconstruction bodies also occurs against a backdrop of increased financial scrutiny in a climate of austerity in the wake of the global financial crisis.

Another of the key institutional responses involves the use of Royal Commissions or Commissions of Inquiry. Commissions are increasingly used in order to forensically examine the events that occur in a crisis, whether a natural disaster or other man made policy failures. Information collected post-event is intended to understand "what drives community behaviour and the effects of certain policies and programs" to inform future behaviour (Bruce, 2015, p. 6). As part of a post-event response, inquiries are often cited as part of the learning and knowledge transfer process that occurs (Prasser, 2006). Inquiries are highly politicised and used as an instrument to forensically examine the activities of key individuals as much as the overall design and implementation of a disaster management system. There is a strong suggestion that inquiries have the benefit of operating from a position of hindsight. Inquiries have the ability to generalise regarding actions which should have been taken with respect to the disasters and highlight mistakes that decision-makers make during the heat of the crisis itself. There is also reflection required on whether commissions are the most appropriate means to assess policy and service delivery success. This comes against a background where inquiries continue to rise in prominence and are increasingly being used as a means to retrospectively 'try' those involved in policy failures. In both cases, understanding events through a framework which looks at the role of commissions of inquiry holds high value, as commissions of inquiry were important in shaping the long term perceptions and narrative of the events.

The case study events did not occur within a vacuum but rather can be seen as the product of the disaster management system. Federalism and its impact on crisis management structures as well as the risk profiles of states means that the set-up of their disaster management arrangements are largely contingent on historical legacy. Accounting for the differences, there are more generic features or characteristics around leadership, communication, coordination and organisational values which transcend the case studies. As a result of the aforementioned, the all hazards approach and its objective to "involve a range of parties acting in co-ordination to achieve a mutual goal" in confronting significant events (McLennan, Weir et al., 2014, p. 22) remains an important guiding principle. The cases can be seen to epitomise the key challenges of managing crises as well as generating new insights and areas for further empirical review.

Complex but not impossible: Final reflections

This book has reviewed the link between whole of government coordination and crisis management by examining the internal relationships which existed within two state governments. The research has provided analysis of key factors to understand whether the commitments to joined up working are matched by actions during the acute response phase. The book has explicitly linked the bodies of literature on whole of government and crisis management, given that to date limited work has been done in connecting these areas. Linking the two bodies of literature has been valuable given that there are significant synergies on issues related to coordination, integration, verticality and horizontality and more generally moves away from command and control and towards networks. As a result, there is scope for further and sustained research to better understand the intersection of the two groups of literature and the translation to disaster management practice. In regards to future research directions, there are a number of areas which merit further investigation including:

1. How do policy and legislative frameworks impact on disaster management responses? Preparation and planning for natural disasters and crisis events remains a significant task at the national level. The 'all hazards' approach provides for responses based on a number of potential threats whether natural disasters or other man made events. In recent years, little empirical work has been undertaken to understand whether the moves towards an 'all hazards' approach has made the task of preparation and planning for eventualities easier or more difficult. Whilst acknowledging the importance of the 'all hazards' approach, limited work has been done to assess its impact on crisis management. Given the current climate around global threats and pandemics, it would be an appropriate time to review the impact of the 'all hazards' approach to better understand the influence that it has had on preparation and planning for disasters. An examination of key preparation and planning mechanisms at the federal and state level would provide an indication of how planning moves from conceptualisation to implementation. The research would also seek to better understand from a public sector perspective the strengths and weaknesses of such an approach in terms of preparing for any contingency.

2. What is the impact of governance on crisis management? Given the complexity of large scale disaster responses, further review of governance arrangements that exist in the recovery phase of a natural disaster is a potential area of research where more depth is needed. Increasingly, it is clear that the long-term recovery and reconstruction from disasters requires the input and capacity of government, non-government and corporate sectors. To date, little academic work has been done on the long-term evaluation of governance arrangements and their relationship to outcomes with respect to recovery and reconstruction. A further and more detailed analysis could be undertaken to better understand the relationships that exist between government and non-government organisations and the corporate sector. Such an approach should help to unravel the complex series of relationships and evaluate their impact on crisis recovery. A particular emphasis could be placed on the role of insurers and their relationship to government, given that there has been sustained attention around the roles of insurers in assisting communities to rebuild and controversies where insurance policies have not been honoured due to legal and definitional issues.

3. How can learning occur from major disaster events and be used to mitigate future crises? Royal Commissions and inquiries have increasingly become an important part of the review of natural disasters. Despite the growing number of inquiries, questions remain as to how their findings are

translated into the mitigation of future events. Little work has been done on assessing whether the findings and recommendations from inquiries have led to long term policy or structural change which better prepares states and their citizens. The review of findings from recent disaster inquiries provides a means of assessing whether final recommendations and outcomes do indeed shape policy changes with regard to natural disasters and represents an important stream of research.

In concluding, this book has reviewed the intersection between whole of government and crisis management by looking at two recent natural disaster events the 2009 Victorian bushfires and 2011 Queensland floods. Examining the conceptual model through cases provides a means to compare and contrast how whole of government played out in two different events in distinct jurisdictions. The research indicates that almost universally whole of government is seen as being extremely important in order to try and leverage the resources and capacity across government to confront key public policy challenges. In reflecting on the research themes, there are clear commitments to implementing whole of government during crisis events. The commitments towards connecting government did not however necessarily mean that the whole of government implementation was successful but did represent a commitment to make this reality. This research indicates that a mere commitment to whole of government is not sufficient but that there must be appropriate support to move towards successful implementation. A crisis situation represents a unique opportunity in which to implement whole of government activities, in many ways it can be seen to typify the instance in which whole of government operates best. In an emergency there is an imperative and urgency to connect government and the traditional enmities which exist in the public service which may be put aside towards the unfolding needs of a disaster. The research has provided new insights into the analysis of whole of government by looking at key thematic areas related to the whole of government management of crisis including: leadership, coordination, organisational culture, social capital and institutions. In both of the case studies, the aforementioned themes have strong explanatory power with regard to the perception of a 'failed' or 'successful' response.

Firstly if we look at leadership, the public have strong expectations around the role that leaders play both at the political and technocratic level as well as at the human level in connecting with those impacted by crisis events. In terms of outcomes, the long-term political outcomes for those politicians involved in the response to crises may not mirror the perception of the success or failure of the response. It is clear that there is uniqueness around a crisis period which may fade over time. As time passes, more routine policy concerns such as education, health, transport and the economy return to their place at the top of the state agenda.

Coordination across government is a fundamental element during the response to crises. A broader conceptualisation which views whole of

government as the intersection between political, bureaucratic and operational levels is necessary to better understand the challenges of integration.
Structural disaster management arrangements which exist in a jurisdiction
play a crucial role in bringing together the key actors in the right way to
ensure dialogue and communication across the different strands of government. In order to underpin and support crisis management structures, the
organisational cultures of departments and agencies involved in the response
to disasters need to be attuned to connected working. In a crisis situation
itself, there is a strong need for horizontal collaboration to meet the challenges
that arise. The individual relationships which exist across government are
also crucial and need to be leveraged at the time of the disaster itself.

With regard to institutional responses, beyond the mandated disaster
response arrangements that exist, two other elements must be acknowledged; commissions of inquiry and reconstruction authorities. Commissions
of Inquiry are seen as a highly proportionate response to events and a means
of reassuring the public that a full and thorough investigation will occur. In
the case studies however, commissions were highly politicised and created a
blame attribution process rather than purely reviewing disaster management
arrangements. The creation of reconstruction bodies during the midst of the
crises itself can be seen as a very powerful symbol. The move towards the
setup of recovery processes shows that governments are reacting promptly
and swiftly to unfolding events and indeed provides recognition that business
as usual is inadequate.

The key thematic areas examined also tell us about the ability to solve
problems and create solutions, to understand horizontality and verticality
and consider what may be ideal vs. practical forms of actions. If we consider
a crisis as a significant and complex problem for government, whole of
government provides a potential solution to address events as they unfold.
At the crux of whole of government issues there are clear debates about
horizontality and verticality given that whole of government seeks to address
issues such as the silo mentality and create a more horizontally integrated
and agile government that can marshal resources across its many departments
and agencies. At the heart of all crisis management lies the understanding
that crises are deeply contested, subject to contextualisation and that perception plays a major part in defining whether a crisis response is seen as
'successful' or 'unsuccessful.' As such, at the centre of key issues lie normative and prescriptive view points on what an idealised response may look
like. Normative views fail however to provide the necessary consideration of
what the practical barriers or impediments to connecting government in
crises may be.

Finally, in the context of the Victorian bushfires and the Queensland
floods, although commitments to whole of government working were reality,
the contexts of the events and their implementation ultimately meant that
Victoria is remembered as a 'failed' response whilst Queensland remains a
case study of 'success.' The outcomes of the events based on joined-up

responses demonstrates the complexity of using connected forms of working across large, complex and disparate government contexts and indicates that whole of government is still rightly considered as highly favourable in the public sector.

References

6, P., Leat, D., Seltzer, K., & Stoker, G. (2002). *Towards Holistic Governance*. Hampshire, UK: Palgrave.

Arklay, T. (2015). What happened to Queensland's disaster management arrangements?: From "global best practice' to "unsustainable' in 3 Years. *Australian Journal of Public Administration*, 74(2), 187–198.

Au, A. (2011). Analysis of command and control networks on Black Saturday. *Australian Journal of Emergency Management*, 26(3), 20–29.

Australian Public Service Commission (2007). *Tackling Wicked Problems: A Public Policy Perspective*. Canberra: Commonwealth of Australia.

Bell, S., & Park, A. (2006). The problematic metagovernance of networks: Water reform in NSW. *Journal of Public Policy*, 26(1), 63–83.

Bridson, W. (2014). Interview with George Carayannopoulos.

Bruce, D. (2015). Post incident research – gaining knowledge after the event. *Australian Journal of Emergency Management*, 30(3), 6–8.

Cavallo, A. (2014). Integrating disaster preparedness and resilience: A complex approach using system of systems. *Australian Journal of Emergency Management*, 29(3), 46–51.

Cherry, N. L. (2014). The frontline: A new focus for learning about leadership. *Australian Journal of Emergency Management*, 29(2), 31–34.

Christensen, T., & Laegreid, P. (2005). Trust in government: The relative importance of service satisfaction, political factors and demography. *Public Performance and Management Review*, 28(4), 487–511.

Collins, R. (2014). Interview with George Carayannopoulos.

Cornall, R. (2005). New levels of government responsiveness for 'all-hazards': The management of natural disasters and emergencies. *Australian Journal of Public Administration*, 64(2), 27–30.

Council of Australian Governments (2011). *National Strategy for Disaster Resilience*. Canberra: Commonwealth of Australia.

Crosweller, M. (2015). How a change in thinking might change the inevitability in disasters. *Australian Journal of Emergency Management*, 30(3), 48–55.

Former Senior Emergency Management Officer (2014). Interview with George Carayannopoulos.

Gibbs, L., Harms, L., Howell-Meurs, S., Block, K., Lusher, D., Richardson, J., et al. (2015). Community wellbeing: Applications for a disaster context. *Australian Journal of Emergency Management*, 30(3), 20–24.

Goode, N., Spencer, C., Archer, F., McArdle, D., Salmon, P., & McClure, R. (2011). *Review of Recent Australian Disaster Inquiries*. Melbourne: Disaster Resilience Unit, Injury Research Institute and the Faculty of Medicine, Nursing and Health Sciences, Monash University.

Grady, B. (2014). Interview with George Carayannopoulos.

Halligan, J. (2007). Reintegrating government in third generation reforms of Australia and New Zealand. *Public Policy and Administration*, 22(2), 217–238.

Heifetz, R. A., & Laurie, D. L. (1997). The work of leadership. *Harvard Business Review*, 75(1), 124–135.

Hood, C. (2005). The idea of joined-up government: A historical perspective. In V. Bogdanor (Ed.), *Joined-Up Government* (pp. 19–42). Oxford: Oxford University Press.

Humpage, L. (2005). Experimenting with a whole of government approach. *Policy Studies*, 26(1), 47–66.

Jones, R. (2013). In search of the 'prepared community': The way ahead for Australia? *Australian Journal of Emergency Management*, 28(1), 15–19.

Kefford, G. (2013). The presidentialisation of Australian politics? Kevin Rudd's leadership of the Australian Labor Party. *Australian Journal of Political Science*, 48(2), 135–146.

Lapsley, C. (2014). Interview with George Carayannopoulos.

Lentini, J. R. (2014). Bracing for the 'new normal': How communities are preparing for disasters. *Australian Journal of Emergency Management*, 29(4), 52–54.

Ling, T. (2002). Delivering joined-up government in the UK: Dimensions, issues and problems. *Public Administration*, 80(4), 615–642.

Management Advisory Committee (2004). *Connecting Government: Whole of Government Responses to Australia's Priority Challenges Summary of Findings*. Canberra: Commonwealth of Australia.

McLennan, B., Weir, J. K., Eburn, M., Handmer, J., Dovers, S., & Norman, B. J. (2014). Negotiating risk and responsibility through law, policy and planning. *Australian Journal of Emergency Management*, 29(3), 22–28.

McLennan, J., Elliott, G., & Wright, L. (2014). Bushfire survival preparations by householders in at-risk areas of south-eastern Australia. *Australian Journal of Emergency Management*, 29(2), 11–17.

Mitroff, I. (2001). *Managing Crises Before They Happen*. New York: American Management Association Press.

Newman, C. (2014). Interview with George Carayannopoulos.

Organisation for Economic Co-operation and Development (2015). *Trust in Government*. Retrieved 15 July 2015 from http://www.oecd.org/gov/trust-in-government.htm

Page, E. (2005). Joined-up government and the civil service. In V. Bogdanor (Ed.), *Joined-Up Government* (pp. 139–156). Oxford: Oxford University Press.

Prasser, S. (2006). *Royal Commissions and Public Inquiries in Australia*. Sydney: Lexis Nexis Butterworths.

Rittel, H., & Webber, M. (1973). Dilemmas in a general theory of planning. *Policy Sciences*, 4(2), 155–169.

Robinson, S., Eller, W., Gall, M., & Gerber, B. (2013). The core and periphery of emergency management networks. *Public Management Review*, 15(3), 344–362.

Rosenthal, U., Boin, A., & Comfort, L. (2001). *Managing Crises, Threats, Dilemmas, Opportunities*. Springfield, IL: Charles Thomas Publishing.

Stark, A., & George, N. (2015). Community resilience and crisis management: Policy lessons from the ground. *Policy and Politics*, 44(4), 591–607.

State Government of Victoria (2010). *Victorian Bushfires Royal Commission: Victorian Bushfire Reconstruction and Recovery Authority Report*.

Svedin, L. (2012). *Accountability in Crises and Public Trust in Governing Institutions*. New York: Routledge.

Wanna, J. (2007). Improving federalism: Drivers of change, repair options and reform scenarios. *Australian Journal of Public Administration*, 66(3), 275–279.

Index